William Henry Green, W. Robertson Smith

Moses and the Prophets: The Old Testament in the Jewish Church

by W. Robertson Smith

Reviewed by Wiliam Henry Green

William Henry Green, W. Robertson Smith

Moses and the Prophets: The Old Testament in the Jewish Church by W. Robertson Smith
Reviewed by Wiliam Henry Green

ISBN/EAN: 9783743310704

Manufactured in Europe, USA, Canada, Australia, Japa

Cover: Foto ©Lupo / pixelio.de

Manufactured and distributed by brebook publishing software (www.brebook.com)

William Henry Green, W. Robertson Smith

Moses and the Prophets: The Old Testament in the Jewish Church

by W. Robertson Smith

Moses and the Prophets:

THE

OLD TESTAMENT IN THE JEWISH CHURCH,

By PROF. W. ROBERTSON SMITH;

THE PROPHETS AND PROPHECY IN ISRAEL,

By DR. A. KUENEN;

AND

THE PROPHETS OF ISRAEL,

By W. ROBERTSON SMITH, LL.D.

REVIEWED BY

WILLIAM HENRY GREEN, D.D.,

PROFESSOR IN PRINCETON THEOLOGICAL SEMINARY.

NEW YORK:

ROBERT CARTER AND BROTHERS,

530 BROADWAY.

1883.

Copyright, 1882,
BY ROBERT CARTER AND BROTHERS.

UNIVERSITY PRESS:
JOHN WILSON & SON, CAMBRIDGE.

PREFACE.

THIS volume does not pretend to discuss all questions pertaining to the Books of Moses and the Prophets. It is simply a reprint, with additions, of articles in review of the works named in the title, which appeared in the "Presbyterian Review," for October, 1881, and for January, 1882, and in the "Princeton Review," for July, 1878. The last is published as originally written, a few pages having been restored which were dropped to bring it within smaller compass. The Preliminary Remarks were delivered in September, 1881, as the opening lecture of the session in Princeton Theological Seminary. A few paragraphs have been added to the article entitled "Professor Robertson Smith on the Pentateuch," for the sake of greater fulness or clearness in the argument. Thus attention is drawn to the fact that the alleged diversity of writers in the Pentateuch, if it could be proved, would not affect its antiquity or authority (p. 46); that the Levitical Law must have been written as well as enacted in the Wilderness (p. 61); that Moses could have spoken of his own meekness with no disparagement to his modesty (p. 61, *note*); that the variant phraseology of Leviticus and of Deuteronomy, in relation to the priests, involves no diversity of authorship or of age (p. 80, *note* 2); and that there is no discrepancy, as is alleged, between Deuteronomy and the Levitical Law in relation to the Passover (p. 118, *note*). A separate chapter has also been devoted to the Worship in High Places, about which the critics hold the most extravagant opinions, and upon which they found their principal arguments against the antiquity of the Laws of the Pentateuch.

The review of Dr. Robertson Smith's recent Lectures on the Prophets of Israel is here published for the first time.

If this little book shall serve in any measure to confirm the faith or to relieve the perplexities of any who have been disturbed by recent critical speculations, the author's highest wishes on its behalf will be realized. With whatever learned ingenuity and skill the unfounded speculations may be contrived, and with whatever boastful confidence they may be put forward, we may rest assured that the established belief of ages will not be unsettled, nor the firm foundations of God's Word be overturned.

PRINCETON, N. J., August 22d, 1882.

CONTENTS.

PREFACE . . . . Page 1

I. PRELIMINARY REMARKS.
Pages 9–32.

Novel aspects of the present agitation, 9; the first impulse was given by English deism, 13; the method of German rationalists, 13; of French infidels, 15; of the unbelieving higher criticism, 16; previously existing barriers are now removed, 23; the peril hence resulting, 27; the duty thus made incumbent, 28.

II. THE OLD TESTAMENT IN THE JEWISH CHURCH.
Pages 33–43.

The volume characterized in general, 33; the text of the Old Testament, 34; the canon of the Old Testament, 39; the meaning of the name Jehovah, 42.

III. PROF. ROBERTSON SMITH ON THE PENTATEUCH.
Pages 44–134.

The view defended by Professor S., 44; history of this hypothesis, 44; its first reception, 48; passages in the Pentateuch affirming Moses' authorship, 49; three groups of laws, 50; extent of the claim of authorship, 51; this claim cannot be false, 54; nor a legal fiction, 56 and *note* ; it is confirmed by the language and tenor of the laws, 57, which shows them to have been both enacted and written in the Wilderness, 61; Moses' use of the third person, 61; and self-laudation, *note;* no analogous example of legal fiction in the Old Testament, 62; laws of Deuteronomy incompatible with the reign of Josiah, 63; direction respecting the future king, *note;* the Levitical Law not post-exilic, 65; it is alleged that the Law cannot all have come from Moses, but must be a development, 67; but Israel at the Exodus not uncivilized nomads, 68; little change required in their laws, 69; necessary changes not prevented by the Mosaic Law, 69; the different codes are alleged to represent distinct stages in the life of the people, 71; fallacy in the method of the critics, 72; no discrepancy in relation to the unity of the Sanctuary, 73; the cities of refuge, 76 *note;* nor the priesthood, 76; Deuteronomy refers to pre-existing laws, and assumes their existence, 77; distinguishes between priests and Levites, 78; its peculiar phraseology involves no discrepancy, 80, is found in books which recognize this distinction, *note* 1, and is readily accounted for, *note* 2; no discrepancy in relation to the provision for the priesthood, 82 *note*, 83; other alleged discrepancies, 84 *note;* traces of the Mosaic Law in the subsequent books of the Old Testament, 85; Joshua and Chronicles arbitrarily excluded, 86; early portion of the period of the Judges, 87; later portion of the same period, 90; the carriage of the Ark, 91 *note* 2; extraordinary sacrifices, 94; infrequent mention of the Sanctuary, 97; God's help not limited to His ordinary methods, 98; regularity of ritual subordinated to spiritual obedience, 99, in the Mosaic history, 100, as in that of the Judges, 101; Samuel's sacrifices, 102; David's alleged infractions of the Mosaic Law, 105 *note;* the worship in high places, 106; the Law of Moses in the Books of Kings, 107; the Davidic Psalms, 109; the dilemma presented by Ps. xl., 110; Hosea affirms the apostasy of Israel from a purer worship, 113, and the existence of a written law, 114 and *note;* both he and Amos speak of an elaborate ritual, 115, and make numerous and even verbal allusions to the laws of the Pentateuch, 116 *note;* the alleged depreciation of sacrifice by the Prophets, 117; the Passover in Deuteronomy and the Levitical code, 118 *note;* the other Prophets, 119; Elijah, 119 *note* 1; Isaiah, 119; the "pillar" in the land of Egypt, 121; Ezekiel claimed on behalf of the new hypothesis, 122; general opposing considerations, 123; the degradation of the Levites, 127; uncircumcised foreigners in the Sanctuary, 127 *note;* priests and Levites distinguished in the previous history, 128, though not in Malachi, 128 *note;* Ezekiel an advance upon the Law, not *vice versâ,* 129; provision for stated sacrifices, 131; purgation of the altar, 131; Day of Atonement, 133.

IV. THE WORSHIP IN HIGH PLACES.
Pages 137–169.

One Sanctuary prior to Samuel and the laws of Moses observed, 137; significance of the loss of the Ark and the slaughter of the priests, 139; return and subsequent privacy of the Ark, 141; the victory at Eben-ezer, 143; plan of the Books of Samuel, 143 *note;* hopeful symptoms destroyed by the rejection of God in asking for a king, 144; Saul disobedient and finally abandoned, 147; David's restoration of the Ark, 148; considering their estimate of the ark, Israel's conduct, 149, and that of Samuel, 150, demand an explanation which is equally consistent with their knowledge of the whole Mosaic Law, 153; why the Ark was not restored to the Tabernacle of Moses, 153; High Places are nowhere sanctioned after Solomon in the Books of Kings, 155, in the Psalms or Prophets, 156; Hosea and Amos, 157; alleged local sanctuaries, 159, shown not to have been such; no known facts of Israel's worship conflict with the Mosaic origin of the laws of the Pentateuch, 167; the Books of Chronicles, 169.

V. KUENEN ON THE PROPHETS AND PROPHECY IN ISRAEL.
Pages 173–251.

Attitude of Dr. Kuenen, 173; premature anticipations of Mr. Muir, 175, and of Dr. Kuenen, 177; naturalistic view of prophecy not historico-critical or organic, 178; classification of predictions, 181; genuineness and date of the prophecies, 182; three groups of alleged unfulfilled prophecies, 184; cities of the Philistines, 184; Tyre, 188; Damascus, 197; Ammon and Moab, 197; Edom, 198; Egypt, 200; Assyria, 213; objection first, from the slow accomplishment of prophecy, and its successive stages, 216; objection second, the avenging of wrongs done to Israel should precede the loss of Israel's national existence, 219; Babylon, 223; the Book of Daniel, 224; judgments upon Israel, 230; the restoration of Israel, 234; the Messiah, 236; prophecies respecting Israel fulfilled in the Christian Church, 240; modes of evading those prophecies whose fulfilment is confessed, 247; prophecies in the historical books, 248; the authority of the New Testament, 250; incredible assumptions required by the naturalistic hypothesis, 251.

VI. DR. W. ROBERTSON SMITH ON THE PROPHETS OF ISRAEL.

Pages 255-353.

The disappointing character of these Lectures, 255; divine and human elements in Scripture, 257; the Lecturer's views of revelation, and of the inspiration of the Prophets, 260; alleged indifference of Elijah to the golden calves, 263; this worship not derived from the time of the Judges, 264 *note;* denounced by preceding Prophets, 265; Elijah's attitude, as conceived by the author of Kings, 266; his opposition to Baal, 267; its political bearings, 268; his silence no sanction, 269; no positive approval of the calves, 270; he adores the God of the Patriarchs, 270; maintains the exclusive godhead of Jehovah, 271; links Baal and the calves, 271; predicts a penalty to be inflicted on the worshippers of the calves, 272; his visit to Horeb, 273; Dr. W. R. Smith's view of the God of Moses, 274, overlooks the Ten Commandments, 277, which gave sacredness to Sinai, 278, and were contained in the Ark, 280; Wellhausen's objections to the Mosaic origin of the Decalogue, 281, from (1) Ex. xxxiv., 282; his critical analysis of Ex. xix.-xxxiv., 283 *note;* (2) image-worship, 288; Kuenen on the Second Commandment, 288, Dillmann, 291, Dr. W. R. Smith, 292, Amos and the calves, 293, Elisha, 295; (3) Israel's religion originally national, not moral, answered by Dr. W. R. Smith, 296; (4) Monotheism could not be the basis of a national religion, 298; the antiquity of the Ten Commandments, 298; inference respecting Elijah, 299; other deductions, 300; alleged separate legal standard of different epochs, 301; time of the Judges and Samuel, 302; Deuteronomy and Leviticus not unknown to the narratives of Elijah and Elisha, 303; nor Levitical Law to the rest of Kings, 306; law of Ex. xx. 24, 310; Mosaic legislation not uninfluential, 313; nor without recognition in the Northern Kingdom, 315; argument from Deut. xxxiii. and Josh. xxiv., 316; according to Hosea and Amos, the Law of Jehovah valid in both kingdoms, 317, while dispensed by priests and prophets, 318, existed in a permanent form independent of their occasional utterance of it, and is traced back to the Exodus, 320; it enjoined duties to men, 321, and to God, 323; prescribed one Sanctuary, 324; and, so far as appears, embraced the whole of Deuteronomy, 331, and the Levitical Law, 332; it was a written law, 338; by whom written, 341; the traditional view, 344; treatment of individual Prophets, 346; prophetic foresight of Amos and Hosea, 347; alleged conflict of Hosea and Elisha, 348; Isaiah and the Prophets of Israel, 350; accuracy of Isaiah's predictions, 351; prophecies emptied of their meaning, or eliminated by criticism, 352.

	PAGE
INDEX OF SCRIPTURE TEXTS	355
ADDENDUM to page 149	170

MOSES AND THE PROPHETS.

PRELIMINARY REMARKS.

ALL the signs of the times indicate that the American Church, and, in fact, the whole of English-speaking Christendom, is upon the eve of an agitation upon the vital and fundamental question of the inspiration and infallibility of the Bible, such as it has never known before. The divinity and authority of the Scriptures have heretofore been defended against the outside world of unbelievers, against pagans, infidels, and sceptics; but the question is now raised, and the supreme authority of the Scriptures contested, within the Church itself. In the controversies which have agitated the churches of Great Britain and of this country heretofore, the infallible authority of Scripture has been admitted as the ultimate test of doctrine by all contending parties. All made their appeal to this standard. The settlement of every question depended upon its interpretation, or upon inferences fairly deducible from it. But now the standard is itself brought into question. Utterances which fill the air on every side, and are borne to us from every quarter, — from professors' chairs, from pulpits, from the religious press, not to speak of what is incidentally woven into general literature and promiscuous conversation, — show abundantly that the burning question of the age is not, What does the Bible teach? It is one yet more radical and fundamental: What is the Bible? In what sense is it the Word of God? Is it a revelation from Him, and divinely authoritative; or is it to be left to the interpreter to say what in it is from God and worthy of our faith, and what is the fallible human element that may be rejected? This question is approached from all sides, and the most diverse and conflicting answers have been given.

It is not a new thing for the Church to have contests without and within. Our Lord himself said: "I came not to send peace on earth, but a sword." The intrusion of a new principle leads, of necessity, to antagonisms, and the strife is not always nor wholly an unmixed evil. It is through struggle and contest that the truth has won its way, and that godliness is purified and strengthened. Nothing is more fatal to true progress than stagnation and quiet indifference. It is something to have attention roused and interest excited, and important subjects narrowly inspected from different sides. Discussion results in clearer apprehensions, juster views, and a more thorough appreciation of all the elements entering into the decision of vexed questions than could otherwise be attained.

According to the sacred record, one providential reason why the Canaanites were not at once destroyed was to teach Israel war. By the conflicts which they were obliged to maintain from generation to generation, Israel was prevented from falling into the supineness, effeminacy, and weakness resulting from too great ease and tranquillity. The need of vigilance, of self-defence and daring deeds, compelled them to develop manly and heroic qualities. Our Saviour said to His disciples: "When ye hear of wars and rumors of wars, be ye not troubled; for such things must needs be." The outward oppressions to which the Church has been subjected, and her inward dissensions and conflicts, disastrous as these sometimes appear upon the surface, have nevertheless invariably been overruled for good. It is in consequence of the vigor with which she has been assailed on every side that the defences of Zion have been made so strong. The skilful and ingenious advocacy of erroneous views has forced the friends of truth to clearer thinking, to more accurate definitions and more correct statements of the doctrines of religion. The adversary who uncovers a weak point in the reasonings or in the formulated statements of orthodox men, really renders them a valuable service by directing attention to what is faulty in position or construction, and compelling its correction.

Truth is many-sided and large, and it is by no means easy to frame exhaustive statements which shall be precisely coincident with the reality at every point,—which shall embrace all the facts, and nothing but what is fact. It is only by a series of gradual approximations that absolutely correct solutions are found of complicated questions. And so long as any element of truth has been overlooked, or has not been assigned its due place in the system, so long will unguarded points be left open to attack, which an adversary will be sure to find out.

This has been the function of heresies and religious controversies from the beginning until now. The Church has come out of each great conflict with a more clearly defined creed, and a better apprehension of the truth that has been brought into question; and this has thenceforth been a substantial acquisition. The creed of evangelical Christendom of the present day is made up of articles which have been brought to their present accuracy and clearness by just this process. From every period of Egyptian oppression the Church comes forth laden with rich substance. The weapons that have been employed against her are converted to her use; and the intellectual wealth and resources, developed by her adversaries, become her own legitimate inheritance.

The special aspect of the conflict, to which we wish to direct attention as now imminent, is the application of historical criticism to the Bible by Christian hands, and, it may be added, by professedly orthodox Presbyterians claiming adherence to the Westminster standards,— the application of criticism to the Bible in a manner to overthrow old established views of the authorship of the books of Scripture, of the meaning and value of the Bible, of the course and character of God's revelation to men.

This is a reflex wave from German critical speculation, which is now surging with startling effect upon English shores. The first impulse to this movement, however, came from England itself, and is traceable to the deism of the 17th century,—the deism of Hobbes and Tindal, Bolingbroke and Hume. The effect of British free-thinking on the continent of Europe can be distinctly traced in the writings of the time. It is enough for the present to say that the combat against the supernatural, which English deists conducted on abstract philosophical principles, has been since carried forward on three distinct lines with direct application to the Bible. Three different methods have been employed to eliminate the supernatural from the Scriptures.

The first is that of the old German rationalists, of whom Eichhorn in the Old Testament, and Paulus in the New, may be mentioned as leaders and representatives. The genuineness and credibility of the books of the Bible were not impugned; but a method of interpretation was adopted which reduced the miraculous to the merely marvellous, and predictions to vague anticipations or shrewd forecastings of the future. The plagues of Egypt, upon this hypothesis, were not immediate inflictions, but simply an accumulation of extraordinary phenomena, the like of which, in lower intensity, are of frequent occurrence. The passage of the Red Sea was not made possible by any divine intervention, but the waters were driven back by a high wind which laid the shallows bare. The manna was not a direct gift from Heaven, but a natural product exuded from a plant still found in the

Arabian Peninsula. The Prophets were men of remarkable sagacity, who had a clear insight into the political combinations of the period and the various tendencies then at work, from which they were able to divine, with singular accuracy, the course of events. Much of the language of the Prophets is mere poetic fancy and highly wrought emblematic descriptions, whose inspiration is that of genius and of the Muses; but it is not in any special sense the very Word of God.

The difficulty with this method was that it assigned to interpretation an impossible task. It is beyond the power of hermeneutics to expunge the supernatural from the Bible, which is so firmly wrought into it at every point that it cannot be separated from it. If the genuineness of the sacred writings be conceded, and any credit whatever for honesty and truthfulness is allowed to the writers, the language which they use and the facts which they record cannot be explained away. No fair sense can be put upon them which will make them consistent with the assumption that there has been no departure from the ordinary course of nature and the regular operation of its established laws. No amount of forcing that can be applied to their language, short of completely setting aside its obvious meaning, can bring down the miracles, which they relate, to the effects of natural causes, or can account for the predictions which have been manifestly fulfilled without transcending the bounds of the merely human. With the most liberal allowance for excited fancy and poetical exaggeration, there will still remain so many extraordinary occurrences and remarkable coincidences, conspiring to an end previously announced, or taking place as was foretold by some man of God, that the miracle, which an attempt is made to escape in one direction, is nevertheless encountered in another.

The supernatural cannot be expunged from the Bible by the method of interpretation. A second method that was tried was that of denying the trustworthiness of the record and the good faith of the writers. The seed sown by the English deists produced upon French soil a harvest of a different description from that which we have just considered. To the frivolity and the godlessness of the period, all religion was accounted a fraud practised upon the masses by a designing and interested priesthood. The populace were the dupes of those who imposed upon their credulity to accomplish their own selfish and ambitious ends. The Prophets and workers of miracles were conscious impostors; the sacred writers falsified the truth of history in order to maintain and perpetuate the cheat. Thus the scoffing crew of Voltaire and his compeers, and the ignoble herd of imitators among ourselves, from Thomas Paine to Robert Ingersoll.

The trouble with this theory of deception is that it accounts for nothing which it professes to explain, while it shocks the moral sense of every thoughtful man. In ridding itself of the supernatural in the Bible, it sweeps away the supernatural altogether, and utterly discards the religious element of our nature. It imputes all religion to fraud, which is not a satisfactory explanation even of the Pagan religions; for the frauds, which have been practised in connection with them, depended for their success upon a prior belief in the supernatural, and could not themselves have produced this belief. Then the circumstances and character of the miracles and the prophecies contained in the Bible are such that the supposition of fraud is preposterous. And that such purity and excellence as characterize the religion of the Bible could be the work of deceivers, or find its support in fraud, is simply inconceivable. The denial of the veracity of the record is of all modes of escaping from the supernatural the most shallow, and to all right-thinking and right-feeling persons it is the most offensive.

The supernatural cannot be abolished by adopting some different interpretation of the Bible which shall bring all its contents down to a level with the operations of natural laws, nor by casting imputations upon the honesty and truthfulness of the sacred writers and thus discrediting their narrative. But one resource remains. It is the method of what has been denominated the higher criticism. The genuineness of the sacred writings is called in question. It is freely confessed that the writers of Scripture really meant to affirm that miracles were actually wrought and that prophecies were uttered. At the same time no charge of dishonesty is brought against them; they doubtless believed themselves that these supernatural events which they record really took place.

But such a length of time had intervened that legendary stories had grown to supernatural proportions, and the writers have simply transmitted to us the mistaken belief of their own times. It is claimed that the miracles of the Bible are not attested by eyewitnesses and contemporaries, but by persons living in an age long subsequent to their alleged occurrence; and that the prophecies, so called, were not committed to writing until after the events in which they have been thought to be fulfilled. The age and authorship traditionally ascribed to them are not correct; a critical examination shows that they must be referred to quite a different origin.

No objection can be made to the demand that the sacred writings should be subjected to the same critical tests as other literary productions of antiquity. When were they written, and by whom? For whom were they intended, and with what end in view? These are questions that may fairly be asked respecting the several books of the Bible, as respecting other books, and the same criteria that are applicable in the one case are applicable likewise in the other. Every production of any age bears the stamp of that age. It takes its shape from influences then at work. It is part of the life of the period, and can only be properly estimated and understood from being viewed in its original connections. Its language will be the language of the time when it was produced. The subject, the style of thought, the local and personal allusions, will have relation to the circumstances of the period, to which in fact the whole and every part of it must have its adaptation, and which must have their rightful place in determining its true explanation.

Inspiration has no tendency to obliterate those distinctive qualities and characteristics which link men to their own age. It is as true of Paul and Isaiah as it is of Plato and Virgil, that their intellectual life and writings received a peculiar impress from their surroundings. It is by the application of this principle that literary forgeries are detected. The attempt to palm off one's own production as the work of one of a different age, and subject to different conditions, is rarely successful. In spite of every precaution, something will leak out to betray the fact that the real circumstances of its origin are different from those that are pretended. If now inspired writings, like others, are in all their literary aspects the outgrowth of their own age, then the most thorough scrutiny can but confirm our faith in their real origin; and if in any instance the view commonly entertained of their origin or authorship is incorrect in any particular, the critical study which detects the error, and assigns each writing to its proper time and place, can only conduce to its being better understood and more accurately appreciated.

But, in applying the principles and methods of literary criticism to the books of the Bible, it must be borne in mind that these books have a character peculiarly their own, as a revelation from God; and a criticism which denies this at the outset, and conducts all its investigations upon this presumption, is under a bias which must necessarily lead to false conclusions. There is a Biblical criticism which is born of unbelief, and there is a Biblical criticism which has sprung from a reverent faith in the Divine Word; and it is not surprising that, proceeding from such opposite principles, they arrive at totally different results.

It is not necessary, in order to vitiate its conclusions, that the unbelieving criticism should formally proclaim the principles on which it proceeds, and the assumptions which lie at the basis of all its investigations. These are no less real, however, for not being announced, and for being hidden under a show of a strictly scientific procedure, by which they who conduct it may be themselves deceived. The latent principle which guides and controls throughout is, nevertheless, the elimination of the supernatural from the Bible. The problem to which it addresses itself is: How can this result be most effectually secured, and by the most plausible method?

That this is really the animus of the movement can be sufficiently shown by a survey of the various hypotheses which have been successively broached, and the arguments by which they have been defended. The only thing common to them all is the end at which they arrive; but this is reached by the most various and opposite routes. They universally agree in so dealing with the different books of Scripture that their testimony to the actual occurrence of miracles and the utterance of real prophecies shall be discredited and nullified; but in the method by which this result is reached in individual cases there is endless discord and disagreement, so that the most effectual reply to these various hypotheses often is to set them over against one another and exhibit their mutual contrariety. In every instance in which the common result can be attained by a diversity of method, we find these different methods employed by one or another of the critics. If the supernatural can be removed in a given case by a process of interpretation in the judgment of any critic, this method will be adopted, and the genuineness of the writing which contains it will be left unassailed; and any arguments that may have been advanced by others to set it aside will be pronounced inconclusive. Other critics employed upon the very same passage, and deeming this method ineffectual, maintain the charge of spuriousness with arguments adapted to the purpose, but just to the length that to their individual judgment seems necessary to compass their end. Where some are satisfied with removing a word or a clause from the text, others make bold to cast away paragraphs, or the entire writing in which they are found; and the arguments for retention or rejection, while apparently satisfactory to each critic's own mind, fail to convince his fellows. So that it is difficult to resist the conclusion that the validity of the arguments employed rests, after all, upon the end to be effected; and that criteria of like nature and of equal weight are admitted here and discredited there, according to the varying exigencies of the hypothesis which the critic is maintaining.

There is accordingly an unbelieving criticism which

may not openly avow its unbelief, or professedly make this the basis of its action, but nevertheless is practically governed in its course and its issues by radical principles that are at war with divine revelation; and there is a believing criticism framed under the opposite principle, of the reality of the supernatural revelation given in the Scriptures. A sense of the need of a divine salvation, and a conviction that the salvation set forth in the gospel of Christ meets this pressing necessity of the individual soul and of all men as it is not and cannot be met elsewhere, produces an inward persuasion of the truth and divinity of the Scriptures that cannot be set aside. He who approaches them in this state of mind, instead of being offended by the immediate divine interventions therein recorded, and being under a temptation to deny their reality or to explain them away, is prepared to accept them, on proper evidence, as kindred to or prognostic of that supreme act of immediate divine interference which achieved the world's redemption.

What the one style of criticism is thus under a constant bias to set aside as unreal and untrue, the other is prepared to accept without difficulty, whenever it is properly attested. The latter consequently disputes the legitimacy of the entire process upon which the unbelieving criticism effects its work of negation and destruction. The antecedent presumption that all testimony which confirms the reality of miracles and prophecy must necessarily be false, leads to the suspicion that the records containing this testimony must be spurious, and to the admission of criteria of spuriousness which would not have been entertained but for this previous suspicion. Ingenious and apparently formidable arguments are derived from a minute and elaborate investigation of points of diction, of style and language, of aim and tendency; and conclusions of the most serious nature are built on these fine-spun arguments, which lie after all wholly in the region of hypothesis, which have no proof from established facts and no basis in known historical data, but are so dexterously contrived as to avoid collision as far as possible with what is indisputable; and thus, on the ground of what is purely conjectural, it is proposed to revolutionize what has always been credibly believed and is supported by an authority which these ingenious processes cannot after all invalidate.

What has now been said casts no reflection upon the motives or the honesty of individual critics. It relates simply to systems and methods of criticism as such. The opposite spirit of these two systems is unmistakable; but it does not follow that each individual critic is aware of, much less that he is invariably penetrated by, the spirit of the system to which he has addicted himself. Earnest believers may be ensnared by the specious character of the arguments employed by an unbelieving criticism, and may not be able to emancipate themselves from its power and hence may adopt its conclusions; just as Christians may be living under a Pagan civilization, or Pagans may be living under a Christian civilization,—the system to which they are attached being the outgrowth of principles most opposite to those which they inwardly adopt, whether they are themselves sensible of this contrariety or not.

The peculiarity of the present crisis, to which we have already adverted, does not consist merely in the fact that critical assaults are made upon the genuineness and integrity of the books of the Bible. Such assaults have been repeatedly made, and have been conducted with great ingenuity and supported by great learning; but the war has hitherto been remote from our shores, only faint echoes of the distant conflict reached our ears, and it awakened little interest or attention among us. The evangelical churches of Great Britain and America have to a great extent been secluded from these critical contests. They have scarcely been affected by the agitation which struggles of this nature have produced in Germany, which has been their chief seat and fountainhead during the present century; and the importance and serious nature of these conflicts have scarcely been appreciated among us. We have not only been sheltered by the remoteness of our position, and by the barrier which a difference of language has interposed, but also, and still more, by the absence of any general or widespread sympathy with the theological bias which these various critical hypotheses betrayed. Religious thought among us was actively turned in quite a different direction. Questions of doctrine, of ecclesiastical organization, or of practical religious life were eagerly discussed; these absorbed the energies of leading minds and engaged the attention of the religious public. These discussions were conducted on the acknowledged basis of the divine authority of the Scriptures. Their integrity and genuineness were regarded as settled beyond dispute.

Some knowledge was indeed maintained of the critical battles which were waging in Germany; but the questions which these raised were not living practical issues among ourselves. They were consequently looked upon as ingenious disputations about matters with which we were but little concerned, and which had little intrinsic probability as judged by Anglo-Saxon common sense; and which, moreover, were urged in the interest of a disbelief in the divine original of the Scriptures, which had gained small lodgment in this quarter.

The various hypotheses which followed one another in quick succession in Germany, each having its brief day of popularity while it was in the ascendant, scarcely found their way here to the public eye, through the medium of translations or by transfusion in our current literature, before they were already antiquated in Germany itself, thrust aside by some more recent and popular novelty, or thoroughly and satisfactorily answered by noble champions of the faith, through whose learned labors Germany was constantly building up a believing Biblical criticism, to match and overturn the unbelieving criticism of which it was likewise the prolific hive; and thus the poison found its antidote already prepared by the time it had reached our shores.

Now however, by a natural reaction perhaps, the period of theological controversy among us seems to be yielding to one of doctrinal indifferentism. Questions affecting the Trinity, the atonement, human ability, the parity of the ministry, the mode of baptism, which have agitated the Christian community by strifes between different denominations, or different factions in the same denomination, no longer engage public attention to anything like the same extent. People are growing impatient of doctrinal and ecclesiastical dissensions, and the tendency of the times is rather toward a Broad Church liberalism, and sinking the differences between hitherto discordant bodies in a more catholic fellowship, if not organic union.

We do not pause here to discuss this prevalent and growing tendency, nor to distinguish the elements of good and evil that enter into it. We simply remark upon its existence as an obvious fact, characteristic of the present in contrast with the recent past.

And concurrently with this indifference to doctrinal distinctions there has arisen a weakening of the strict religious sentiment which has heretofore pervaded the Christian community. There is not the same reverence for the absolute authority of Scripture, nor the same sense of the imperative need of the objective supernatural salvation which it reveals. The distinctive doctrines of grace are less urgently and prominently set forth in the instructions of the pulpit. In various prominent and influential quarters the shallow and self-sufficient view of man's estate is coming to be more and more distinctly formulated, which finds in men's moral instincts an adequate guide, and which looks to the forces of human nature to work out its own salvation.

We have now reached a juncture when the general sense of the need of infallible guidance in the Scriptures has been somewhat shaken by a growing confidence in men's own powers, and the fact of that infallible guidance has been assailed from the most diverse quarters; when students of physical science claim that the facts of nature are irreconcilable with the Bible account of the creation, the flood, and the dispersion of the human race; when antiquarians affirm that the monumental records of Egypt or of Assyria are in conflict with the alleged facts of the sacred history; when philosophers, who have made a study of Comparative Religion, deny that there is anything of consequence in the religion of the Bible which does not find illustrative parallels elsewhere and cannot be accounted for on purely natural principles; when moralists bring into question its solutions of moral problems and challenge its alleged divine decisions as indefensible; when socialistic schemers oppose the Bible because it stands in the way of their disorganizing theories; and the wayward heart is now as ever restive under its restraints and penalties, and ready to avail itself of any pretext to escape them. The antagonism directed against the divine infallible authority of the Bible from these and other quarters, while it does not shake the citadel of its strength, nevertheless has by persistent repetition had its influence on the public mind. Doubts and insinuations are freely uttered by those who venture on no positive assertions discrediting the Scriptures. And even professed friends of the Bible have said that there must be some abatement of its claims and some modification of its defences, that something must be yielded to its antagonists in the hope of saving what remains.

In this condition of things, induced by the causes now described, doubts and misgivings, from alleged critical discoveries, find an opportunity for lodgment such as has not existed in the Christian community of Great Britain and America at any former period. Hence the peculiar peril of the position in which the Church in these lands finds itself at this moment, and of which the case of Prof. Robertson Smith, in the Free Church of Scotland, is one of the most characteristic and illustrative incidents. The barriers of distance and of language, in which we found our safety from the critical battles that have raged in Germany, are suddenly thrown down and the conflict is at once transported to our own shores, with no interposed check or hindrance, and in the very acme of the struggle.

The particular critical hypothesis, which has within the last few years risen to a sudden popularity and just now is in the ascendant, met with no favor whatever when it was first suggested less than fifty years ago. In falling in with this novel scheme the Biblical critics have reversed all their previous hypotheses as suddenly and completely as was done a few years since by natural philosophers in their hypothesis of the origin of man, — when from disputing the unity of the human race and the possibility that the several races of mankind could have sprung from a common source, they suddenly swung to the opposite extreme of maintaining a common origin not only for men but for the inferior animals as well.

The adoption of these views would be attended with very far-reaching consequences. It would render necessary a complete reconstruction of Old Testament history; it would alter our views entirely as to the mode and the nature of God's revelation to Israel. It would compel a revision of the question: In what sense can the Scriptures be regarded as the Word of God, and what measure of authority can be attributed to them?

We are thus, by the necessity of the case, set to grappling with the most fundamental inquiries. We must dig down to the very foundations, and re-examine the basis upon which our Christian faith reposes. And this necessity is not laid upon us a whit too soon. It is providentially ordered that at this very time, when a lax theology is drifting away from the strict standard of the Scriptures, and is disposed to govern its faith by the moral intuitions of men rather than by the positive statements of the Word of God, we should be summoned to a most thorough sifting of this whole matter,—that we should be driven to a most minute and thorough inspection of the inspired volume, and led to employ the most searching tests that can be applied to it, in order to discover whether it really is what it has hitherto been credited to be.

It is under the circumstances just recited that we are now living, and they speak to us in tones which should not be disregarded. The soldier is expected faithfully to execute his drill and evolutions, and to train himself in all the martial exercises demanded of him, even in times of profound peace, in order that he may gain the knowledge and practised skill which properly belong to his vocation. But a new responsibility rests upon him in time of actual war; there is a fresh demand for diligence when he may soon be summoned to the field of strife, and the issue of the conflict turn upon the valor and dexterity of the troops engaged.

The venerable Dr. Hodge, who was for nearly threescore years the glory and the strength of Princeton Seminary, was called upon for some remarks in the Week of Prayer at the beginning, I think, of the last year of his life. The subject before the meeting was the Conversion of the World. It was his habit on such occasions to present a cheering view derived from the progress which the Gospel had made or was making, or from the accomplished work of redemption which is the assured basis of the world's salvation, or the unfailing promises of God which make the issue certain; but at the time referred to he recited, in long and formidable array, the various forms of opposition which are directed against the Gospel within the bounds of Christendom itself, — the materialistic philosophy, the oppositions of science, the socialistic excesses, and showed in what various ways unsanctified learning, power and influence in irreligious hands, and unchristianized masses stand as barriers to the progress of truth and holiness. His aim was not to discourage, but to present a truthful and sober view of the actual aspect of the world, and of the forces which are at war against the progress of the Gospel. It was the trumpet-call of the veteran, who had fought his battles and won his victories, summoning new recruits to the Holy War, and uttering loud notes of warning, that the strife was by no means ended, that there are many and fierce battles yet to fight, and that others must take up the weapons which he was laying down.

We are coming now, as it would seem, to the culmination of the struggle. The battle rages around the citadel. No drones or cowards are wanted now. It is not the incompetent and the unfaithful who can serve the Church in such a crisis. She can well afford to spare the idlers and stragglers and faint-hearted from her ranks. The times emphatically demand those who shall be prepared to acquit themselves like men.

He has a very low conception of the work of the ministry, of the solemn duties and the momentous responsibilities which it involves, who can suffer himself to be slack and negligent in his preparation for it, or inactive and half-hearted in his discharge of it. And he gives little evidence of being called of God to the office, and little prospect of usefulness and success in it, who does not engage, whether in his preparatory studies or in the actual labors of the ministry, with a holy enthusiasm, throwing himself into them with all the energy of his nature, — resolved by the aids of divine grace to make the most of the powers and faculties which God has given him in the special line of this high calling; seizing with eagerness every opportunity within his reach, and training himself by all available methods to the highest measure of fitness he can secure to be entrusted with the care of souls, to be an ambassador of God to men, to be a steward of the mysteries of the Kingdom of Heaven. If a charge so weighty and so sacred as this will not stir the energies of a man to the utmost, the least that can be said is, that he shows that he has no appreciation of this high and holy office, and no fitness for it.

But besides this general demand which is always laid upon all ministers and all candidates for the ministry, to use the utmost zeal in the whole round of their professional or preparatory studies, there is a call to special diligence and thoroughness now in the circumstances which have already been recited. If supineness were ever admissible, there is a loud call for alertness at the present time. There is a demand now, as never before, for high Biblical scholarship, for well-trained exegetes and critics, — for men well versed in the critical and speculative attacks made upon the Word of God, and who are well prepared to defend it. The present phases of critical and speculative assault upon the Scriptures need create no alarm, as though they were more formidable than their predecessors; but though these should be repulsed and prove short-lived, that will not end the strife. The assault will be renewed at some fresh point, or in some other form. And now that the critical battle is brought to our own doors, it will not do to wait till defenders of the faith in other lands work out a solution for us. We must have an English and American scholarship that is fitted to grapple with these questions as they arise. We need, in the ranks of the pastorate, men who can conduct Biblical researches and who can prosecute learned critical inquiries; who can do, in their own chosen field of Scripture study, what German evangelical pastors have done, — such as Baehr in his " Symbolism of the Mosaic Cultus," and Ranke in the critical defence of the genuineness of the Pentateuch, and Fuller in the interpretation of the Prophet Daniel, and Keil, who published his learned defence of the books of Chronicles and Ezra when he was only a licentiate.

THE OLD TESTAMENT IN THE JEWISH CHURCH.[1]

THESE lectures, originally prepared for popular delivery, are eminently adapted for their purpose. Their author has a remarkable faculty for presenting subjects, that are commonly regarded as dry and technical, in a lucid and attractive manner, — with such clearness of statement, such aptness of illustration, and such a close logical connection from first to last, that the interest is maintained to the end, and his readers cannot fail to gain a satisfactory comprehension of the conclusions reached, and the general nature of the grounds upon which they rest. No one can rise from the perusal of this volume without a high respect for the learning and ability of the author, and a profound impression that Biblical Criticism offers a very wide and important field for study; an impression that will be deepened in most minds, probably, by the startling character of some of the opinions here confidently announced, as though they were the undoubted results of the latest and most thorough scholarship. It is exceedingly unfortunate that a volume which has so many excellent points,

[1] The Old Testament in the Jewish Church: twelve lectures on Biblical Criticism. By W. Robertson Smith, M. A. New York: D. Appleton & Co. 1881. 12mo, pp. 446.

and which, from the peculiar circumstances attending its publication, naturally attracts so much attention, does not discriminate between facts and theories; but — after the method of the German critics, who must speak oracularly, if at all, and to whom the self-consistency of an ingenious hypothesis sufficiently recommends it, in the absence of any evidence to support it — the purely conjectural is propounded as though it were of the same unquestionable certainty with that which is really known.

These lectures throughout challenge the accuracy of the Jewish transmission of the Old Testament in respect to its text, its canon, and the constitution of its separate books. The train of investigation pursued relative to these various points opens questions of the highest consequence, both bringing to light a large amount of valuable information, and suggesting lines of inquiry that still remain to be explored; nevertheless, from the deplorable fault already alluded to, it is so conducted as to leave an exaggerated or thoroughly false impression.

It is readily conceded that, notwithstanding the substantial unanimity of Hebrew manuscripts, the Masoretic text is not immaculate. There are some obvious mistakes, in certain books, which prove this; and the discrepancies in various parallel passages, and the incompleteness of a few acrostic poems, though largely explicable otherwise, may be partly due to faulty transcription. But it is an immense and unwarranted stride from these premises to the assumption that — though the Hebrew text, as it existed in the first Christian century has been transmitted with unparalleled precision — "in earlier ages Hebrew MSS. differed as much as, or more than, MSS. of the New Testament" (p. 73). The allegation (p. 78), "that the early guardians of the text did not hesitate to make small changes in order to remove expressions which they thought unedifying," is wholly unfounded. Of the eighteen so-called *Tikkûnê Sophcrîm* (Corrections of the Scribes) which are adduced in proof, Professor Smith himself admits that fifteen are irrelevant. The fact is that, in the judgment of the best critics, the entire series are mere rabbinical conceits, and warrant no suspicion whatever of any tampering with the text. Ishbosheth may be a contemptuous nickname which the son of Saul "would never have consented to bear;" but who can certify us that it was not current in the rival kingdom during his lifetime, or that it was not so written by the author of the Books of Samuel, but was an alteration by some copyist in later times? The forced interpretations, which the scribes confessedly put upon the Law,[1] are no evidence that they wilfully changed the written text, but the reverse; if the Law could have been accommodated to their usages by altering its expressions, they would

---

[1] The censure impliedly cast on the author of the Books of Chronicles (p. 64) is quite gratuitous. King Joash directed a temporary assessment from year to year for the repair of the Temple, and fixed its rate by the example of Moses. (Note that the italic words in the English version of II. Chron. xxiv. 6, form no part of the text.) It is hard to see what this has to do with a voluntary arrangement in the time of Nehemiah for a different purpose, or how it appears that the Chronicler was under a mistake about it.

have been under no temptation to do violence to its language. It is puzzling to account for the concurrence of all existing manuscripts in obvious mistakes, or in such an arbitrary notation as the extraordinary points, suspended letters, and the like; but there is nothing to require or to justify the assumption of "a rigorous suppression of discordant copies" (p. 75), or of a serious dissonance at any time among Hebrew manuscripts.

Professor Smith complains (p. 74) that our present Old Testament text cannot be traced back beyond the fall of the Jewish State. This is to be regretted, doubtless; but it is simply due to the lack of any adequate sources of information. If, as he says of the antecedent period (p. 98), "there is not a particle of evidence that there was a uniform Palestinian text," and its existence is "a pure hypothesis," neither is there, on the other hand, a particle of evidence of a discrepant text at all approaching the "variations and corruptions found in MSS. of the New Testament." This too is a pure hypothesis, only with the difference that all the probabilities and the inferences deducible from known facts are against it, and establish beyond reasonable doubt that there never was any wide divergence of manuscripts, and that we now possess a text which is not indeed absolutely faultless, but yet substantially and even astonishingly accurate.

The only accessible witnesses to the state of the text in the pre-Christian period, outside of the line of Palestine tradition, are the Samaritan Pentateuch and the Septuagint version. Gesenius's careful analysis of the former has put an end to all thought of correcting the Hebrew text by the Samaritan; and the variant "ages assigned to the patriarchs" (p. 73) are clearly due to systematic and intentional alteration and not to the errors of transcribers; they must therefore be classed with the arbitrary changes characteristic of the Samaritan recension. We are very far from any disposition to undervalue the Septuagint, or to refuse such critical aid as can fairly and legitimately be derived from it. Let it be noted that the question between the Masoretic and the Septuagint text is one of form rather than substance. If the latter were to be substituted for the former throughout, which Professor Smith is very far from proposing, it would involve no peril to the Christian faith. This may be fairly inferred from the free use made of the Septuagint by the inspired writers of the New Testament; and it would be difficult to point out any appreciable change that would have resulted in the belief of the early Greek Church, had the Fathers been conversant with Hebrew instead of being limited in the Old Testament to the use of the Septuagint. The matter involved is simply verbal precision and minute textual accuracy.

And here the Professor correctly informs us that — in consequence of mistakes of the translators [1] (p. 87), the license which they allowed themselves in various

---

[1] Prof. W. R. Smith gratuitously links copyists with translators, as though the former took the same liberties with the text as the latter; but the cases are not analogous. Translation naturally led to elucidation, while the work of the scribe was simply to reproduce word for word and letter for letter.

ways (pp. 88-90), and the manifold corruptions that have since crept into the text of the Septuagint (p. 103), — "it is an affair of the most delicate scholarship to make profitable use of the Alexandrian version for the confirmation or emendation of the Hebrew." The statement that the "readings of the Septuagint offer a fair measure of the limits of variation in the early history of the text" must accordingly be taken with very large abatement; and the formula, by which it is proposed to determine which reading is to be preferred in the illustrations given (p. 90), viz. "in cases of this sort the shorter text is obviously the original," is by no means so settled a rule, or of so wide application, as the Professor would have us believe.

In its application to the book of Jeremiah, it is particularly unfortunate, as the elaborate discussion of Wichelhaus abundantly shows. On this point we will not venture to quote Keil, whose unfavorable judgment of the Septuagint text is so summarily set aside (p. 85). But Graf, the *coryphæus* of the latest critical speculations, will perhaps be heard with more respect. After a careful comparison of the Greek and Hebrew text of Jeremiah, he says, in the Introduction to his Commentary (p. li.), "after what has now been shown there can no longer be any doubt that the form of the text yielded by the Greek translator is a mutilated and corrupted one, which arose out of the text preserved to us in the Hebrew, and at a much later time." This is the more noteworthy as he tells us (*Vorwort*, p. ix.): "I began the work with the most favorable opinion of the Septuagint, but was soon led to the opposite view by the convincing power of the facts," which satisfied him that "the suspicion which has been expressed against the genuineness of certain passages in the book, particularly the prophecy respecting Babylon, chaps. l. li. [which Prof. W. R. Smith appears to be prepared to surrender, pp. 112, 121], as well as the hypothesis of a double recension of the book, which has obtained almost universal prevalence in recent times, is utterly without foundation." And Delitzsch, who is certainly indulgent enough in questions of criticism, says of "the transpositions occurring in the Book of Proverbs," to which our author also refers (pp. 121, 122): "These remind one of the transpositions in Jeremiah, and rest, as they do, upon a mistake as to the true relations of the subject-matter," (*Spruchbuch*, p. 39.) And Jeremiah, ch. xxvii., which is adduced to exemplify the superiority of the Greek text, affords a signal proof of the reverse; for ver. 7, whose presence in the Hebrew and absence from the Greek is one of the points remarked upon (p. 115), was certainly in the text when Chronicles was written, as appears from the manifest allusion to it, II Chron. xxxvi. 20.

The obscurity which overhangs the final collection and arrangement of the Old Testament canon, opens a fresh opportunity for theorizing, in which a modicum of facts is mingled with a large infusion of doubtful conjectures. The presence of apocryphal books and sections in the Septuagint is appealed to in evidence that the extent of the canon was fluctuating and uncertain, while yet Professor Smith confesses that these books have no proper claim to be regarded as canonical, and that they never were accepted as such by the Jews in Alexandria or elsewhere. They were valued as aids to religious edification, but not esteemed authoritative. His notion of the process by which the Old Testament was gradually brought to its present compass is substantially as follows. The canon of Ezra was the Pentateuch alone. The divine authority of the Prophets was recognized, but only as books for private edification. There was no standard edition of individual Prophets, and no fixed collection of the Prophets as a whole, till their use in the public worship of the synagogue made it necessary at a comparatively late date. It already existed "in the time of Daniel" (Dan. ix. 2), that is, as may be inferred from a critical opinion cited with apparent approbation on p. 168, the period of the Maccabees. "The Psalter, the hymn-book of the second temple," did not reach its finished form till a still later date, and was added subsequently, together with Job and Proverbs. This is the undisputed portion of the canon, whose authority has always been practically acknowledged, and to which the sanction of the New Testament is given. The remainder of the Hagiographa is the region of the *antilegomena*, books whose authority was more or less contested, but which gradually worked their way to canonical recognition, though the full and final settlement in their favor was not reached till the end of the first Christian century. And he thinks it matter of thankfulness that the determination of the canon was not made sooner, or "the principles of the Scribes and Pharisees" would have led to a most unsatisfactory result.

It will not be necessary to review the whole course of this discussion. It is enough to refer to one outstanding fact, which cannot be set aside. The express testimony of Josephus assures us that the twenty-two books of the Jewish canon, which are universally admitted to be identical with the present Hebrew Bible, constituted a determinate body of writings "justly believed to be divine," and which had been for ages sundered from all other books and ranked above them. This statement of Josephus, whatever question may be raised about its accuracy in details, unquestionably represents the current belief of his time. And this is utterly inconsistent with a canon still fluctuating during the life of our Lord and His Apostles. The Scriptures to which they make their appeal were the Old Testament as we now have it, as well defined and settled as it is at present. The case is no more affected by the disputes in Jewish schools, than the canonicity of the Epistle of James is shaken by the doubts expressed by Luther. These casuistical questionings — or, as they might rather for the most part be called, these contests of rabbinical subtlety — did not touch the historic basis on which the canon rested; and such as they were, they were directed not merely against Esther, Canticles, and Ecclesiastes, but, as Prof. W. R. Smith has to allow, against what he calls the undisputed portion of the canon likewise, *e. g.*, Ezekiel (p. 410) and Proverbs

(p. 170). And the omission of Esther from the catalogue of Melito in the second century, and from those of Athanasius and Gregory Nazianzen in the fourth, certainly lends no support to the Professor's view; for, on his own showing, the canon was then settled and Esther was in it.

The most significant discussion in the volume before us, however, and that for which all that preceded was designed to pave the way, is that concerning the constitution and date of the Pentateuch. This cannot be considered at the close of a notice already sufficiently extended, but must be treated in a separate article.

In conclusion, we are compelled to say that the Professor, with all his brilliancy and learning, seems to be deficient in well-balanced judgment. How easily he is misled by the *ignis fatuus* of novel and ingenious speculations, conspicuously appears from his adoption of the whimsical conceit that Jehovah means "*He who causes* rain or lightning *to fall* upon the earth" (p. 423). This is not only giving the preference to a rare and somewhat doubtful meaning of the verbal root, above that which it uniformly has everywhere except in a single poetical passage (Job xxxvii. 6), — and a meaning which, if allowed, contains in itself no special reference to rain or lightning, but would more naturally, when other derivations are taken into the account, suggest the sense "*He who causes to fall* to destruction and ruin," *i. e.*, the Destroyer, — but it involves an amazing lack of apprehension of what is really characteristic of the religion of Israel, to imagine that the one name of God, in which this religion reaches its highest expression of the object of worship, could possibly mean nothing more than the Giver of Rain. If the profound meaning sanctioned Ex. iii. 14, and adopted by the best philologists, was to be discredited at all hazards, the suggestion of Kuenen and others, "*He who causes to be*," *i.e.*, the Creator, would have vastly more in its favor. And if a crude notion of the Deity was perforce to be wrung out of the Israelitish conception, there would be more plausibility in the allegation, baseless as it is, that light and fire, which are such frequent emblems of the divine being or attributes, gave shape to their earliest thoughts of the Most High, than that they thought of Him simply as the One who made it rain.

PROFESSOR ROBERTSON SMITH ON THE PENTATEUCH.

PROFESSOR ROBERTSON SMITH tells us, on p. 216 of his recently published lectures on Biblical Criticism,[1] that "the discrepancy between the traditional view of the Pentateuch, and the plain statements of the Historical Books and the Prophets, is marked and fundamental." This view is accordingly discarded by him, and another commended to us as representing "the growing conviction of an overwhelming weight of the most earnest and sober scholarship." He asks us to believe that Deuteronomy made its first appearance in the reign of Josiah, and that the Levitical Law was not in existence until the time of Ezra.

The hypothesis which the Professor has undertaken to unfold and defend has only very recently attracted any serious attention. Professor Reuss of Strasburg claims the credit of having given the original impulse to this newest school of Pentateuch criticism, by propounding this view in his lectures as early as 1833. His pupil, K. H. Graf, elaborated it more fully in his treatise "De Templo Silonensi" (1855), in his "Pro-

[1] The Old Testament in the Jewish Church; twelve lectures on Biblical Criticism. By W. Robertson Smith, M.A. New York: D. Appleton & Co. 1881. 12mo, pp. 446.

phet Jeremiah" (1862), and in his "Geschichtliche Bücher des Alten Testaments" (1866). As proposed by him, however, it was burdened with fatal inconsistencies which were speedily pointed out by its antagonists. The divisive critics, who parcelled out the Pentateuch among different writers, had previously conducted their analysis and based their conclusions upon literary considerations chiefly, — the style and diction, and quality of thought and acquaintance shown with other parts of the work. Graf drew his arguments from legislative considerations, the supposed development of laws, and the order in which successive enactments may be thought to have been made; and conceiving the legislation of Deuteronomy to be simpler and more primitive, and that of Leviticus to be more complicated and developed, he inferred, contrary to the prevailing sentiment of preceding critics, that Deuteronomy is of earlier date than Leviticus, and belongs to a prior stage in the history of the people. Meanwhile he allowed the conclusions of the critics in relation to the narratives of the Pentateuch to remain undisturbed, conceding a higher antiquity to the Elohistic portion, which is in the closest affinity with Leviticus, than to the Jehovistic portion, to which Deuteronomy attaches itself. This self-contradiction Kuenen undertook to remove by reversing the relation of the Elohist and the Jehovist, thus boldly challenging the position which all preceding critical investigations had been supposed to settle beyond peradventure.

To disinterested spectators of these hostile critical

camps, this looks very like a fresh demonstration of the precarious and inconclusive nature of their entire process of argument. Experiments without number have been made of running the dissecting knife through the Pentateuch; and each fresh operator has pronounced, with the utmost positiveness, upon the age of each separate portion, and has pointed out the influences under which it was written and the condition of affairs when it was produced. And now everything has been thrown into a fresh jumble again; the whole order of production, confidently insisted upon before, is suddenly declared to be a mistake; everything must be reconstructed on a new basis. In the midst of this jargon of voices, clamoring on the one hand for the priority of the Elohist, and on the other for the priority of the Jehovist, it may be safe to wait awhile before attaching ourselves to either party. Possibly the next critical discovery may be that they were contemporaneous.

Of course we cannot here enter upon the interminable question as to the real existence of the various writers among whom the critics propose to parcel the Pentateuch, and fortunately it is quite unnecessary for our present purpose. So far as its decision depends upon alleged peculiarities of style and diction it is a purely literary question, which no more affects the antiquity and authority of the books of Moses in general, or of the laws of Moses in particular, than the fact that a given law of Congress was not drafted throughout by the same pen, but that certain words or clauses or paragraphs can be traced to different members of that body, detracts from its authenticity or validity. The composite character of the Pentateuch, supposing it established, would not prove the post-Mosaic date of the Pentateuchal legislation in its present form, unless this could first be proved for one or more of its constituent parts. The several dates of the assumed documents, and the order of their production, are alone pertinent to the matter now at issue. And here the critics are confessedly at sea.

We cannot deny to the authors of this latest hypothesis the praise of a high degree of ingenuity in its construction, of consummate dexterity in adapting it to the emergencies of the case and in marshalling all available materials for its support, and of unflinching intrepidity — or rather a veritable audacity — in pushing it to its last results, so that it is absolutely beyond the reach of the *reductio ad absurdum* argument; for the most preposterous conclusions are accepted without hesitation, and paraded as genuine discoveries. Kuenen and Wellhausen have shown us by what clever tricks of legerdemain they can construct Castles in the Air, and produce histories which have positively no basis whatever but their own exuberant fancy; while Lagarde makes the practical application of their principles by demanding the overthrow of the Christian Church and its institutions, as the mere outgrowth of Pharisaical superstition. The temporary applause which has followed upon the performance of these novel feats is no augury of its abiding popularity, much less of its assured success. The boastful claims of its advocates will not disturb the equanimity of those who remember with what rapidity hypothesis has succeeded hypothesis, and one phase of criticism has grown up after another, in the fruitful soil of German speculation.

It is substantially a revival of ideas which were almost simultaneously suggested by Vatke, George, and Von Bohlen, in 1835, but which then fell utterly flat. De Wette,[1] in his review of these "three young critics," dryly suggested that there was a reason for this hypothesis coming to the surface, inasmuch as the criticism of the Pentateuch could only thus complete the entire round of possible assumptions. And he said of the reconstruction of Israelitish history upon the basis proposed, that "the only thing lacking to make it attractive is truth;" that "whether from a dread of individualism inspired by the Hegelian philosophy, a predilection for development and self-impelled struggles upward, or a love of paradox, they have linked the history of Hebraism not with the fixed point of the grand creations of Moses, but have suspended its beginnings upon airy nothing." Hupfeld[2] repudiated in the strongest terms the distinctive principle of their hypothesis (as of Graf's and Kuenen's) that Deuteronomy is the earliest instead of the latest portion of the Pentateuch, — calling it "a monstrous error that turned everything topsy-turvy, and perverted and entangled the questions at issue, but did not solve them." Riehm,[3] in 1854, considered it

---

[1] "Studien und Kritiken" for 1837, pp. 955, 981.
[2] "De Primitiva Festorum Ratione," 1851, p. 1.
[3] "Die Gesetzgebung Mosis im Lande Moab, Vorrede," p. v.

a "critical or rather uncritical view," which was already "antiquated" and unworthy of attention. And there is little likelihood that this hypothesis, even in its most recent phase, will win its way to universal favor, when critics such as Riehm, Dillmann, Kleinert, Marti, Delitzsch, Klostermann, Bredenkamp, and D. Hoffmann[1] have pronounced against it, not to speak of the assaults made upon it from the rear by those who charge it with a timid conservatism and with not being thorough-going enough in the work of demolition. It is apparent that this hypothesis affords us no firm footing, were we to embrace it. If all that has thus far been asked were to be conceded, no guarantee is or can be given against fresh demands in the same direction. It is only the arbitrary pleasure of the critics, and nothing in the nature of the case, which leads them with their principles and methods to stop where they do.

In five passages in the Pentateuch (Ex. xvii. 14, xxiv. 4, xxxiv. 27; Num. xxxiii. 2; Deut. xxxi. 9, 22, 24), as Prof. Robertson Smith correctly informs us, Moses is said to have written down certain things.

---

[1] Riehm reviewed Graf's positions in the "Studien und Kritiken" for 1868 and 1872; Dillmann, "Die Bücher Exodus und Leviticus," 1880; Kleinert, "Das Deuteronomium und der Deuteronomiker," 1872; Marti, "Traces of the so-called Grundschrift of the Hexateuch in the Pre-exilic Prophets of the Old Testament," in the Jahrbücher für Protestantische Theologie, 1880; Delitzsch, a series of articles in "Luthardt's Zeitschrift für Wissenschaft und Leben," 1880; Klostermann, in the "Zeitschrift für Lutherische Theologie und Kirche," 1877; Bredenkamp, "Gesetz und Propheten," 1881; D. Hoffmann, "Magazin für die Wissenschaft des Judenthums," 1876–80.

The express statement of his authorship in these cases does not exclude it in others, any more than it follows, from Isa. viii. 1 and xxx. 8, that Isaiah wrote nothing but what is referred to in those verses. The natural presumption, on the contrary, is that if he wrote those scraps of the History and those sections of the Law, he also wrote others which it was quite as important to have recorded. These recognitions of the fact that whatever was memorable should be committed to writing for safe preservation, and that Moses was the proper person to write it, would rather lead us to expect that Moses would record the history and the legislation in which he bore so prominent a part, and incline us to believe that "the book," to which reference is made (Ex. xvii. 14 *Heb.*), is such a comprehensive work upon which he was then already engaged, or which at least he intended to prepare.

But we shall lay no stress upon presumptions. We shall concern ourselves simply with duly certified facts; and as the discussion of Prof. W. R. Smith relates merely to the laws of the Pentateuch, we shall confine ourselves to these. And here we adopt the appropriate division, which he gives us (pp. 316, ff.), into "three principal groups of laws or ritual observances, in addition to the Ten Commandments," viz: 1. The Collection, Ex. xxi.–xxiii. 2. The Deuteronomic Code, Deut. xii.–xxvi., as distinguished from what is purely hortatory and historical in the book. 3. The Levitical Legislation, which does not form a compact code like the preceding, but is scattered through several parts of Exodus and the books of Leviticus and Numbers. Three of the passages above adduced speak of Moses as writing laws. In Ex. xxiv. 4 he is said to have written "all the words of the LORD." This the Professor (p. 331) would restrict to the Ten Commandments. But after God had uttered these by His own voice, and the terrified people had asked that Moses should henceforth speak with them, and not God, the LORD gave them His commands through Moses (Ex. xx. 22 ff.), including a body of judgments or ordinances (ch. xxi–xxiii.). Then (xxiv. 3) Moses came and told the people all the words of the LORD, — of course not merely the Ten Words which they had themselves heard Him speak, but all that God had charged him to say to them, and particularly "the judgments," which are therefore separately specified. "And all the people answered with one voice, and said, All the words which the LORD hath said, will we do." Now, unless any one is prepared to maintain that the people here promised obedience to the Ten Commandments only, and not to the judgments which Moses had just repeated to them from the mouth of God, he must admit that both are included in the words of the LORD, which the very next verse declares that Moses wrote, and which (ver. 8) entered into the covenant then formed between Jehovah and Israel. It could not be more explicitly stated than it is, that this first collection of laws dates from the time immediately following the exodus. It was then reduced to writing, formally read in the audience of the people, their submission to it pledged, and the covenant of God with Israel ratified on the basis of it with appropriate ceremonies. It even claims priority to the tables of the law deposited in the Ark, whose authenticity and antiquity are vouched for in the most unimpeachable manner, and are not disputed by Prof. W. R. Smith.

Again, at the renewal of the covenant after the sin of the Golden Calf, Moses is directed to write certain words, which are not "expressly identified with the Ten Words on the tables of stone," but are, on the contrary, expressly distinguished from them (Ex. xxxiv. 27, 28). The ambiguity arising from the omission of the subject of the verb in the last clause of verse 28 is removed by a comparison of verse 1. It was the LORD, not Moses, who wrote the Ten Commandments upon the tables which were carried to the summit of Sinai for this purpose. Moses wrote upon some material, not indicated, the words contained in Ex. xxxiv. 10–26, which is substantially repeated, from the Book of the Covenant (Ex. xx. 23, xxiii. 12–33), being the specifications there given respecting the service of God, and the pledge on His part to subdue the Canaanites before them. They had grossly violated their duty to God, which wrought a forfeiture of His pledge to them. Hence these portions of the Covenant are singled out and enforced upon the people afresh. The rewriting of these extracts is an additional confirmation of the existence of the Code from which they were taken, and is equivalent to a new assertion of its Mosaic origin.

In Deut. xxxi. 9, we read " Moses wrote this law: "

and (vers. 24–26) "When Moses had made an end of writing the words of this law in a book, until they were finished, Moses commanded the Levites .... saying, Take this Book of the Law and put it in the side of the Ark." If it is possible for words to convey the idea that the entire code of laws here spoken of, which cannot be less than Deut. xii.–xxvi., was written by Moses, this idea is here expressed; and no amount of arguing about the variety of meanings that may be given to the term *law* can make it different. The fact that "all the words of this law" were to be written on plastered stones on Mount Ebal (Deut. xxvii. 3) can create no difficulty. This statement finds abundant illustration in the walls of tombs and temples in Egypt, and its numerous monuments written all over with hieroglyphical legends. And it surely requires no great effort to believe it feasible to trace these laws in plaster as a symbolic declaration that they were thenceforth the laws of the land. Written in letters five times the size of those in ordinary Hebrew Bibles, they could all be embraced in the space of eight feet by three. The famous Behistûn inscription of Darius, in its triple form, is twice as long as this entire Code, besides being carved in bold characters on the solid rock, and in a position difficult of access on the mountain side.

And the whole book of Deuteronomy purports to be a series of discourses delivered by Moses to the people in the plains of Moab, inculcating and enforcing this Law. The Professor reminds us that these were not "taken down by a shorthand reporter;"

and he queries whether it is certainly the meaning of Deut. xxxi. 24 that we have this body of laws "word for word" as it was written down by Moses. But under cover of this regard for absolute precision, it will not do to fritter away the entire record. That Moses in his oral discourse uttered in every case exactly the words reported to us, just those and neither less nor more, we are not concerned to affirm; but that he did deliver such discourses, and that they are here preserved in their substantial import, is fully certified, unless the credibility of the book can be impeached. And this code of laws is substantially as it came from the pen of Moses, if any reliance can be placed upon the record.

So, too, the Mosaic origin of the Levitical laws is abundantly declared by the formulas with which they are introduced, and which recur over and over again: The LORD spake unto Moses, or the LORD spake unto Moses and Aaron; and the formulas, by which they are often followed, *e. g.*, Lev. vii. 37, 38; xxiii. 44; xxvi. 46; xxvii. 34. The occasion is recited upon which particular laws were delivered; and the circumstances connected with these enactments are inseparably united with the historical narrative of the time.

Now as to the origin of these several codes of laws there can be no possibility of mistake. It is not merely affirmed in a credible history, of whose truth we have abundant guarantee, but the nature of the case precludes falsehood or error. An accepted system of legislation, whose authority is confessed and submitted to, has, in that fact, the strongest possible proof of its genuineness. No forged body of laws could ever be imposed upon any people. No supposititious code, issued in the name of Moses in a subsequent age, could have been accepted without inquiry, and established as the law of the land. It is indeed supposable that the current laws and usages of any given period might be popularly supposed to be more ancient than they really were. But this is not what we are asked to believe. We are told that the first that is known of the book of Deuteronomy is that it was found in the Temple in the days of Josiah. It claims to be the work of Moses, but it never emanated from him. Its enactments had never been in force before. No such laws were known at any time during the history of the people. They were not in harmony with existing customs or with prevailing ideas, but were in some essential points directly antagonistic to them. It was prepared with the view of inaugurating a new departure, of carrying into effect reforms which Hezekiah had made a vigorous attempt to introduce, but had failed. Such was the hostility of the masses, and such the influence of parties interested in opposing them, that "a violent and bloody reaction" followed under Manasseh, and "in Josiah's time the whole work had to be done again from the beginning" (p. 244). And yet a newly found book, purporting to be the Law of Moses, but which "had no external credentials" (p. 351), and which, if the facts be as alleged, every one must have known was not what it claimed to be, was at once accepted by Josiah, "to whom it was of no consequence to know the exact date and authorship of the book" (p. 363). One, at least, of its provisions was unwelcome to the priests (p. 362), but they raised no question as to the origin of a code so mysteriously discovered; and under its potent influence, regulations were readily carried into effect, which had been so stubbornly resisted before. And Ezra, it seems, met with similar success in introducing the Levitical Code after the exile. If Mr. Gladstone could but find some law-book in Dublin which had never been heard of before, how easily and amicably the whole Irish question might be settled!

But this use of the name of Moses, we are told, is simply "a legal fiction;" "in Israel all law was held to be derived from the teaching of Moses" (p. 385). Such a notion could not have arisen unless Moses really was the great legislator of the nation, and something more than the Ten Commandments was directly traceable to him. This of itself creates a presumption in favor of the Mosaic origin of the codes ascribed to him, unless there be good reason to the contrary. The instances which are adduced to show that customs or statutes of a later date were imputed to Moses, admit of no such interpretation, and could only be distorted to this end by one intent upon making out a case.[1]

[1] Prof. W. R. Smith says (p. 387): "A peculiarly clear case of this occurs in the law of war. According to I. Sam. xxx. 24, 25, the standing law of Israel as to the distribution of booty was enacted by David, and goes back only to a precedent in his war with the Amalekites who burned Ziklag. In the priestly legislation the same law is given as a Mosaic precedent from the war with Midian (Num. xxxi. 27)."

> The style in which the laws are framed, and the
> terms in which they are drawn up, point to the sojourn

The fact is, that Moses gave no law upon the subject whatever. It is simply related, as one of the incidents of the battle with Midian, that the prey was divided into two parts between them who went out to battle and all the congregation. The circumstances were peculiar, and no general rule was enacted. David did not divide the booty into two equal parts, but ordered that the two hundred who guarded the baggage should individually have like shares with the four hundred who engaged in the conflict; and the division was not, as Moses directed, between the army on the one hand and the people on the other, but between the two divisions of his little army, while to the people at large he simply sent presents. A more exact precedent is found in Josh. xxii. 8, though even in that instance no law was enacted. David made the first statute in relation to the matter; though some critic may be able to discover that even this is only a "legal fiction," that being attributed to David which was really originated by Judas Maccabeus, who gave an equal share of the spoils of the enemy to the feeble and needy classes (II. Macc. viii. 28, 30). In Ezra ix. 11, "where a law of the Pentateuch is cited as an ordinance of the Prophets" (p. 310), the Prophets are inclusive of Moses (Deut. xviii. 18; Hos. xii. 13), not distinguished from him.

It is further alleged (pp. 319, 432) that there are conflicting statements respecting the position of the Tabernacle with respect to the camp of Israel, only one of which can be true history, while the other must be later law veiled in historic form; but the apparent discrepancy is due to the interpreter, not to the text. It is brought about by the fashionable method of dissecting the Pentateuch, and then viewing the separate paragraphs in their isolation and without regard to their connection, or only so much regard to it as will choose variance, where that is possible, in preference to harmony. We protest against the entire procedure, notwithstanding the eminence and ability of those who indulge in it. It opens a boundless field for the display of the critic's ingenuity, but it is not rational interpretation, and would as easily create the semblance of self-contradiction in any author to whom it should be applied. If a meaning be given to Ex. xxxiii. 7–11 which it cannot bear in the connection in which it is found, but which it is assumed that it might have had in some other imaginable connection, — and especially if, with Dillman, the sense of vers. 1–6 be altered by

in the wilderness, prior to the occupation of Canaan, as the time when both the Levitical and the Deuter-

leaving out words or clauses *ad libitum*, — it may be made to appear that according to this passage, and a few others, the Sacred Tent stood outside of the camp; whereas it is elsewhere spoken of as pitched in the centre of the camp. But if we discard imaginary possibilities, and give to these verses their obvious sense as they stand, the alleged discrepancy disappears. Immediately after the ratification of God's covenant with Israel, Moses went up into the Mount and received direction to make a sanctuary in which God might dwell among His people. The sin of the Golden Calf ruptured the covenant and put an end to all proceedings under it. Without going on to construct the Tabernacle according to the specifications given him, he sets before the eyes of the people a visible sign of their altered relation to the Lord by pitching a provisional tabernacle outside of the camp, and at a distance from it, to signify that God would not remain in the midst of them (Ex. xxxiii. 3). It is called "*the* tabernacle" (ver. 7) because it is definitely conceived by the writer as the one used for the purpose, and which was well remembered by him and by his readers. (Compare the use of the Hebrew article in Ex. ii. 15; Num. xi. 27; Hab. ii. 2.) And it is possible, as the Septuagint assumes and many commentators have supposed, that *the* tent referred to is the one which had already attained a sacred character from its having been occupied by Moses in his capacity of the representative of God to the people, — to which they had come to inquire of God, and from which he had delivered the divine responses, adjudications, and laws (Ex. xviii. 13-16). Joshua, Moses' servant, though an Ephraimite, remained in the Tabernacle when Moses left it (xxxiii. 11), since the Levites had not yet been set apart to the service of the sanctuary. The Tabernacle is in this passage spoken of as the place of divine revelation (vers. 7, 9, 11), and no mention made of sacrifice for the simple reason that the Levitical ceremonial was not instituted at the Tabernacle until the structure for which directions were given on the Mount had first been built and set up (Ex. xl., Lev. i.). In Num. xi. 24, 26, 30; xii. 4, 5, persons are said to go out of the camp unto the Tabernacle, and out of the Tabernacle into the camp; but this does not prove the Tabernacle to have been outside of the camp. If a gentleman goes out of his yard into his house, it does not follow that his house is not in his yard. The camp considered as the abode of the people had its limits within as well as without. An open space, such

onomic codes were produced (Lev. xviii. 3; Deut. xii. 9). The standing designation of Canaan is, " The land which the Lord giveth thee to possess it" (Deut. xv. 4, 7; xxi. 1, 23). The laws look forward to the time "when thou art come into the land, etc., and shalt possess it"[1] (Deut. xvii. 14; Lev. xiv. 34, xix. 23, xxv. 2), or "when the Lord hath cut off these nations, and thou succeedest them and dwellest in their cities" (Deut. xix. 1), as the period when they are to go into full operation (Deut. xii. 1, 8, 9). The place of sacrifice is not where Jehovah has fixed His habitation, but "the place which Jehovah shall

as reverence required, separated the tents of the people from the Tent of God; and this must be traversed in passing from one to the other. It was just as natural under the circumstances for an Israelite to distinguish the camp from the sacred enclosure of the Tabernacle, as it is for a person in New York City to speak of driving out to Central Park, which is nevertheless within the city limits. So that all that the Professor tells us about early sanctuaries being outside of cities, and Ezekiel paving the way for the sanctuary being located in the midst of the people, is quite irrelevant. Num. x. 33 is adduced to prove that the Sanctuary was outside the camp when the people were on the march; but it makes no mention of the Sanctuary; it simply says that the Ark went before them, when they left Sinai, as their guide. And this is not in conflict with ver. 21. (Compare iv. 15-21.) To suppose such a contradiction within the compass of a few verses is to impute the most extraordinary heedlessness to the writer, or, if any prefer, the compiler of the book. While the Tabernacle and the sacred vessels had their place assigned them between the tribes as they moved forward, the Ark, which was the symbol and the seat of God's presence, was singled out, as we are expressly told, to lead the way.

[1] This is the case even in Deut. xix. 14, where the last clause of the verse makes it apparent that the setting of the landmarks did not precede the enacting of the Law. The Hebrew for "they of old time" means simply "first," and is applicable to those who originally marked the boundary, at whatever date.

choose to place His name there" (Deut. xii. 5, 10 ff., xiv. 23 ff., xvi. 2, 6 ff.). Israel is contemplated as occupying a camp (Lev. xvi. 26, 28, xxiv. 10, 14, 23; Num. v. 2–4, xii. 14, 15), and living in tents (Lev. xiv. 8; Deut. xvi. 7), and in the wilderness (Lev. xvi. 21, 22). The bullock of the sin-offering was to be burned without the camp (Lev. iv. 12, 21); the ashes from the altar were to be carried without the camp (vi. 11). The leper was to have his habitation without the camp (xiii. 46); the priest was to go forth out of the camp to inspect him (xiv. 3); ceremonies are prescribed for his admission to the camp (ver. 8), as well as the interval which must elapse before his return to his own tent. In slaying an animal for food the only possibilities suggested are that it may be in the camp or out of the camp (xvii. 3). The law of the consecration of priests respects by name Aaron and his sons (viii. 2 ff.). Silver trumpets were made to direct the calling of the assembly and the journeying of the camps (Num. x. 2 ff.). The ceremonies of the red heifer were to be performed without the camp (Num. xix. 3, 7, 9), and by Eleazar personally (vers. 3, 4). The law of purification provides simply for death in tents and in the open fields (vers. 14, 16). How differently laws are worded when framed specifically for a time of settled abodes may be seen from (Lev. xiv. 34 ff.) "house," "walls," "stones," "plaster," "without the city," etc. All this, and much more of the same sort, we must suppose to be "legal fiction;" but it would be too "artificial" (p. 321), in the Professor's view, to imagine that Moses could speak of himself in the third person, as Isaiah (vii. 3 ff.), Jeremiah (xxxvi. 4 ff.), Hosea (i. 2 ff.), and the evangelists Matthew (ix. 9) and John (xiii. 23) have done.[1]

This peculiarity of these laws carries with it the evidence that they were not only enacted during the sojourn in the wilderness, but that they were then committed to writing. Had they been preserved orally, the forms of expression would have been changed, insensibly, to adapt them to the circumstances of later times. It is only the unvarying permanence of a written code that could have perpetuated these laws in a form which no longer described directly and precisely the thing to be done,

[1] The Professor demands proof "that Moses would write such a verse" as Num. xii. 3. If Paul could say, comparing himself with the other apostles, " I labored more abundantly than they all," and John, without any imputation upon his modesty, could call himself "the disciple whom Jesus loved," is it altogether insupposable that Moses, who frankly relates his own backwardness to obey God's call (Ex. iv. 10 ff.), his neglect to circumcise his child (vers. 24-26), and the sin which excluded him from the Promised Land (Num. xx. 12), should refer with equal impartiality and in no boastful spirit to the unexampled meekness displayed by him under circumstances of extraordinary provocation? But if any deem it impossible that Moses could have penned such a statement about himself, however necessary to his own vindication and to the truth of history, it surely does not follow that Moses is not the author of the Pentateuch. Least of all can they, whose own theory rests on the assumption of an extended series of interpolations, and of emendations and additions *ad libitum*, by successive editors, object with any show of reason to the hypothesis that, in a very few instances, a word or a clause or a paragraph may have been inserted in the writings of Moses by some competent and duly authorized person for the sake of explanation, or of greater completeness of the record.

but must be mentally adapted to an altered state of affairs before it could be carried into effect.

But suppose that we yield our assent to this notion that the Israelites had the singular custom of issuing all their laws in the name of Moses, and that they continued to do so down to the time of Josiah and after the Exile, still expressing them as though Israel were encamped in the wilderness of Sinai or on the plains of Moab. It is true that no instance of the kind is recorded in any historical book of the Old Testament. David and Solomon and Jehoshaphat and Hezekiah issue their orders and enforce their regulations in their own name and by their own authority. Ezekiel, who, we are told, represents an intermediate stage between Deuteronomy and Leviticus, makes no pretence of Mosaic authority in all that he says respecting the Temple and its worship and the Holy Land. The idea of a legal fiction never dawned upon the author of the Books of Kings, who records the finding of the Law in the Temple, but has no suspicion of its recent origin. Let us, however, waive all objection on this ground. But the further insuperable difficulty remains that, by the hypothesis under consideration, laws are attributed to a period for which they have no meaning or fitness. Legislation, as Prof. W. R. Smith himself insists, and this is, in fact, the basis on which his whole argument professedly rests,— legislation must be adapted to the times in which it is issued. Its aim is practical; it concerns matters of present obligation, and its statutes are enacted with the view of being enforced and obeyed. Laws are never issued to regulate a state of things which has passed away ages before, and can by no possibility be revived. What are we to think, then, of a hypothesis which assigns the code of Deuteronomy to the reign of Josiah, or shortly before it, when its injunction to exterminate the Canaanites (xx. 16-18) and the Amalekites[1] (xxv. 17-19), who had long since disappeared, would be as utterly out of date as a law in New Jersey at the present time offering a bounty for killing wolves and bears, or a royal proclamation in Great Britain ordering the expulsion of the Danes? A law contemplating foreign conquests (xx. 10-15) would have been absurd when the urgent question was whether Judah could maintain its own existence against the encroachments of Babylon and Egypt. A law discriminating against Ammon and Moab (xxiii. 3, 4), in favor of Edom (vers. 7, 8), had its warrant in the Mosaic period, but not in the time of the later kings. Jeremiah discriminates precisely the other way, promising a future restoration to Moab (xlviii. 47) and Ammon (xlix. 6), which he denies to Edom (xlix. 17, 18), who is also to Joel (iii. 19), Obadiah, and Isaiah (lxiii. 1-6), the representative foe of the people of God. The special injunction to show no

[1] An insignificant remnant of this once powerful people seems to have survived in the secluded fastnesses of Mount Seir (I. Chron. iv. 42, 43), which five hundred Simeonites were competent to destroy. The date of this incident is not stated. It is mentioned in connection with a fact belonging to the reign of Hezekiah (ver. 41) and is probably to be referred to the same period; but the Amalekites had ceased to be formidable from the time of Saul and David.

unfriendliness to Egyptians (Deut. xxiii. 7) is insupposable in a code issued under prophetic influence at a time when the Prophets were doing everything in their power to dissuade the people from alliance or association with them (Isai. xxx. 1 ff., xxxi. 1 ; Jer. ii. 18, 36). The allusions to Egypt imply familiarity with and recent residence in that land; an impressive argument for obedience is drawn from the memory of bondage in Egypt (Deut. xxiv. 18, 22 ; compare ver. 9), or of deliverance from it (Deut. xiii. 5, 10, xx. 1 ; Lev. xix. 36, xxvi. 13 ; Num. xv, 41) ; warnings are pointed by a reference to the diseases of Egypt (Deut. vii. 15, xxviii. 60). And how can a code belong to the time of Josiah, which, while it contemplates the possible selection of a king in the future (Deut. xvii. 14 ff.), nowhere implies an actual regal government, but vests the supreme central authority in a judge and the priesthood (xvii. 8–12; xix. 17) ; which lays special stress on the requirements that the king must be a native and not a foreigner (xvii. 15), when the undisputed line of succession had for ages been fixed in the family of David, and that he must not " cause the people to return to Egypt " (ver. 16), as they seemed ready to do on every grievance in the days of Moses (Num. xiv. 4), but which no one ever dreamed of doing after they were fairly established in Canaan?[1]

[1] It would not be surprising, even on natural principles, for Moses to have anticipated that the people might some time desire a king, and to prohibit, in that event, the display and luxurious indulgence which characterize Oriental courts. That Samuel disapproved of the people's hankering after a king under circumstances which implied an un-

And it is quite as incongruous to place the Levitical law after the Exile. Professor Dillmann, though he conceives that "the Book of the Law did not receive its final form and arrangement until after the Exile and in the time of Ezra," nevertheless protests against the hypothesis as "irrational" that "the priestly laws and those of the cultus were first committed to writing, or actually first framed, in the Exile or in Babylonia, where no cultus whatever existed."[1] And then there are detailed accounts of the Mosaic Tabernacle, reciting the contribution of materials for its construction,[2] with minute specifications of the number and

timely setting aside of himself and a want of confidence in God (1. Sam. viii. 7, 8; x. 18, 19), does not imply that the law in Deuteronomy was unknown to him. On the contrary, the author of the Book of Samuel plainly shows that it was then in existence, or that he believed that it was, by the allusions to it, or the adoption of its language, in this very narrative: *e. g.*, 1. Sam. viii. 3, "took bribes and perverted judgment," (compare Deut. xvi. 19); ver. 5, "make us a king . . . like all the nations," (compare Deut. xvii. 14); x. 24, "him whom the LORD hath chosen," (compare Deut. xvii. 15); xii. 14, "obey his voice and not rebel against the commandment of the LORD" (compare Deut. ix. 23; i. 43). The Hebrew expressions in these several passages are identical, even where the English version varies. Solomon's violation of the law only shows how men may and do transgress known law under strong temptation. And he may have palliated his offence as not contravening the real spirit and intent of the statute. His numerous alliances gave stability to his kingdom, and assurance of peace with surrounding nations, and he could surely avoid the snare of their idolatry. He amassed silver and gold, but he spent vast sums on the Temple. He multiplied horses for the sake of adding to his military strength, but he had no thought of taking the people back to Egypt. Compare Isaiah's description of a like state of things under Uzziah (Isai. ii. 6, 7).

[1] "Die Bücher Exodus und Leviticus," Vorwort, p. viii.

[2] Delitzsch, in his Preface to Professor Curtiss's valuable treatise on "The Levitical Priests," notes the interesting circumstance that the

dimensions of its boards, their sockets and tenons and bars, of its various coverings and the mode of their preparation, and how they are to be joined by loops and taches, of its various articles of furniture, and the instruments of the service, and precise directions as to the manner in which they should be wrapped, and by whom they should be carried, and what place they should have in the ranks during the journeyings through the wilderness. All this is stated with the utmost precision, and every particular insisted upon as of real consequence. And we are asked to believe that this is all a fiction of the time of Ezra and of the Second Temple, when it could serve no imaginable purpose. Prof. W. R. Smith tells us (p. 357), "It is very noteworthy and, on the traditional view, quite inexplicable that the Mosaic sanctuary of the Ark is never mentioned in the Deuteronomic Code." It is mentioned in Deut. x. 1–8, not to speak of xxxi. 9, 25, 26; and, by the common consent of critics, the whole book of Deuteronomy is one in its language, its character, and its aims. But why any one should expect the Ark to be mentioned in a code which had no occasion to speak of it, we are not informed. It is, however, much more inexplicable, on the Professor's own hypothesis, that the Ark is described in such detail and such prominence given to it in the Levitical Code (Ex. xxv. 10–22, etc.), if this was prepared for the guidance of

original words for "fine linen, purple, and scarlet," which reappear so often in the Mosaic description of the sanctuary, are the ancient Hebrew terms, and not their Aramaic equivalents which are found in writings after the Exile.

the priests and the conduct of the ritual in the days of Ezra; whereas the Ark perished in the destruction of the First Temple, and was not reproduced subsequently. And why should directions be given about the Urim and Thummim (Ex. xxviii. 30; Num. xxvii. 21), which had ceased to be of any practical account (Ezra ii 63; Neh. vii. 65)?

Now, what is there to hinder us from believing the laws of the Pentateuch to be the production of Moses, as they claim to be, and as their style and contents declare them to be? Prof. W. R. Smith, enlightens us upon this point (p. 333):—

"It is a very remarkable fact, to begin with, that all the sacred law of Israel is comprised in the Pentateuch, and that, apart from the Levitical legislation, it is presented in codified form. On the traditional view, three successive bodies of law were given to Israel within forty years. Within that short time many ordinances were modified, and the whole law of Sinai recast on the plains of Moab. But from the days of Moses there was no change. With his death the Israelites entered on a new career, which transformed the nomads of Goshen into the civilized inhabitants of vineyard-land and cities in Canaan. But the divine laws given them beyond Jordan were to remain unmodified through all the long centuries of development in Canaan, an absolute and immutable code. I say, with all reverence, that this is impossible."

The idea of development is in the air; and yet it is possible that it may be applied to some things that do not call for it and will not admit of it. The "nomads of Goshen" had been settled for more than four centuries under the government of the most highly civilized and the most thoroughly organized empire in the ancient world. They were employed in building treasure-cities for Pharaoh (Ex. i. 11), in the manufacture of brick (Ex. v. 7 ff.), in masonry, and in all manner of service in the field (Ex. i. 14). They were skilled in working metals, carving wood, and engraving gems (Ex. xxxi. 2 ff., xxxv. 30 ff.), in spinning, weaving, and embroidery (Ex. xxxv. 25, 26). Their familiarity with the cultivation of the soil is attested not only by such statements as Num. xi. 5, xx. 5 and Deut. xi. 10, but by the express provisions of what the Professor himself regards as their oldest extant code of laws (Ex. xxii. 5, 6), including the regulations respecting first-fruits (xxii. 29, xxiii. 19), the weekly Sabbath (xxiii. 12, xxxiv. 21), the sabbatical year (xxiii. 10, 11), the festivals of the harvest and the ingathering (xxiii. 15, 16), not to speak of the requirement of the shew-bread and of the meat and drink offerings. The Israel of the exodus could not, therefore, have been at so great a remove from "the civilized inhabitants of the vineyard-land and cities in Canaan." Even though the Mosaic Tabernacle were to be remanded to the region of fable, it would still be true that tradition attributed the arts employed in its construction to the generation that left Egypt, and the monuments of that land lend this abundant corroboration. But enough besides remains to rivet our conclusion, which even the wildest criticism must respect, unless it would destroy the whole basis on which it can rest itself, and deny that there is any certainty as to the condition of the Israelites under Moses, in which case the entire objection is admitted to be groundless.

And where habits and manners remain fixed, as they proverbially do in the East, there could be little reason for change in the laws of the simple agricultural population of Palestine, eschewing as they did all foreign trade or travel, and holding so limited intercourse with other nations. Even through all changes in the national government, the tribal organization continued at least until the time of the Exile, the usages of society underwent little alteration, and the affairs of each community were managed very much in the same manner from age to age.

But the objection is completely neutralized when we consider further that the Mosaic Code leaves abundant room for all the modifications that could be demanded by the progressive life of the people. It is not, and was not intended to be, a complete system of political institutions; and objections have been made to it on this very ground of its lack of completeness, urging that it could never have been put in actual operation without the supply of some important gaps in the legislation. The fact is, that the Mosaic regulations presuppose and were super-induced upon an already existing political constitution and customs that had the force of laws. The aim of Moses simply was to establish and perpetuate the covenant relation between Israel and Jehovah. It was not to give fixity to one particular system of civil administration, but to incorporate and express religious ideas in the national life. Hence, some of his laws are purely ethical, and were not intended to be enforced by the magistrate: (Ex. xxii. 21–24, xxiii. 2, 3, 9; Deut. xv. 5, 6, xvi. 20, xix. 8, 9, xxiv. 13, 15). The specific regulations which they contain were adopted or modified, as the case might be, from pre-existing usages. And all that was not expressly ordained by divine sanction was left free either to remain as it was, or to shape itself as circumstances might require or as the principles of the Mosaic religion and constitution might suggest. There was abundant flexibility here, and all the opportunity for development that could be desired. Thus submission to rulers is inculcated (Ex. xxii. 28) without prescribing any definite form of government. The authority of elders (Num. xi. 16), princes (Num. xxxii. 2, xxxvi. 1), and other existing officials is recognized, but there is nothing to require that public functionaries should preserve this unvarying type. A monarchy was contemplated in the future, but was not enjoined; it was left entirely to the wishes of the people and the course of events; and when the time arrived, the transition was made without a jar. Moses, acting under a present necessity, created judges and based his appointment on a decimal division of the people (Ex. xviii. 21, 22); but this particular form of organization is not once mentioned in his codes of laws, much less perpetuated by express divine sanction. In Ex. xxi. 6, xxii. 8, 9, to come before the legitimate tribunal is to come before God; but who should be clothed with judicial functions, and how

these should be exercised, is not specified. The
Deuteronomic Code directs that there shall be judges
in every city (xvi. 18), and that the ultimate decision
of controversies shall lie with the priests and the
judge at the religious centre of the nation (xvii.
8–12); but the terms are general, and Jehoshaphat
was not hindered from enlarging the judiciary in accordance with the needs of his own time (II. Chron.
xix. 5, 8).

The three codes of law above mentioned belong,
it is claimed, to different periods in Israel's history,
and represent distinct grades of social culture and
development, and, particularly, successive stages in
their religious advancement. Prof. W. R. Smith tells
us that "in the first legislation the question of correct ritual has little prominence" (p. 343), and it
"presupposes a plurality of sanctuaries" (p. 352).
The Law of Deuteronomy, on the other hand, is "a
law for the abolition of the local sanctuaries, as they
are recognized by the first legislation" (p. 353).
"The first legislation has no law of priesthood, no
provision as to priestly dues." It "assumes the right
of laymen to offer sacrifice," and "presupposes a
priesthood whose business lies less with sacrifice than
with the divine Torah, which they administer in the
sanctuary as successors of Moses, — for the sanctuary
is the seat of judgment." This priesthood consisted
of the entire body of the Levites, who were "priests
of local sanctuaries" throughout the whole land (pp.
358, 359). "Deuteronomy also knows no Levites
who cannot be priests, and no priests who are not

Levites;" and, in abolishing the local sanctuaries, it makes provision for the priests who had previously ministered in them (p. 360). But "Deuteronomy knows nothing of a sacrificial priestly Torah" (p. 371), such as the Levitical Code. According to this hypothesis, then, these three codes severally represent three periods in the religion of Israel. The first sanctions various local sanctuaries where laymen offer sacrifice, and where the Levites — who are indiscriminately clothed with priestly prerogatives — administer judgment. Deuteronomy, which belongs to a later time, restricts worship to one sanctuary, whose priests consequently rise to new dignity, while the Levites previously ministering elsewhere are now thrown out of occupation, and, in the need to which they are reduced, special provision must be made for their support. The fully developed ritual of Leviticus belongs to a period later still.

This is about as rational as though some critic were to deal with the Constitution of the United States in a similar manner, erecting its several articles into distinct codes, assigning them to different periods of the national history, and inferring from them that different forms of government have successively prevailed. The article upon the Executive treats only of a President and Vice-President as entrusted with power, and seems to represent a sort of elective monarchy in which rude tribes summon one of their chieftains to the supreme command. Then the article upon the Judiciary places control in a body of judges, who hold office during life or good behavior, and thus represents a later aristocratic stage. And, finally, the article which confers legislative authority upon Congress must have originated at a still later date, when popular ideas came into vogue, and the government was lodged with representatives elected by the people. This method of treating a system of laws, whose different parts are mutually supplementary, as though they were distinct and independent codes, can only lead to distortion and misconception.

It is the fashion now to ridicule the harmonistic treatment of the Mosaic laws, and the development theory is all the rage. Nevertheless, every one must concede that if, upon any fair interpretation of their language, these laws can be shown to be mutually consistent and harmonious, this is entitled to the preference over any view which represents them as incompatible and conflicting. And even where the law has been changed in any of its provisions, and a later statute abrogates or modifies another given previously, this may still be consistent with the Mosaic record, provided it admits of a satisfactory explanation from the different times and circumstances under which the law was given, and the different ends which it was intended to subserve. Unless variations should be found which it is impossible to account for in any other way, it is gratuitous and unwarrantable to assume that any of the laws ascribed to Moses are really of later date.

To prove that a plurality of sanctuaries is presupposed in the first legislation, appeal is made to

Ex. xx. 24, 25 and to xxii. 30. The former of these passages can only afford an argument by putting a sense upon it which the words do not require, which is at variance with every other utterance of Hebrew law upon the subject, and which disregards the circumstances under which these words were spoken. It is the primary law of the Hebrew altar, given at Sinai, before the Tabernacle was built, as preliminary to concluding the covenant between Jehovah and Israel (Ex. xxiv. 4). It directs the erection of an altar of earth or stone, and promises God's presence and blessing, not wherever they might choose to erect such an altar, but in every place[1] where God should record His name, that is, make a manifestation of His being. (Compare Deut. xii. 5, etc.) This was their warrant for building an altar at Sinai, where He had so conspicuously manifested Himself, and at every future place of supernatural revelation, including the Tabernacle which they carried with them in their journeyings through the wilderness; for the wooden frame described Ex. xxvii. 1 ff. took its name from the altar of earth which it enclosed. It is not coexisting sanctuaries in Canaan, but altars successively reared at different places in the Wilderness, that are contemplated by the passage under consideration. Unless it can be shown that God "recorded His name" in various places at once, no sanction is here given to a multiplicity of altars. It was so even in

---

[1] The plural form in the authorized version (Ex. xx. 24) "in all places," which might seem to lend some color to plurality of sanctuaries, does not accurately represent the Hebrew.

patriarchal days, in the Holy Land itself. Abraham, Isaac, and Jacob built altars and offered sacrifices at their successive places of abode; but they did not establish rival sanctuaries to be simultaneously occupied.

And Ex. xxii. 30 is quite as little to the purpose: the firstling of ox or sheep " shall be seven days with his dam; on the eighth day thou shalt give it Me." This is commonly understood to mean that it was sufficiently mature for sacrifice by its eighth day (Lev. xxii. 27). Its presentation at the Sanctuary, though admissible on that day, may have been postponed to one of the annual feasts, perhaps the Passover, with which it is associated in Ex. xxxiv. 18–20, which is universally admitted to belong to the most ancient legislation. The law before us will then be substantially identical with that in Deut. xv. 20, which enjoins that it should be eaten at the Sanctuary year by year. If, however, this very natural explanation be rejected, and it be insisted that the first legislation differs from Deuteronomy in requiring that the firstling should be sacrificed on its eighth day, still there is no need of supposing a reference to local sanctuaries in Palestine, accessible to every neighborhood. The law was given at Sinai, and regulated the presentation of the first-born in the wilderness, where all Israel was encamped in the vicinity of the Tabernacle. When they were about to enter Canaan the old law was replaced by one in Deuteronomy, adapted to the changed circumstances. And while there is nothing in the first legislation implying a plurality of sanctuaries, the three annual pilgrimages enjoined to "the House of the LORD" (Ex. xxiii. 17, 19), on the contrary, very decidedly imply its unity.[1]

It is further charged that there is a serious discrepancy between Deuteronomy and the Levitical Law in respect to the priesthood: that according to the former all Levites are priests, and have an equal right to perform priestly functions and share the priestly revenues (pp. 360, 436), while in the latter none are priests but Aaron and his sons, and the Levites are servants or attendants upon the priests. All that is plausible in this representation arises from the assumption that Deuteronomy is a body of laws complete in itself; whereas it is really attached to and co-ordinated with the legislation of the preceding books. The mutual relations of priests and Levites and the special functions of each are developed at length in the Levitical Law, which made it unnecessary to repeat the same things in Deuteronomy. Prof. W. R. Smith freely concedes the difference in subject and aim between these two bodies of legislation.[2]

---

[1] The allegation that "the asylum for the man-slayer, in Ex. xxi. 12-14, is Jehovah's altar," whereas "under the law of Deuteronomy, there are to be three fixed Cities of Refuge," can hardly be seriously meant in the face of the distinct reference to the future appointment of Cities of Refuge in the passage in Exodus.

[2] "The first legislation and the code of Deuteronomy take the land of Canaan as their basis. They give directions for the life of Jehovah's people in the land He gives them. The Levitical legislation starts from the Sanctuary and the priesthood. Its object is to develop the theory of a religious life which has its centre in the Sanctuary, and is ruled by principles of holiness radiating forth from Jehovah's dwelling-place. The first two legislations deal with Israel as a nation; in

All that specially relates to the ordinances of worship and the ministers of religion finds its place in the former rather than in the latter.

In matters of this description Deuteronomy makes explicit reference to pre-existing laws. In xxiv. 8, 9 there is direct allusion to the Law of Leprosy previously given (Lev. xiii., xiv.), with an injunction to obey it, and mention of the case of Miriam which had arisen under it (Num. xii.). The introductory portion of Deuteronomy is filled with arguments and earnest exhortations based upon the antecedent history of Israel, which find their only illustration in the preceding books. Deut. x. 8, 9; xviii. 1, 2, speak of duties previously assigned and support allotted to the tribe of Levi, with specific reference in each case to former declarations on the subject, and a verbal quotation from Num. xviii. 20, the context of which clearly defines the relative status of priests and Levites. Deut. xi. 6 appeals to the overthrow of Dathan and Abiram (Num. xvi.), which the critics have not yet succeeded in disentangling from the uprising of the Levite Korah against the special prerogatives of the Aaronic priesthood. The removal (Deut. xii. 15) of the restriction requiring every animal slain for food to be presented at the Sanctuary, is a plain allusion to the law (Lev. xvii. 3 ff.) which could only have been enacted in the Wilderness, as its very terms imply, and was an important safeguard against idolatry

the third, Israel is a church, and as such is habitually addressed as a Congregation ('*ēdah*), a word characteristic of the Levitical Law" (p. 318).

as the people were then situated. It was obviously impracticable in Canaan,[1] however, and is therefore formally abrogated before their entrance into the promised land. The blessing of Levi (Deut. xxxiii. 8–11) abounds in allusions to the preceding history and enactments. Deuteronomy thus, by its own express statements, recognizes the existence and binding authority of a more detailed antecedent legislation respecting matters to which it only alludes in a brief and summary manner.

It is to be observed further that Deuteronomy does distinguish between priests and Levites. In xviii. 1 "all the tribe of Levi" is a superfluous addition to the standing phrase, "the priests the Levites," if it is simply co-extensive in signification. (Compare Neh. xi. 20: "Israel, the priests, the Levites.") The intention manifestly is to affirm, both of the priests and of the entire tribe to which they belong, that they are without inheritance. Accordingly in the following verses statements are made respecting first the priest (vers. 3–5), then the Levite (vers. 6–8). And throughout the entire book, wherever priests are spoken of, the functions ascribed to them are either those assigned to the priests in the Levitical Law, or are entirely consistent with them; while on the contrary,

---

[1] Even the local sanctuaries, by which the Professor seeks to account for it, would not render it tolerable. And a plurality of sanctuaries is inconsistent with the express requirement of the law in question (Lev. xvii. 4, 5), which recognizes but one sanctuary, "the Tabernacle of the Congregation," and places offering sacrifices there in contrast with offering them elsewhere. If the unity of the Sanctuary is insisted upon anywhere in the Levitical Law, this is the case here.

the Levite is in repeated passages (*e. g.*, xiv. 29) associated with needy or dependent classes as like them an object of generous beneficence. The distinction between Levitical priests and Levites generally is also made in xxvii. 9, 12, 14. The priests of this book, as all admit, are those of the tribe of Levi who discharge priestly functions, and are distinguished from those Levites who do not. But who in the tribe are privileged to be priests? Deut. x. 6 tells us that Aaron was priest, and his son succeeded him. The Levitical Law declares that the priesthood was limited to Aaron's family. The critics infer from Deut. xviii. 6 that any Levite, who is disposed to do so, may become a priest by presenting himself at the Sanctuary and claiming the right to exercise priestly functions. We think it more reasonable to understand the verse in a manner which is equally consistent with its language, and is moreover in harmony with the Levitical Law, viz: that any Levite, whether belonging to the seed of Aaron or not, is privileged to go to the Sanctuary and perform such ministrations as are allowed to Levites of the same grade; if of priestly stock, he may act as priest; if not, he may perform those subordinate offices which are allowed to Levites.[1]

The characteristic expression for the priests in the Book of Deuteronomy is "the priests the Levites," or rather, as the words should be rendered, "the Levitical priests" (xvii. 9, 18, xviii. 1, xxiv. 8, xxvii.

---

[1] Ministering to the LORD was a function of the Levites as well as the priests (1. Chron. xv. 2; see also 1. Sam. ii. 11, 18, iii. 1).

9). In Leviticus and Numbers this phrase is never employed, but we find instead "the priests, the sons of Aaron" (Lev. i. 5, 8, 11, ii. 2, iii. 2, xiii. 2, xxi. 1; Num. iii. 3, x. 8). This striking difference, however, involves no real discrepancy, for the sons of Aaron were of course Levites; and " Levitical priests " no more proves that priests and Levites are convertible terms than " Egyptian priests " would imply that all Egyptians were or, if they chose, might be priests. This expression is, moreover, found in books where the distinctions of the Levitical Law are plainly recognized.[1] The occurrence in the preceding books of the Pentateuch of the expression "the priests the sons of Aaron," along with such phrases as "Aaron the priest," "the sons of Aaron the priest," "Eleazar the priest," etc., is altogether natural, because these were the persons who filled the office at the time, and to whom the divine directions were immediately given; just as we read in later times of " Eli the priest," " the sons of Eli the priest," etc. (1. Sam. i. 3, 9), when these are the persons intended. In Deuteronomy, however, which gives no personal directions to individuals, but contemplates the priests of the future as a body, a general designation, such as Levitical priests, was more appropriate.[2]

---

[1] Thus Josh. iii. 3, viii. 33 (compare xxi. 4 ff., "the children of Aaron the priest which were of the Levites"); also II. Chron. v. 5 (where the Professor accepts the reading, "the Levite priests," in preference to that in the parallel passage, I. Kings viii. 4, "the priests and the Levites," p. 436), xxiii. 18, xxx. 27, where the sense plainly shows the insertion of "and" to be inadmissible.

[2] That there is nothing in this phraseology to warrant the conclu-

That priestly functions should be attributed to the
sions which the critics would have us draw from it, is apparent from a simple inspection of the facts of the case. In the Book of Leviticus "priest" occurs without any qualifying epithet or any name in apposition with it 176 times, the plural "priests" four times, and "high priest" once. In Lev. viii.–x., the consecration of Aaron and his sons, and the penalty inflicted upon Nadab and Abihu for their transgression, "priest" does not occur, but we find instead "Aaron" fourteen times, "Aaron's sons" seven times, "Aaron and his sons" thirteen times, evidently for the reason that these are the persons whom the narrative concerns. In Lev. xvi., the institution of the Day of Atonement, after an allusion to the death of Aaron's two sons, Aaron is mentioned eight times as the person charged with conducting the services of the day. It is only at the close of the chapter, ver. 32, that "the priest who shall be anointed, and shall be consecrated to minister in the priest's office in his father's stead," is spoken of as the future celebrant. In Ex. xxvii.–xxxi. we read constantly of "Aaron" (fifteen times), "Aaron's sons" (twice), or "Aaron and his sons" (twenty-two times); "Aaron and his sons shall order the lamp," "holy garments for Aaron and his sons," "Aaron shall bear the names of the children of Israel," etc.; only once "Aaron the priest," xxxi. 10, and once "that son that is priest in his stead," xxix. 30. In Lev. i.–vii. "Aaron and his sons" (ten times) and "Aaron's sons" (six times) interchange with "the priest," the writer passing readily and naturally from the names of those who held the office to the term descriptive of the office itself. It would not have been surprising if he had combined the name and the office more frequently than he has done; but the fact is, that in the entire Book of Leviticus "Aaron the priest" occurs but three times, "the priests Aaron's sons" five times, "the sons of Aaron the priest" once, and "his sons" (meaning Aaron's) joined with "priest" or "priests" twice. The form of expression is evidently governed by the fact that the persons then composing the priestly order were present to the writer's thoughts. And laws drawn up in this form thereby give evidence that they were both enacted and committed to writing in the lifetime of Aaron and his sons.

In the Deuteronomic code "priest" or "priests" with no qualifying epithet occurs seven times; and "the priests the Levites" (or "the sons of Levi") five times, or (if we include xxvii. 9 and xxxi. 9, which are outside of the code proper as defined above) seven times in the tribe of Levi[1] (x. 8, xxxiii. 8, 10), because they were entrusted to a particular family in that tribe, is by the entire book. In Moses' final address, which looks forward over the entire future of Israel, it would have been out of place to speak of the individual priests then living. Why should he say Eleazar or Ithamar or Phinehas the priest, when the priestly order for all time was meant? and he could not say Aaron the priest, for Aaron was already dead. What was more natural under the circumstances than that the priests should simply be referred to the sacred tribe to which they belonged? There is nothing here that requires for its explanation the peculiarities of a distinct writer, nor a change in the constitution of the priesthood. The character of the address of Moses, and the circumstances under which it was delivered, amply account for the difference between the language used in it and in Leviticus. If the late Emperor of the French, in his attempt to reorganize the Mexican government by placing the Archduke of Austria upon the throne, had drawn up a paper for his personal guidance, in which he was throughout spoken of as "Maximilian" and "a descendant of Charles V.," and in his convention with Mexico upon the subject had simply styled him "the Emperor of Mexico," without adding his personal name, what would there be in this difference of designation to cast suspicion upon the authenticity of either document, or to warrant the inference that they belong to different periods of time?

[1] The Professor is mistaken in saying (p. 437) that according to "Deut. xviii. 1 *seq.* the whole tribe of Levi has a claim on the altar gifts, the first fruits, and other priestly offerings." This belongs to the priests, as explicitly appears from vers. 3-5; the Levites have a share in the Lord's inheritance (ver. 1). What this embraces is not defined here, but is assumed as known from the Levitical Law. When the Lord promises to be their inheritance, He surely does not design that the only subsistence of the entire tribe, except those who were on duty at the Sanctuary, should be such occasional invitations as they might receive to religious festivals (Deut. xvi. 14, xxvi. 11, 12). This necessarily implies the Levitical tithe, of which the Professor says "Deuteronomy knows nothing;" and "the patrimony" referred to in ver. 8 implies the Levitical cities, notwithstanding the fact that at the date to which he has seen fit to assign Deuteronomy they "lay outside the kingdom of Judah." The list given of these cities in Josh. xxi., the Professor tells us, is "really part of the Levitical Law," which on

same familiar use of language as, in Gen. xlix. 10, the sceptre is ascribed to Judah because wielded by the royal line of David; or as we might speak of the house of Hanover as reigning in England because a member of that family is seated on the throne; or of the American troops at the siege of Yorktown, without naming the particular colonies which were represented there.

"The increased provision for the priesthood," which, we are told (p. 440) is "one of the chief innovations of the Ritual Law," is a sheer creation of the critics. If by one section of a law a given officer is allowed certain fees for specific services, and another section assigns him a regular salary, critics of the modern school would infer that these sections are separate laws which were in operation at differ-

his theory is post-exilic; only he does not explain the puzzle that thirty-five cities are assigned to the Levites, and but thirteen to the priests, though, as he informs us in another place (p. 383), "on the return from captivity very few Levites in comparison with the full priests cared to attach themselves to the Temple (Neh. vii. 39, *seq.*)." That Gezer, though assigned to the Levites, was not conquered till the time of Solomon (p. 441), only shows what appears equally from other cases, that the entire land was divided among the tribes before all of it had been wrested from the Canaanites. That citizens of other tribes were joint occupants of some of these cities with the Levites, merely proves that the latter were not numerous enough to fill all the places allotted to them. That Abiathar could own a field in Anathoth, and Jeremiah buy one, is no infraction of law (p. 428), whether a plot of ground in the city is meant (Lev. xxv. 33), or a field in the suburbs, which could not indeed be sold so as to be even temporarily alienated from the tribe (ver. 34), but may, for all that we know, have been to a greater or less extent parcelled amongst individual owners, as was the case in the priestly city of Beth-shemesh, 1. Sam. vi. 14, 18; Josh. xxi. 16.

ent periods, and that the latter belongs to a time when these officials were more generously dealt with than they had been previously. The proper legal provision for the priests and Levites is fully stated in the Levitical Law. Deuteronomy does not deal with this subject in any professed or formal way; it only incidentally makes mention of certain perquisites which they should receive, or attentions which should be shown them.[1] And he who can find a

[1] It is not surprising if we find it difficult to adjust some of the particulars in a system of legislation belonging to so remote a period, and to a state of things so different from our own. Jurists are sometimes in doubt as to the precise meaning of legislators in modern times; but in such cases they never admit a discrepancy if there is any rational way of avoiding it. If critics would adopt the same rule, which is a simple dictate of common sense, they would find fewer perplexities. In Num. xviii. 18 the flesh of the firstlings is the priests'; in Deut. xv. 19, 20 the offerer is to eat it before the Lord with his household, "the priest of course receiving," as the Professor correctly suggests, "the usual share of each victim." In this class of victims the priest received the whole; but why might he not return to the offerer all that was needed for his sacrificial meal? The direction to the offerer to hold such a festival is an injunction to the priests to supply him with what was requisite for the purpose. There is a difference, however, which, in the Professor's judgment, "cannot be explained away, for according to Deut. xiv. 24 the firstlings might be turned into money, and materials of a feast bought with them; but in Num. xviii. 17, it is forbidden to redeem any firstlings fit for sacrifice." But the thing prohibited and the thing allowed are quite distinct. The owner would "redeem" his firstling if he paid an estimated sum and retained the animal himself; this might be a temptation to cupidity, to cheapen the estimate, and thus pay an inadequate sum. But where the distance from the Sanctuary was so great as to make literal transportation of the animal thither impossible or onerous, its alienation by an honest sale freed the owner from any selfish temptation, and the consecration of its equivalent in money fulfilled the spirit of the statute. The alleged discrepancy in tithes is removed by observing that the tithe spoken of in

discrepancy in this, must have a very keen critical sense.

But it is alleged that there are no traces of the Pentateuchal Law in the historical and other books of the Old Testament until ages after the death of Moses; and that both the facts of the history and the statements of the sacred writers are inconsistent with the existence of Deuteronomy before Josiah, or the Levitical Law before Ezra. Of course if this is so, the Mosaic authorship of the Law must be abandoned; but, on the other hand, if that Law is distinctly traceable through all the post-Mosaic history and writings, its genuineness is completely vindicated.

How, then, stands the evidence? The Professor begins his investigation by summarily ruling out two

---

Deuteronomy is quite distinct from that in Leviticus and Numbers. It was additional to it, and was appropriated to a different purpose. The Jews paid both tithes, as there is abundant evidence; a burden to which they would not have submitted, if this had not been believed to be the meaning of the law, whether it was enacted after the Exile or was ordained by Moses. "The priest's share of a sacrifice in Deuteronomy consists of inferior parts." But this, so far from conflicting with the more ample provision made for them in the Levitical Law, necessarily implies the existence of that provision. The distinguished position assigned to priests in Deuteronomy, as the Lord's ministers and the highest judicial authority in the land, forbids the idea that a miserable pittance was doled out for their support. The perquisite in Deut. xviii. 3 is a special allowance from every animal slain for sacred purposes; the phrase rendered "offer a sacrifice" has a broader meaning than the regular sacrifices properly so called, and has even been supposed by some to embrace all animals slain for food. It is probably intended to indemnify the priests for the change made (Deut. xii. 15) in the Law of Sacrifice, as a substitute for what they received as their due when no animal was allowed to be slain even for domestic purposes elsewhere than at the Sanctuary.

important witnesses (p. 218): "I exclude the Book of Joshua, because it, in all its parts, hangs closely together with the Pentateuch." It is our only source of information respecting the period immediately succeeding the life of Moses; but, as it carries the "legal fiction" through another generation, it is untrustworthy and must be abandoned. "And, on the other hand, I exclude for the present the narrative of Chronicles, which was written long after the reformation of Ezra, and has not the character of a primary source for the earlier history." It claims to be based on early contemporary records, which Prof. Robertson Smith admits to be the case with "the historical books from Judges to Kings." It names its sources, which were still accessible to its readers, and appeals to them in verification of its statements; so that its acceptance under these circumstances as a reliable history, and especially its admission to the canon, assure us that there has been no tampering with the facts. Chronicles, written after the Exile, when the people were zealously engaged in restoring the institutions of their fathers, concerns itself largely with the history of worship. Samuel and Kings, though covering the same period of the history, were written with a different aim, and omit much upon this subject which Chronicles records. Does the silence of the former outweigh the positive declarations of the latter, and justify their being set aside as pure invention or as Levitical sermonizing [1] (p. 420)?

[1] We cannot here turn aside to answer the specific objections made to the truth and reliability of Chronicles further than to say that they

However, let Joshua and Chronicles be excluded; what is the testimony of the remaining books? And first let us inquire respecting the period immediately succeeding Joshua — that of the Judges. In Judg. xix. 18 the Levite says, "I am going," not to one of the houses of the Lord, but " to the House of the Lord," as if he knew of but one; and this was near his residence " in the recesses of Mount Ephraim." From xviii. 31 we learn more definitely that "the House of God was in Shiloh," where " the Tabernacle of the Congregation " had been set up in the time of Joshua (Josh. xviii. 1, xix. 51), and where it had accordingly continued since. It is not here stated with exactness how much longer it remained there, — other passages give information upon this point, — but that it was a considerable period, appears from its measuring the duration of the worship of Micah's graven image in Dan. "The Feast of the LORD"[1] was also

all rest on the unproved assumption that the only sources accessible to the writer were the books of Samuel and Kings; so that everything additional to or varying from their statements falls under the suspicion of being inference, conjecture, or pure invention.

[1] Interpreters have not been agreed whether this was the Passover or the Feast of Tabernacles. Prof. W. R. Smith says of it (p. 257): "This appears to have been a vintage feast, like the Pentateuchal Feast of Tabernacles, for it was accompanied by dancers in the vineyards (Judg. xxi. 21); and, according to the correct rendering of 1. Sam. i. 20, 21, it took place when the new year came in, that is, at the close of the agricultural year, which ended with the ingathering of the vintage (Ex. xxxiv. 22)." If the considerations which he adduces have any force, it was so very "like the Pentateuchal feast" as to be identical with it. The characteristic expression borrowed from Ex. xxxiv. 22 implies acquaintance with that law of the three Mosaic festivals, and makes it strange that the Professor should say, in the very same para-

annually observed in Shiloh (xxi. 19). The people came to the Ark to inquire of the LORD (Judg. xx. 27; compare Ex. xxv. 22). This most sacred article of the Mosaic Tabernacle (Ex. xxv. 10 ff.) is called by its ancient name "the Ark of the Covenant" (Num. x. 33, xiv. 44), implying that it contained the Tables of the Covenant (Ex. xxxiv. 28), as Moses had directed (Ex. xxv. 21; Deut. x. 1–5). It had been taken to Bethel (wrongly translated "the House of God," Judg. xx. 18, 26, 31, xxi. 2), temporarily as appears from xx. 27, that it might be near the scene of conflict at Gibeah (ver. 31), as was done in later times in the battle with the Philistines (1. Sam.

---

graph, that Shiloh was visited "not three times a year according to the Pentateuchal Law, but at an annual feast." Especially as on a subsequent page (341) he affirms in evidence of the existence and operation of the first legislation at this very time: "The annual feasts — at least that of the autumn, which seems to have been best observed — are often alluded to. . . . The proof that this law was known and acknowledged in all its leading provisions is as complete as the proof that the Levitical Law was still unheard of." We think it is a great deal more complete. But let that pass. The first legislation enjoins the three annual feasts (Ex. xxiii. 14 ff.) as explicitly and emphatically as the law of Deuteronomy and Leviticus. Either the three festivals were observed at this time, and then his suggestion of a departure from Pentateuchal Law is gratuitous, or the neglect of some of the festivals on his own admission does not disprove the existence of the law requiring them. The Professor may choose either alternative. When he says of the feast at Shiloh, "It had not a strictly national character, for in Judg. xxi. 19 it appears to be only locally known, and to have the character of a village festival," all the seeming plausibility of his remark arises from an inaccuracy in the Authorized Version. "There is a feast of the Lord" should be "The feast of the Lord is," etc. The idolatrous parallel in Shechem (Judg. ix. 27) is nothing to the purpose.

iv. 3), in the hope that the words of Moses (Num. x. 35) might be verified in their experience. The Ark was in priestly custody, as the law required; and the priest who " stood before " it (Deut. x. 8) was Phinehas, the son of Eleazar, the son of Aaron. Sacrifices were freely offered in the presence of the Ark, though Bethel was only a provisional place of worship *pro hâc vice;* hence it was necessary to build an altar for the purpose (Judg. xxi. 4), and as soon as the war was ended the camp was removed to Shiloh (ver. 12).[1]

The events recorded Judg. xvii.–xxi. belong, as is universally allowed, to the early part of the period

[1] The failure to exterminate the Canaanites, with its natural result of alliances with them and the worship of their gods, to which all the troubles of the period are traced in the Book of Judges, was an offence against both the first legislation and the Law of Deuteronomy, to both of which there are many verbal allusions. The historical references are also frequent (see particularly Judg. xi. 13 ff.). Technical expressions also occur, borrowed from the language of the Law. The term for the "congregation" gathered for the sacred war against Gibeah (Judg. xx. 1, xxi. 10, 13) is the one which Prof. W. R. Smith tells us (p. 318) is "characteristic of the Levitical Law." Another, equally characteristic, is rendered "lewdness." (Judg. xx. 6; see Lev. xviii. 17, xix. 29, where it is translated "wickedness.") The phrase "put away evil from Israel" (Judg. xx. 13) is frequent in Deuteronomy and peculiar to it (Deut. xiii. 5, xvii. 12, etc., etc.), and the punishment of Gibeah for its gross crime was in obedience to Deut. xiii. 12 ff. "Wrought folly in Israel" (Judg. xx. 6, 10, xix. 23, 24) is from Deut. xxii. 21. Judg. xxi. 17 alludes to Deut. xxv. 6, not only in thought, but with a verbal correspondence that does not appear in the English Bible; so Judg. x. 14 to Deut. xxxii. 37, 38. The law of the Nazirite (Num. vi. 1–5) was in force (Judg. xiii. 4, 5, 14, xvi. 17; I. Sam. i. 11); the vow of irremediable destruction (Judg. i. 17, xxi. 11; compare Deut. xx. 17; Lev. xxvii. 29); the irrevocable character of a vow (Judg. xi. 35, 36; compare Deut. xxiii. 21–23.)

of the Judges. And then, as we have seen, there was but one House of God and there was an Aaronic priesthood. The opening chapters of Samuel will tell us how it was at the close of that period. "The House of the Lord" (I. Sam. i. 7, 24) was still in Shiloh.[1] In it was the lamp of God (iii. 3), which burned nightly (Ex. xxvii. 20; xxx. 8), and the Ark with its cherubim (1 Sam. iv. 4). Thither Elkanah

---

[1] But says Prof. W. R. Smith (p. 258): "We find glaring departures from the very principles of the Pentateuchal Sanctuary. The Ark stood, not in the Tabernacle, but in a temple with door-posts and folding-doors, which were thrown open during the day (1. Sam. i. 9, iii. 15). Access to the temple was not guarded on rules of Levitical sanctity." And this in the face of ii. 22, where the Shiloh Sanctuary is called "the Tabernacle of the Congregation," identifying it with the old Mosaic Tent of Meeting (Ex. xxix. 4), and of II. Sam. vii. 6, where God says to David, "I have not dwelt in any house since the time that I brought up the children of Israel out of Egypt, even to this day, but have walked in a Tent and in a tabernacle." The Mosaic Tent had been the sole Sanctuary throughout this entire period, until the Ark was removed to Zion. During its long abode at Shiloh, more solid structures would naturally be erected in and about the court for the accommodation of the resident priests, the reception of offerings, and other purposes of convenience, like the chambers subsequently in the Temple (1. Kings vi. 5; Jer. xxxv. 2, 4). The doors and door-posts were no doubt those of the court or the entire sacred enclosure. To throw open the innermost part of the Temple to public view would be an inconceivable profanation, not only to Israelitish, but to Pagan ideas. Because Samuel slept in the Temple where the Ark of God was,—slept, that is, in one of the chambers already adverted to,—the Professor seems to think that he made a bedroom of the Holy of Holies. If he were told of some servant who blacked boots in the mansion where President Garfield lay sick, we suppose he would straightway infer that this menial occupation was carried on by the President's bedside. And upon the basis of such perversions as this he concludes, "These things strike at the root of the Levitical system of access to God."

went up yearly to worship and sacrifice (i. 3). Shiloh was visited with this view, not, as the Professor tells us (p. 257), "by pilgrims from the surrounding country of Ephraim," but by all Israel (ii. 14, 22, 29). This was the one prescribed place of sacrifice (ii. 29).[1] Here there was an Aaronic priesthood, — Eli and his sons (i. 3) being descended from Ithamar, the son of Aaron (I. Chron. xxiv. 3; I. Sam. xxii. 20; I. Kin. ii. 27). And this was the only lawful priesthood; for God says (I. Sam. ii. 27, 28) of his father Aaron, to whom He had appeared in Egypt, in Pharaoh's house: "I chose him out of all the tribes of Israel to be My priest, to offer upon Mine altar, to burn incense, to wear an ephod before Me; and I gave unto the house of thy father all the offerings made by fire of the children of Israel." And no other priesthood than that of Aaron is recognized at any subsequent time under the Old Testament; not a priest is named who was not descended from Aaron; and no other can be shown to have performed any priestly function at the Sanctuary. The position of the Levites in the time of the Judges is also that which is assigned to them by the Law. They are spoken of as sojourners (Judg. xvii. 7–9, xix. 1), because they had no inheritance like other tribes (ch. i.). They took down the Ark of the Lord,[2] when

---

[1] This passage flatly contradicts the extraordinary comment which the Professor makes (p. 288) upon Jer. vii. 22, "It is impossible to give a flatter contradiction to the traditional theory that the Levitical system was enacted in the Wilderness." He might as well quote Luke xiv. 26 in proof that the Gospel prohibits filial affection.

[2] Prof. W. R. Smith (p. 427) finds an "irregularity" in the fact

sent back by the Philistines (I. Sam. vi. 15), while the men who looked at the Ark were smitten by a great slaughter (ver. 19), and Uzzah was smitten for presuming to take hold of it (II. Sam. vi, 7; compare Num. iv. 15, 20). Beth-shemesh being a priestly city (Josh. xxi. 16) must have contained those who could rightfully offer sacrifices on the arrival of the Ark. Samuel, who was a Levite [1] (I. Chron. vi. 28) — notwithstanding the fact that his father is called an Ephrathite (I. Sam. i. 1) in consequence of his residing within the bounds of Ephraim (compare Judg. xvii. 7) — performed subordinate ministries

that "according to the Levitical Law it is the function of the Levites to carry the Ark; in the history the Ark is borne by the priests (Josh. iii. 3, vi. 6, viii. 33; I. Kings viii. 3)." But this is no "irregularity" whatever. The priests, being themselves Levites, and of the family of Kohath (Num. xxvii. 58, 59), had of course a legal right to do whatever was performed by the latter (Num. iv. 15). Hence, on occasions of special solemnity, priests were bearers of the Ark; while on all ordinary occasions the Levites were competent. Accordingly II. Sam. xv. 24, 29 where "the Levites aid the chief priests in carrying the Ark" does not need for its explanation the unfounded suggestion "that before Ezekiel priests and Levites are not two separate classes." Conveying the Ark in a cart (II. Sam. vi. 3) was in violation of the Law, and led to a disastrous issue (vers. 6, 7); this was recognized and corrected (ver. 13).

[1] Samuel did not become a priest, as Prof. W. R. Smith affirms (p. 259). The ephod which he wore is not that "which the Law confines to the high-priest," for it was a "linen ephod" (I. Sam. ii. 18), while that of the high-priest (Ex. xxviii. 6) was of more costly materials. Nor is it true that he wore "the high-priestly mantle." One article of the high-priest's dress was a mantle (Authorized Version, *robe*) made as is described (Ex. xxviii. 31, ff.). But others besides priests wore mantles; so that when Samuel's mother made him a little one (Authorized Version, *coat*) year by year, she did not invade the high-priest's prerogative. Thus "the startling irregularities" after all amount to nothing.

at the Tabernacle (1. Sam. ii. 11; compare Num. viii. 22).

The alleged departures from the ritual law at Shiloh were not really such. Eli's sons "made irregular exactions, and, in particular, would not burn the fat of the sacrifice till they had secured a portion of uncooked meat (1. Sam. ii. 12 *seq.*). Under the Levitical ordinance this claim was perfectly regular . . . (Lev. vii. 30 *seq.*, x. 15); but at Shiloh the claim was viewed as illegal and highly wicked" (p. 258). The sin of Eli's sons, and that which so disgusted the worshippers, was that they forcibly insisted on having their share before the LORD had His; and further, they claimed over and above what the Law allowed. Their legal portion was a matter of course, and is not particularly spoken of; but when the servant, with his flesh-hook, seized upon whatever he could get without leave or license, this was both offensive and unauthorized. And when the priestly perquisite was demanded before the fat was given to God upon the altar, and violence was threatened if this was not conceded, the worship of Jehovah was plainly subordinated to priestly gain. The abominable character of the proceeding cannot be glossed over by any reference to the Levitical requisitions.[1] Resistance to such impiety and selfish greed

---

[1] The ritual of the peace-offering, as given (Lev. iii. 1 ff), required the presentation of the victim, laying on of hands, slaying the animal, removing the fat and burning it upon the altar as a sweet savor unto the LORD. A supplemental law (vii. 28 ff.) specifies the portion to be given to the priests and the religious ceremonies to be observed in connection with it; but it affords no justification for the atrocious

is not fitly spoken of as "attaching importance to details."

But what is to be thought of the sacrifices offered elsewhere than at the Sanctuary in the period of the Judges, and by others than priests the sons of Aaron? Two facts are obvious upon the surface which regulate this whole matter. The first is, that there is no mention in the entire Book of Judges, from beginning to end, of any legitimate sanctuary but that at Shiloh, or any lawful priest not descended from Aaron. In every instance of reputed irregularity, it appears by the record that there was no stated or continuous departure from Levitical rules, but only a deviation strictly limited to the occasion which called it forth. A second fact, equally apparent, is that these deviations are invariably linked with immediate divine manifestations. In the lamentable condition to which the people were reduced, Jehovah, or the Angel of Jehovah, appeared from time to time on their behalf. In every such instance sacrifices were offered on the spot by those to whom the LORD thus appeared; and in the absence of such a theophany, sacrifices were never offered except at Shiloh, or in the presence of the Ark, and by priests of the house of Aaron. Wherever God appears the place becomes, for that moment, holy ground (Ex. iii. 5; Josh. v. 15; II. Sam. xxiv. 16, 18). It possesses, for the time, the sanctity of the Tabernacle. And the law that restricts sacri-

claim that the priestly portion should have precedence over that which was destined to the altar, or that these should ever be ranked on a par.

ficial worship, in ordinary times, to the place where God statedly manifests Himself, cannot forbid due worship being paid to Him in any other place which He may make the scene of an extraordinary revelation. To this extent only Ex. xx. 24 authorizes altars elsewhere than at the Sanctuary. Similarly, the divinely appointed priests alone were authorized ordinarily to draw near to God and officiate at His altar. Other men could approach Him acceptably only through their intervention. But if God Himself sees fit, in any case, to dispense with sacerdotal mediation, the man to whom He comes near, by an immediate gracious manifestation, is thereby warranted to present his homage directly to Him in whose presence he stands.

Thus (Judg. ii. 1–5) the angel of the LORD appeared to the people at Bochim, and they sacrificed there unto the LORD; so to Gideon, with a like result (vi. 20–22); a second appearance to Gideon, with explicit directions, which he obeys (vers. 25 ff.); a supernatural manifestation to Manoah, and a sacrifice (xiii. 16 ff.). And these are positively all the instances of irregular sacrifice in the Book of Judges which are not distinctly stigmatized as idolatrous. No one of these places was subsequently a place of sacrifice; and Gideon and Manoah are nowhere said to have sacrificed again. The altar of Gideon, said to be still remaining in Ophrah (Judg. vi. 24), was in all likelihood a monumental altar, as Ex. xvii, 15; Josh. xxii. 26 ff. It does not appear that Gideon ever offered upon it. When directed to make a sacrifice, immediately after (ver. 25), he built another altar. Much less does it appear that it was used for sacrifice after his time. If a writer were to tell us that the fort of Ticonderoga is there to this day, we need not infer that the ancient hostilities are still continued. Judg. xi. 11, " Jephthah uttered all his words before the LORD in Mizpeh," east of the Jordan, and (xx. 1) "the congregation was gathered together unto the LORD in Mizpeh," west of Jordan; these statements do not imply that either Mizpeh was a sanctuary. There is no allusion to sacrifices in either instance. "Before the LORD" simply implies a solemn recognition of God's presence (Gen. xxvii. 7; Ex. vi. 12, 30; 1. Sam. xxvi. 19; Ps. cxvi. 9). That they who bring a sacrifice are said to "offer" it (Judg. xxi. 4; 1. Sam. ii. 13), does not imply that every one could perform priestly functions; for like expressions are used in the Levitical Law itself (Lev. xix. 5). We do not suppose that the Professor will dispute the reality of the divine appearances recorded in Judges, but if he did this would not disturb our argument. For the theophanies and the sacrifices are firmly linked together; and if there is no evidence that the former took place, there is none that the latter were offered.

But the Professor tells us (p. 256) that

— " all God's acts of grace mentioned in the Book of Judges, all His calls to repentance, and all the ways in which He appears from time to time to support His people . . . . are connected with this same local worship. The call to repentance is never a call to put aside the local sanctuaries, and worship only before the Ark at Shiloh. . . . . If the Pentateuchal programme of worship, and the rules which it lays down for the administration of the dispensation of grace, existed in these days, they were at least absolutely suspended. It was not according to the Law that Jehovah administered His grace to Israel during the period of the Judges."

There were no "local sanctuaries," as we have seen, except the idolatrous shrines; and every call to forsake Baal and Ashtoreth and return to Jehovah, was a summons to abandon them, and worship in Shiloh; and their cries unto the LORD (Judg. iii. 9, iv. 3, etc.) doubtless found expression at the altar and the Sanctuary. The infrequent mention of the Sanctuary in Shiloh in the course of this period can throw no doubt upon its continuity; for we find it at the end of the period just where and as it was at the beginning, and as it had been from the days of Joshua. The regular operation of established institutions is taken for granted by historians, and seems to demand no special record. And the writer of Judges professedly devotes himself to reciting the instances of apostasy, punishment, and deliverance (ii. 11–19), while the intervals of rest and pious obedience are passed over with a simple mention of their existence (iii. 11, 30, viii. 28, etc.). But if Shiloh was the religious centre of the true worshippers of Jehovah, why was it not the fountain-head of religious power, the spring of every religious movement? Why did not the trumpet-call to repentance issue from its priests, and each recurring revival spread from Shiloh outward? Why this seeming paralysis of the regularly instituted ordinances and means of grace, and of the duly authorized ministers of religion? The Church may well ask, and hang her head in shame. With all the deduction for the unrecorded influence that emanated from the Sanctuary, and this was doubtless great at this as at every epoch, it must be still confessed that things are not altogether as on theory might have been expected. Nor were they when the Redeemer came to His own and His own received Him not. Nor were they at the Reformation of Luther.

But how does this discredit the existence of a central sanctuary and an Aaronic priesthood? The body is nourished and strengthened by its ordinary food, and nothing more might seem requisite when it is in a healthy condition; and yet remedies may become necessary which are quite aside from the regularly prescribed diet. The people had no other medium of acceptable approach to God, of expressing their homage or obtaining His saving help, than by the established ordinances of worship. But God was not limited to these in His dealings with His people. His grace is broader than the channels through which it ordinarily flows. Special divine influences were not restricted to the Sanctuary even in the days of Moses (Num. xi. 26–29). The Romish error of an external Church as the sole dispenser of grace finds no sanction under the Old Testament more than under the New.

And no exposition of the Levitical institutions, which places regularity of ritual observance upon a par with the spirit it was designed to express, can make them tally with the history of Israel, the devout breathings of the Psalmists, or the teachings of the Prophets. The ritualism of the Law may be emphasized to such a degree as to bring Leviticus into disharmony with the abundant inculcations of spiritual obedience in Deuteronomy; to make it antagonistic to the declarations of Isai. i. 11 ff., Amos v. 21 ff., and Micah vi. 8 (p. 287); and to represent it as the grand essential of a religious reformation under the Law "to re-establish the stated burnt-offering, and the due atoning ritual before the Ark in the hands of the legitimate priesthood, and on the pattern of the service in the Wilderness" (p. 263). And then the fact may be established that no such system is traceable in Israel before the rise of post-exilic Pharisaism. But the question will recur, Is it Leviticus that is at fault, or the wrong interpretation which has been foisted upon it? Is Leviticus post-exilic, or has Professor Robertson Smith simply misconceived the spirit of the Law and the method of its administration? He tells us (p. 213), "The Israelite had no right to draw a distinction between the spirit and the letter of the Law." He was obliged to do this on numberless occasions. David and his men, in danger of perishing with hunger, ate the shew-bread. The priests in the Temple profaned the Sabbath and were blameless. The rites of burial were defiling. Ezekiel threatens Israel that they shall be compelled to eat defiled bread among the Gentiles. Aaron, in his grief, burned the sin-offering instead of eating it in the Holy Place, and was justified in so doing (Lev. x. 19, 20).

Hezekiah prayed (II. Chron. xxx. 19) that the good LORD would pardon every one that prepareth his heart to seek God, the LORD God of his fathers, though he be not cleansed according to the purification of the Sanctuary. The Law, whose fundamental tenets are (Lev. xix. 2) "Ye shall be holy, for I the LORD your God am holy," and (ver. 18), "Thou shalt love thy neighbor as thyself," not only makes the spiritual meaning the essential thing in every rite, but puts that spiritual meaning above any external rite whatever. Samuel is a true interpreter of it when he says (I. Sam. xv. 22) : " Hath the LORD as great delight in burnt-offerings and sacrifices as in obeying the voice of the LORD? Behold, to obey is better than sacrifice, and to hearken, than the fat of rams."

When Israel sinned with the Golden Calf and broke their covenant with God which had just been ratified, the offence was not atoned nor the breach repaired by any ritual. On the contrary, the Tabernacle was removed outside of the camp (Ex. xxxiii. 7). There was no demand of sacrifice or lustration, but only of repentance and humiliation (vers. 4 ff.) The people were sorely punished (xxxii. 27, 35), but at Moses' earnest intercession they were forgiven (vers. 30 ff.) When they sinned at Kadesh by refusing to go into the Promised Land, not a word was said of sacrificial expiation or of greater zeal in the ceremonial. The Tabernacle and the altar and the ritual drop out of sight as completely as if they did not exist. It was upon Moses' fervent intercession (Num. xiv. 11 ff.) that the people were spared from instant destruction, though still condemned to perish in the Wilderness; and, as appears from Josh. v. 5 ff., the rite of circumcision was suspended, the breakers of the covenant being deprived of its seal. According to Lev. xxvi. and Deut. xxviii. the transgression of the people will be visited by ever increasing judgments, culminating in exile from the LORD'S land; and the return of God's favor is suspended (Lev. xxvi. 40 ff.; Deut. iv. 29), not upon a punctilious observance of rites and ceremonies, but upon confession of their iniquity and the humbling of their uncircumcised hearts.

The principles thus outlined in the Law itself govern the Book of Judges. It records the inflictions by which the LORD from time to time recalled the offending people to a sense of their duty and their need of divine help. These were enforced by communications from "the Angel of the LORD" (Judg. ii. 1 ff. etc.), as promised (Ex. xxiii. 20 ff.), and by Prophets. (Judg. iv. 4, vi. 8., etc. See Deut. xviii. 15 ff.) It was not to be expected that the leaders raised up to judge and to deliver the people would be from the sacerdotal tribe. Moses' own successor was from the tribe of Ephraim. That Gideon and Samson were called to their extraordinary mission not by a summons from the Sanctuary, but by an immediate divine manifestation at their homes, is in accordance with the analogy of the call of Moses. And yet neither these judgments nor these leaders effected a genuine and thorough reformation. The people were gradually sinking from the days of Joshua and the elders that overlived him (Judg. ii. 7) to the time of Jephthah and Samson; and the priesthood, it must be added, fell from the level of Phinehas, the grandson of Aaron, to that of his namesake, the son of Eli. The first effective measures for a true religious reform had their source in Shiloh; they were the work of Samuel, who was trained at the Sanctuary.

But the Professor tells us (p. 263): "Samuel did not know of a systematic and exclusive system of sacrificial ritual confined to the Sanctuary of the Ark" (p. 261); "He continued to sacrifice at a variety of shrines; and his yearly circuit to Bethel, Gilgal, and Mizpeh, returning to Ramah, involved the recognition of all these altars." The LORD declares through Jeremiah (vii. 12, 14, xxvi. 6), that He has abandoned Shiloh, "where He set His name at the first," on account of the wickedness of His people Israel, and He will do the same to His house in Jerusalem, "which is called by His name." Ps. lxxviii. 60, 68: "He forsook the Tabernacle of Shiloh," and "chose Mount Zion." The Prophet and the Psalmist know of but two sanctuaries in Israel, successively sanctioned by the LORD,—Shiloh and Zion. As the Tabernacle was removed from the midst of the camp in consequence of the idolatry at Sinai (Ex. xxxiii. 7), so, for a like reason, Israel was bereft of the Ark, which was sent into captivity in the land of the Philistines (1 Sam. iv. 11). God had no sanctuary in Israel from that day forward. The Ark was restored again by the discomfited Philistines; but the slaughter of the men in the priestly city of Beth-shemesh showed that Israel was not prepared to have Jehovah fix His residence among them; and it was an embarrassing question how to dispose of the Ark, which only spread terror in Israel as it had done among the uncircumcised. It was finally placed provisionally in the obscurity of a private house, and guarded, so far as appears, by a pious layman (1. Sam. vii. 1).

Here is a novel and most extraordinary state of affairs. The Ark, which as the symbol and pledge of Jehovah's presence has always hitherto been the confidence and the glory of Israel, is now a source of alarm. It was not taken back to Shiloh, nor was it taken to Nob, when the Tabernacle was carried thither (1. Sam. xxi. 1, 6). It was not put in any sanctuary. It was simply sheltered in the dwelling of an ordinary Israelite. No priest or Levite ministered before it. No sacrifices were offered where it was. No pilgrimages were made to it (1. Chron. xiii. 3).[1] And during its long abode in Kirjath-jearim, "all the house of Israel lamented after the LORD" (1. Sam. vii. 2). The covenant between Jehovah and Israel was severed, and they knew it. The LORD no longer had a dwelling-place in the midst of them.

Now the one purpose of Samuel's life was to bring Israel back to God, and thus restore these ruptured relations. And absolutely the Professor thinks (pp. 262, 263) that the thing for him to have done was to

---

[1] In 1. Sam. xiv. 18, as Prof. W. R. Smith correctly informs us (p. 94), there seems to be an error in the Hebrew text; and there is much to recommend the reading of the Septuagint, which substitutes "ephod" for "ark."

have taken the Ark to Nob,—"for the distance between these towns is only a forenoon's walk,"—and to have set up the Levitical service under the conduct of the Aaronic priesthood! And because he did not do this, the Levitical Law could not have been in existence! Such reasoning betrays the most astonishing misconception of the relation between Jehovah and Israel, and of the ritual institutions by which that relation was expressed and maintained. Outward regularity in the prescribed ceremonial had nothing in it that was acceptable, so long as the hearts of the people were alienated from God. Leaving the people in their profound but salutary grief at the loss of the Sanctuary, and of God's visible presence among them, he sought "to have them return unto the LORD with all their hearts," "to prepare their hearts unto the LORD and serve Him only" (1. Sam. vii. 3). The worship which he conducted was sacrificial, of course; that was the symbolic form by which penitence and consecration were expressed. But the sacrifice was without a sanctuary and without a priesthood. Samuel officiated, not because he was a regular priest, for he was not; nor by virtue of his being a Levite, which would have given him no legal right to offer sacrifice; but in his prophetic character as God's ambassador and representative. But that this function was an extraordinary one appears from the fact that it was limited to Samuel alone (1. Sam. ix. 13). There is, from the time that the Ark was laid up at Kirjath-jearim till David removed it to Zion, scarcely a recorded instance of sacrifice when Samuel[1] was not present, — except the rash and luckless act of Saul, which brought upon him Samuel's stern reprobation and the loss of his kingdom, in spite of his apology that he was forced to do as he did by the unavoidable pressure of circumstances (1. Sam. xiii. 8–14). Samuel is plainly the centre of the religious life of the period. The presence of God, so far as its gracious manifestation to Israel is concerned, is for the time linked with the Prophet, not with the Ark.

The new religious fervor awakened by the ministry of Samuel found expression as it could. In the absence of any divinely authorized sanctuary we read of men going up to God to Bethel (x. 3), where God had met with Jacob; of a high place at Gibeah (x. 5), visited by a company of prophets and established probably on account of its proximity to their residence; of a yearly sacrifice of David's family (xx. 6) at their home in Bethlehem. These are the only instances of the sort which are mentioned, except the sacrifices conducted by Samuel himself. All the ado made about "local sanctuaries," prior to the reign of David, dwindles down to this; and in it there is no departure even from the strict letter of the Law (1. Kings, iii. 2).[2]

---

[1] In 1. Sam. vii. 9, 17; ix. 12, 13; x. 8; xi. 14, 15; xvi. 2–5, Samuel is distinctly named as the offerer, or at least sanctioned the sacrifice by his presence and participation. Saul built an altar (xiv. 35), and he spoke (xv. 15, 21) of the people's proposing to sacrifice the spoils of the Amalekites in Gilgal; but he cannot have thought of offering in the absence of Samuel after the rebuff which he had already received.

[2] What is said of David's "want of orthodoxy" (p. 264) seems for

The worship in high places was irregular and illegal after the Temple was built; but the fact that they were tolerated by pious princes, who contented themselves with abolishing the emblems and practices of idolatry found there, only shows that they

the most part captious. David did not wear "the priestly ephod" (II. Sam. vi. 14) but a linen ephod, which was worn by priests but was no part of their prescribed dress; and, as shown by this instance and that of Samuel when a child (I. Sam. ii. 18), might be worn by others on sacred occasions. "He offered sacrifices in person" (ver. 13), and so Prof. W. R. Smith tells us (p. 248): "Solomon officiated at the altar in person (I. Kings, ix. 25)"; and by a like principle of interpretation it might have been added that he built the altar with his own hands. If Solomon really "offered two and twenty thousand oxen and an hundred and twenty thousand sheep" in person at one time, he must have had a weary task (I. Kings, viii. 63). "He blessed the people as a priest in the name of Jehovah" (ver. 18), where "as a priest" is without any warrant in the text. "David's sons were priests (II. Sam. viii. 18)"; but though this is the usual sense of the word, it must have a different meaning here, since the priests properly so called had already been named in the verse preceding. In I. Chron. xviii. 17 it is paraphrased "chief about the king," which is justified by the primary sense of the term, and perhaps by the consideration that this high and confidential office was commonly entrusted to priests. (Compare *eunuch*, Gen. xxxix. 1, not in its proper sense, but as an official title.) That he weakly allowed Absalom to visit Hebron under pretence of a sacrificial vow, may be justified by I. Kings, iii. 2. His marriage with a princess of Geshur (II. Sam. iii. 3) is not a violation of the letter of the Law, but offends as much against the spirit of the first legislation (Ex. xxxiv. 15, 16) as against that of Deuteronomy; and, as this was Absalom's mother, the history records the dreadful penalty he incurred. "Solomon, building new shrines for the gods of his wives" (p. 248), could not plead ignorance of the Law, on the Professor's own theory (Ex. xxii. 20, xxiii. 24). The Professor further proves that the priest received his consecration not from Jehovah but from the people, by the case of Micah (Judg. xvii. 5, 12), the idolater, who stole his mother's money (ver. 2), and by the case of Eleazar, son of Abinadab (I. Sam. vii. 1), who was not a priest at all (p. 264).

did not do their whole duty, — not that the Law which had ruled ever since the days of Moses did not exist. They may very easily have persuaded themselves that the spirit of the Law was maintained if only the abuses were rectified, that if God was sincerely and piously worshipped in these local sanctuaries there could not be much harm in suffering them to remain. How much of the New Testament must have been written after the Reformation of Luther, if the habitual disregard of its teachings is to be accepted as evidence against their existence, and especially if the " popular religion " is made the measure of primitive Christianity! How plain it is, upon these principles, that the doctrine of Justification by Faith could never have been formulated by the Apostle Paul, if it was not apprehended in its integrity by the early Fathers and the theologians of the Middle Ages! Hezekiah's admitted reform (II. Kings, xviii. 4) recognized the binding obligation of the Deuteronomic Law a century before the book was found in the Temple. That book — according to the explicit testimony of the author of Kings — was no recent production of the reign of Josiah. It was " The Book of the Law " (II. Kings, xxii. 8), *i.e.*, the well known volume so designated (compare Josh. i. 7, 8, viii. 31, xxiv. 26), which was found " in the House of the Lord," — just where it might have been expected to be (Deut. xxxi. 9, 26). It is further characterized as " the Law of Moses " (II. Kings, xxiii. 24, 25), and is, as Prof. Robertson Smith acknowledges, the standard of judgment which the writer of the Book of Kings applies to all preceding reigns. The people and their rulers do right or do evil in the sight of the LORD as they heed or disregard its injunctions. This Law is expressly referred to (II. Kings, xxi. 7–9), as known and disobeyed by Manasseh, and, in fact, as enjoined by the LORD upon David and Solomon; also as obeyed by Hezekiah (xviii. 6) and by Joash (xiv. 6), where the very words of the statute are quoted from Deut. xxiv. 16. "The testimony" given to Joash at his coronation (II. Kings, xi. 12) was a copy of the written Law as directed by Deut. xvii. 18 (compare Ps. xix. 7, lxxviii. 5). It is appealed to by Solomon in his prayer at the dedication of the Temple (I. Kings, viii. 53, 56), as well as implied throughout in the language of his supplication; and is commended by David to Solomon for the rule of his life (ii. 3). It is represented as equally binding on the Ten Tribes as upon Judah; and their transgression of the covenant of the LORD and the commandments of Moses led to their overthrow (II. Kings, xviii. 12). The idolatrous corruptions of the Northern Kingdom, which the Professor is at great pains to show (p. 230) were "not a mere innovation due to the schism of Jeroboam," are expressly and in detail imputed to him (I. Kings, xii. 26 ff., xiii. 33, xiv. 8, 9), so that his standing designation is "Jeroboam, the son of Nebat, who made Israel to sin" (II. Kings, x. 29, etc.). And what the Professor persists in calling "traditional worship,"— under which head he heaps together all the idolatries and glaring violations of the Mosaic Law that are recorded at various times,—

the sacred historians with one voice denounce as defections from the true worship of their Covenant God, and as due to criminal association with the nations around them. If they are not to be trusted in so fundamental a point as this, they are not to be trusted in anything. It would be better to remand the entire history of Israel to the region of fable, and to confess that we have no positive knowledge about it, than to attempt this revolutionary process of reconstruction, which is professedly based upon authorities that are perpetually discredited.

But if historians may have incorporated their own ideas with their narrative, and committed the mistake of transferring the institutions of their own day to antecedent periods, contemporaneous writings will be free from this error, and represent truly the state of things in which they were produced. Let us turn, then, to these. The Book of Psalms, as the Professor with all his distrust of their titles confesses, contains some ancient songs. He admits that tradition — in imputing the first portion of the Psalter (Ps. i.-xli.) almost without exception to David — "doubtless expresses the fact that these are the oldest Psalms, belonging to the early age of Hebrew psalmody, from David downward" (p. 202). Now in all these Psalms, as in the entire collection in fact, Zion is God's earthly dwelling-place; no other is once alluded to. The Professor does not indicate which Psalms in particular are to be accounted David's. Hitzig, that prince of doubters, regards Pss. iii.-xix. as the genuine Davidic kernel, with the exception of Pss. v., vi., xiv.

Prof. W. R. Smith excepts to Pss. ix., x. Suppose that we content ourselves with the modest residuum. We still find that Jehovah's abode is in His Holy Hill (iii. 4), His Tabernacle (xv. 1), His Temple or Palace, which applies to the Sacred Tent as the residence of the Great King (xi. 4, xviii. 6); and mention is made of the winged cherub attached to His Throne (xviii. 10), also of Jehovah's Law (xix. 7-10), and His Judgments and Statutes (xviii. 22), with expressions in Pss. xv. and xix. borrowed from legal phrases and ideas, not to speak of the historical allusion in Ps. xi. 6, and the abundant references to the Pentateuch in Ps. xviii., whose composition by David is attested by II. Sam. xxii.

We do not know what the Professor thinks of Ps. xl. It is in its title ascribed to David; but Smend — to whose commentary he refers us (p. 377) for "the detailed proof that in every point Ezekiel's Torah prepares the way for the Levitical Law, but represents a more elementary ritual" — remarks on Ezek. xl. 39, "Sin-offerings and trespass-offerings are here mentioned for the first time outside of the Priest-codex." If Ezekiel is the inventor of sin-offerings, Ps. xl. 6[1] must have borrowed them from him or from the Levitical Law, which he pioneered. Such language, when found in Micah vi. 8, Jer. vii. 22, is interpreted (p. 288) as affirming that "Jehovah has not enjoined sacrifice," that He has, in fact, given no law upon the subject; the Levitical

---

[1] "Sacrifice and offering Thou didst not desire, . . . burnt-offering and sin-offering hast Thou not required."

Law was consequently still unknown. But if Ps. xl. 6 can speak thus after Ezekiel's Law, or the Levitical Law, had been announced, Micah and Jeremiah could do the same; and then, for all that appears, the Levitical Law may antedate their utterances.[1] Or if

[1] This conclusion cannot be evaded by imputing to Ps. xl. 6 a sense which the Professor (p. 416) follows Hitzig in attributing to Ps. li. 16, 17: "At present, says the Psalmist, God desires no material sacrifice. . . . But does the Psalmist then mean to say, absolutely and in general, that sacrifice is a superseded thing? No; for he adds that when Jerusalem is rebuilt the sacrifice of Israel (not merely his own sacrifice) will be pleasing to God. He lives, therefore, in a time when the fall of Jerusalem has temporarily suspended the sacrificial ordinances." Hitzig thinks Ps. xl. to be pre-exilic and ascribes it to Jeremiah. Olshausen, who is for sweeping everything into the Maccabean period, places it during the persecution of Antiochus Epiphanes, when the Temple-worship was interdicted. But these passages in the Psalms, as well as Ps. l. 8–15, are so clearly akin to Hos. vi. 6, Isai. i. 11 ff. etc., that they must be interpreted on the same principles. If, as is confessed, there is no absolute discarding of sacrifice in Ps. li., neither is there in Ps. xl., nor in those passages of the Prophets which are quoted to show that sacrifice, if not actually disapproved, was yet in itself a matter of indifference. And the Psalmists declare, just as plainly as the Prophets, God's permanent attitude toward sacrifice. There is nothing in the language of Ps. li. to suggest the thought which it is proposed to put into it, viz., that sacrifices are not required "at present" because providentially rendered impossible. And the prayer in the last two verses of the Psalm, "that God will build the walls of Jerusalem," does not refer so manifestly to the period of the "captivity" as the Professor seems to suppose. Nebuchadnezzar could speak (Dan. iv. 30) of "this great Babylon which I have built," without its being necessary for us to suppose that it did not exist or was in ruins when his reign began. To "build" a city in Scripture phrase, is not merely to construct it *ab initio*, but to strengthen or enlarge it (Josh. xix. 50; I. Kings, xii. 25, xv. 17; II. Kings, xiv. 22; II. Chron. viii. 2; Mic. iii. 10; Hab. ii. 12, etc.) Solomon built "the wall of Jerusalem round about" (I. Kings, iii. 1, ix. 15), though his father had not left it defenceless, and no victorious foe had dismantled it; and, as Delitzsch suggests,

Ps. xl. was prior to the time of Ezekiel, the sin-offering was not introduced by him; though not mentioned elsewhere it was part of the pre-exilic ritual, and Moses may have ordained it after all. And then still further, the Psalmist speaks (ver. 7) of all this as written in a book-roll, which he identifies (ver. 8) with the Law of God, — a written law respecting peace-offering and meat-offering, burnt-offering and sin-offering, which lays its supreme stress not upon the presentation of the animal required, but upon the surrender to God of the person of the offerer. The Professor tells us (p. 364) — and we preserve his italics — "The old Israelite *consecrated himself* before a sacrifice." By an "old Israelite" he plainly means, in the connection, one who lived under "the first legislation" and prior to the time of Isaiah. The author of this Psalm was then an "old Israelite," and may have been David, as the title declares. And accordingly David, or the "old Israelite," had a written law, embracing precisely the forms of sacrifice included in Leviticus; moreover, he understood it in a very different sense from the rigid ritualism which Prof. W. R. Smith insists upon finding there.

From the Psalms we turn to the Prophets. Hosea and Amos are among the earliest from whom we have any writings. They prophesied in the North-

David's prayer found in this a partial accomplishment. There is no reason, therefore, for setting aside the title of this Psalm, which at least represents a very ancient and credible tradition of its origin. And no person, surely, who is untrammelled by a hypothesis, would ever dream of dating the grateful thanksgiving for divine benefits in Ps. xl. 1–5 from either the Babylonish captivity or the Syrian persecution.

ern Kingdom, which had been severed from Judah for nearly 200 years. In casting off subjection to the house of David, the Ten Tribes had abandoned the Temple at Jerusalem, its priesthood, and its worship. The separatist worship of the calves, the Professor tells us, was regarded by the people as perfectly legitimate. "They still believed themselves loyal to Jehovah" (p. 231). They were simply maintaining their old ancestral forms. The Law, which they are charged with violating, had as yet no existence in Judah; and the Ten Tribes went into exile long before it was enacted. The Prophets were the real innovators. Leaving out of view that Israel's idolatrous worship was in open violation, not only of the Deuteronomic and Levitical codes, but likewise of the Ten Commandments which are admitted to be Mosaic, and the basis of Jehovah's covenant with His people, in violation, too, of the first legislation (Ex. xx. 23), which even on the theory of Prof. W. R. Smith antedated this period, what do the Prophets say about it?

Hosea constantly sets forth the relation between Jehovah and Israel under the emblem of a marriage covenant (ii. 19, 20), a form of representation borrowed from the books of Moses (Ex. xx. 5, xxxiv. 15, 16; Lev. xvii. 7, xx. 5, 6; Num. xiv. 33). His ever reiterated charge is that Israel is an unfaithful wife, who had responded to her Lord in former days, when she came up out of Egypt (ii. 15), but had since abandoned Him for other lovers (i.–iii., etc.), Baal and the calves (xiii. 1, 2). She has broken her covenant, has dealt treacherously (v. 7, vi. 7), has backslidden (iv. 16, xi. 7, xiv. 4), is repeating the atrocity of Gibeah (ix. 9, x. 9). The prevalent sacrificing on the hills and under shady trees is a shameless and criminal desertion of her lawful husband for a base and profligate prostitution (iv. 13). Nothing certainly can be further from the Prophet's conception, than that this was Israel's original and hereditary worship. If the Professor is right, Hosea is radically mistaken. His language is not that of one who is seeking to lift a people to purer and more spiritual ideas, from gross and degrading superstitions in which they have always been involved. His effort is to reclaim those who have apostatized from God's true service to the standing from which they have fallen. The "knowledge of God," whose absence he deplores (iv. 1), is not a theoretical apprehension of His being and attributes, as though his hearers had never been instructed about Him, but, as appears from its concomitants, that practical acquaintance with the Most High which is synonymous with true piety, and which had wellnigh vanished from the land.

It appears from Hos. viii. 12,[1] that Israel had a

[1] Prof. Robertson Smith translates this verse hypothetically, as is done by several critics and commentators who seek thus to evade its explicit testimony. To this there are serious objections. But even thus it would establish the existence of a detailed and copious law embracing the subject of sacrifice, and which the Prophet held to be from God, and charged both priests and people with neglecting. "Though I wrote to him the ten thousand precepts of my Torah" (not "my Torah in ten thousand precepts," as Professor Smith has it) by the very hypothesis avers that there is such a Law to write. But the past tense of the verb in the second clause stands in the way of the hypothetical construction, and makes it, if not absolutely certain, yet

written law of very considerable extent. This must have related in part, as the connection implies, to altars and sacrifices, and no doubt embraced the duties which the people are elsewhere charged with violating. (Compare also Hos. iv. 6, viii. 1; Am. ii. 4.) We learn from Hos. ii. 11, ix. 5, xii. 9; Am. v. 21, viii. 5, that the annual feasts, new-moons, Sabbaths, and festive assemblies were observed in Israel, and held in high esteem, and that they occupied a prominent place in the life of the people, so that their abolition would be reckoned a serious disaster. We read also (Am. v. 22; Hos. viii. 13) of burnt-offerings, meat-

highly probable on grammatical grounds alone that it is historical, and that the future in the first clause is to be explained as in Ps. ciii. 7. To this add the incongruities which attend the hypothetical explanation. Why speak of imposing *ten thousand* requirements, as though these would be more likely to secure obedience than a smaller number? and why of *writing* instead of enjoining or declaring the Law? The very mode of putting the hypothesis implies that written law was a familiar idea, that law to have its highest validity should be in written form; and such a notion could only be begotten of usage. So that Smend gives up the hypothetical construction as untenable ("Moses apud Prophetas," p. 13): "The words of Hosea prove that the Ephraimites had many written laws in the eighth century, which, whether contained in one or more books, although they were neglected by a large part of the people, were yet known to all, and in the judgment of the Prophet demanded the obedience of all, since they were of divine obligation, as much so as if written by Jehovah himself." Nowack, one of the most recent commentators on Hosea, confesses that this verse is not hypothetical, but seeks to bend it to the views of the latest critical school, by giving to the first verb a progressive sense, *I am writing*, as implying that the legislation was not given at one time in the age of Moses, but was gradually produced from that time forward. Perhaps he infers from the *creating*, in Isai. xlii. 5, that in the Prophet's estimation the work of creation was still progressing, and that he thus anticipated the cosmical-development hypothesis.

offerings, peace-offerings; (Am. iv. 5) thank-offerings, free-will-offerings; (Hos. ix. 4) drink-offerings; (Am. iv. 4) the daily morning sacrifice. Hos. iv. 8 alludes to the law of the sin-offering; Hos. ix. 3, 4 to the law of clean and unclean meats. Instead of the simplicity of worship, which the Professor finds represented in the first legislation and in Deuteronomy, and which he would have us believe prevailed until the Babylonish exile, they must have had an elaborate ritual closely corresponding to the Levitical institutions. So that Smend himself says ("Moses apud Prophetas," p. 75): "It is sufficiently evident that the cultus of Jehovah, as it existed in the time of the earlier Prophets, and doubtless long before, is by no means at variance with the character of Leviticus. Whatever judgment may be formed of the age of this book, the opinions hitherto entertained of the birth, growth, and maturity of the religion of Israel will undergo no change."

In Hos. vi. 6 ("I desired mercy and not sacrifice,") the very next clause shows that the negation is not absolute, ("and the knowledge of God more than burnt-offerings").[1] This affords a very simple key to

[1] It is remarkable how many allusions to the Deuteronomic and Levitical codes there are in Hosea and Amos, and even striking coincidences of language. In addition to those already cited in the text, the following may be mentioned as among the most obvious. The law of the unity of the Sanctuary is presupposed in charging them with sin for multiplying altars (Hos. viii. 11, xii. 11); the prohibition of removing landmarks (Deut. xix. 14, xxvii. 17) is referred to Hos. v. 10; iv. 4, the final reference of causes in dispute to the priest, refusal to hear whom was a capital offence, (Deut. xvii. 12); viii. 13, ix. 3, penalty of a return to Egypt (Deut. xxviii. 68); ix. 4, defilement from the dead

the passages with which the Professor confronts us on page 287, and which he interprets to mean that in the judgment of the Prophets " sacrifice is not necessary to acceptable religion." "Amos proves God's indifference to ritual by reminding the people that they offered no sacrifice and offerings to Him in the Wilderness during those forty years of wandering which he

(Num. xix. 14, 22; Deut. xxvi. 14); ix. 10, Baal-peor (Num. xxv. 3, 5), which is a Levitical passage (p. 433); x. 11 (compare Deut. xxv. 4), the ox not to be muzzled when treading out corn; vi. 11, Am. ix. 14, "return the captivity," (Deut. xxx. 3). Amos though delivering his message in Bethel, knows but one sanctuary, that in Zion (i. 2); ii. 7, the law of incest (Lev. xx. 11; Deut. xxii. 30); ii. 11, 12, Nazarites, (Num. vi. 2, 3), and Prophets (Deut. xviii. 15); iv. 4, triennial tithes (Deut. xiv. 28, xxvi. 12), for which in their excess of zeal they may substitute tithes every three days; viii. 5, falsifying the ephah, shekel, and balances (Lev. xix. 36; Deut. xxv. 13, ff.); ii. 7, "to profane My holy name" (Lev. xx. 3); ii. 9, compare Num. xiii. 32, 33; v. 11, ix. 14, compare Deut. xxviii. 30, 39; vi. 14, "entering in of Hamath" (Num. xxxiv. 8); ix. 13 compare, Lev. xxvi. 5. Prof. W. R. Smith deduces from Hos. iii. 4 the inference (p. 226) that "sacrifice and *maççēba*, ephod and teraphim, were recognized as the necessary forms and instruments of the worship of Jehovah." This finds its sufficient reply in his own note upon this passage (p. 423), according to which Jehovah "breaks off all intercourse *between Israel and the Baalim*" as well as between Israel and himself. That teraphim are spoken of in connection with Jacob, and were found in David's house, only shows that their wives were not free from superstitious practices. That Micah had them in his idolatrous sanctuary (Judg. xviii. 14, ff.) can surely create no embarrassment. And if Micah's Levite, as he adds in the same connection (p. 227), was really a "grandson of Moses," this is no more damaging to the great legislator than it is to Luther that his descendants have deserted the Protestant faith, or than it is to Isaiah that he once summoned the priest Urijah as a witness to certify a fact (Isai. viii. 2), — whence the Professor dignifies him (p. 253) with the title of Isaiah's "friend," — though he had "co-operated with King Ahaz" in a change of altars.

elsewhere cites as a special proof of Jehovah's covenant grace (Am. ii. 10, v. 25). Micah declares that Jehovah does not require sacrifice; He asks nothing of His people but 'to do justly, and love mercy, and walk humbly with their God' (Mic. vi. 8). And Jeremiah (vii. 21, *seq.*) says in express words, etc., etc." (Compare also Isai. i. 11, *seq.*; Am. v. 21, *seq.*). Am. v. 25 is a greatly disputed passage and has been very variously understood. It is unnecessary to go into a discussion of its meaning here. If we accept the sense which the Professor puts upon its terms, it will simply mean that the Mosaic system of sacrifice did not go into full and developed operation in the Wilderness; a fact of which we have hints elsewhere (*e. g.* Deut. xii. 8, 9), and which is implied in the language of several of the laws themselves (Ex. xii. 25, xxxiv. 12; Lev. xiv. 34, xxiii. 10, xxv. 2, etc. etc.) But the Professor's deduction from these passages is too sweeping for his own theory. If they are irreconcilable with the idea that any divine law of sacrifice then existed, they will not only abolish Leviticus, as he contends, but the first legislation as well (Ex. xxii. 30, xxiii. 14-18, xxxiv. 19, 25), and Deuteronomy (xii. 6, 11, 27, xv. 19, xvi. 2, etc.),[1] of which Jere-

[1] The Professor thinks that the mode of observing the Passover underwent a change between the time of the Deuteronomic Law and the Levitical Code as represented in Ex. xii. 3 ff. He says that under the former (p. 371) "the paschal victim itself may be chosen indifferently from the flock or the herd (xvi. 2), and is still, according to the Hebrew of xvi. 7, presumed to be boiled, not roasted, as is the case in all old sacrifices of which the history speaks." The simple solution of which is, that at the Passover there were sacrificed not only the paschal lamb with which the feast began, but (Num. xxviii. 19, 24)

miah is the acknowledged champion, some adventurous critics having actually claimed that he wrote it himself; and even nullify the plea which the Lord directed Moses to urge with Pharaoh as a reason for leaving Egypt "that we may sacrifice to the LORD our God" (Ex. iii. 18), which is not classed among the Levitical passages (p. 432).

Our space will not permit us to trace the Mosaic codes through the rest of the Prophets. But one view is common to them all,—Jehovah's seat is in Zion[1] (Joel ii. 15, ff., iii. 21; Mic. iv. 1, ff.). Isaiah leaves us in no doubt as to the place of Jehovah's Sanctuary.

"two young bullocks and one ram and seven lambs" day by day on each of the seven days during which the festival lasted. The same Hebrew word is translated "roast" (Deut. xvi. 7) and "sodden" (Ex. xii. 9), being in fact a general term applicable to any style of cooking. But there is no discrepancy in the statements made. According to the passage in Exodus, it was not to be "cooked in water, but roast with fire," not boiled, therefore, but subjected to the direct action of the fire. According to Deuteronomy it was to be "cooked," *i. e.*, not raw, but the mode of preparation is not more particularly specified. That the term employed includes roasting is, however, obvious from II. Chron. xxxv. 13, where "cooked with fire," *i. e.* roast, stands opposed to "cooked in pots and in caldrons," *i. e.* boiled.

[1] The sole prophetic utterance which bears the semblance of approving a plurality of sanctuaries is the complaint of Elijah, "They have thrown down thine altars" (I. Kings, xix. 10). But in the anomalous condition of the Northern Kingdom, cut off from access to the Temple at Jerusalem, it is not surprising if the fearers of Jehovah maintained his worship in local sanctuaries. And the hostility to Jehovah's service, which overthrew these altars, was not palliated by the fact that, from a strictly legal point of view, they were unauthorized. We might be indignant at an infidel government for suppressing the Roman Catholic worship, without approving of the celebration of the Mass. Elijah's own sacrifice at Carmel was by immediate divine direction (I. Kings, xviii. 36).

Not only in the reign of Hezekiah, to whose reform he doubtless contributed, but from the outset of his ministry under Uzziah he declares his mind on this subject in unambiguous language. Zion is the Mountain of the LORD, which shall be so conspicuously exalted, and shall be the resort of all nations, and from which God's Law shall go forth (ii. 2, 3). It is upon Zion that He shall create a cloud and smoke by day and a flaming fire by night, a glory and a defence (iv. 5). In the year that King Uzziah died he had the sublime vision of Jehovah, whom he saw in the Temple, and his lips were purged by a coal from the altar (vi. 1, ff.). It was when Sennacherib presumed to shake his hand against the Mount of the Daughter of Zion that his doom was sealed (x. 32; compare, II. Kings, xix. 34). Zion is " the city of our solemnities " whose protection is secured by the presence of Jehovah (xxxiii. 20). He repudiates a plurality of altars (xvii. 8), which with him has only idolatrous associations; such an altar has no sacredness beyond mere chalk-stones (xxvii. 9). He predicts the time when there shall be "an altar to Jehovah in the midst of the land of Egypt" (xix. 19), as a symbol that this land shall be as truly as Canaan the Lord's land, and its people the Lord's people. Like Mal. i. 11, it is one of the prophetic intimations of the passing away of the local and national restrictions of the former dispensation. But that Isaiah had no thought of a separatist worship appears from ii. 3, where the same truth is clothed in the more strictly Old Testament form of all nations making their pilgrimages to Zion. The Lord cannot tolerate ritual observances as an offset to wicked lives (i. 11, ff.); but He has the same disgust for prayer (i. 15) and the language of the lips (xxix. 13) similarly offered. There is no depreciation of sacrificial worship in this, for the acceptable service that Egypt will one day render unto God is described by saying, "They shall do sacrifice and oblation; they shall vow a vow and perform it" (xix. 21).

But does not Isaiah in the same connection predict "a pillar" (*maççēba*) in the land of Egypt, the very symbol which Deut. xvi. 22 forbids? "This passage," says Professor Smith (p. 354), "gives a superior limit for the date of the Deuteronomic Code." "Isaiah could not refer to a forbidden symbol as a *maççēba* to Jehovah." There is a slight confusion of ideas here. In the first place, it proves too much. This symbol was prohibited likewise by the first legislation (Ex. xxiii. 24, xxxiv. 13, where for "images" read "pillars"), which required the destruction of Canaanitish altars and pillars, not their purification and rededication to the service of God. Secondly, the thing forbidden was the erection of pillars in the neighborhood of altars with the view of worshipping them (Lev. xxvi. 1; Deut. xvi. 21, 22). Moses himself had set up twelve pillars about the altar at the ratification of the covenant with Jehovah (Ex. xxiv. 4), each tribe, as it were, erecting its memorial on that solemn occasion. Stone monuments to commemorate God's goodness or to mark signal events were repeatedly erected in post-Mosaic times. When this was done with no view to sacrifice or adoration, it was no violation of the Pentateuchal statute. The monumental pillar, of which the Prophet speaks, at the border of Egypt, had no connection with the altar which was to be in the midst of the land. It simply marked the sacred character of Egypt, and was not intended for any idolatrous purpose.

But Ezekiel is the great stronghold of the hypothesis which we are considering. Here, we are told, we can see the very process of the formation of the Levitical Law. The Prophet is convinced, by the failure of all his predecessors to reclaim the wayward people, that a new departure must be made. A barrier must be erected to shut out heathen influence, and to confine Israel rigidly to the service of Jehovah. Acting on this idea, he lays down (chs. xl.–xlviii.) a ritual to be observed on the return from Exile, in which the worship which had hitherto been spontaneous and free is reduced to a fixed and unvarying form, and all the ceremonies are described in minute detail. This scheme of the cultus at the Sanctuary was enlarged and modified by Ezra, and thus arose the Levitical Law, which he brought forward in its completed form, and which thenceforth became the law of Israel's worship. Ezekiel's projected system represents a stage between the simplicity of the former cultus and the greater complexity of the Levitical legislation.

These closing chapters of Ezekiel, where it is proposed to find the key to the origin of the middle books of the Pentateuch, have always been a puzzle to commentators. And a hypothesis which professes to relieve them of all mystery (p. 374), to accept them in their most obvious sense, and to suggest a sufficient reason for those various regulations and an important purpose to be answered by them, thus converting what has seemed like a barren waste into a fruitful field, can scarcely fail to attract attention if it has the slightest plausibility. Some perplexities, however, force themselves upon us in advance.

1. There are items in Ezekiel's description of the Sanctuary, the worship, and the Holy Land of the future, which can scarcely have been intended to be literally understood, but seem to have been introduced for the sake of giving an ideal character to the entire section. Zion could not possibly be called " a very high mountain " (xl. 2), unless with a view to the exaltation promised Isai. ii. 2, and assumed Ezek. xvii. 22, 23. Its utmost extent could not afford a site for a sacred enclosure measuring 500 reeds or 3000 cubits, *i. e.*, nearly a mile on each of its four sides (xlii. 16 ff.). The critics have been at great pains to correct " reeds " into " cubits," in order to bring it within some reasonable probability; but this is directly in the face of the repeated statements of the text. The entrance of Jehovah's glory into the House represents a spiritual fact, not an occurrence in the form exhibited in the vision (xliii. 2–4). The stream flowing from the Sanctuary (xlvii. 1–12), swelling as it advanced, and carrying life, fertility, and healing even to the desert and the Dead Sea, is manifestly symbolical, and can no more represent an

actual river than its counterpart in Rev. xxii. 1 ff. The symmetrical division of the land parcelled among the tribes in parallel strips, with a holy oblation unto the LORD in the centre, is as unpractical as possible, and, in the case of the tribes located to the south, assumes a complete reclaiming of the arid desert. It is as plainly ideal as the uniform numbers of the tribes in Rev. vii. 5 ff., or as the resurrection of the dry bones (Ezek. xxxvii. 1 ff.) and the destruction of Gog (xxxix. 9 ff.), which are preliminary to these closing chapters.

2. These directions of Ezekiel were not in fact obeyed by the returning exiles, which shows that their intention, as understood by those immediately addressed, was not to guide the present but to forecast the future. The temple of Zerubbabel was not built by Ezekiel's plan; nor did its cultus or the partition of the land correspond with the model sketched by him.

3. If the Levitical Law was based upon that of Ezekiel, why did it not adopt the regulations given by him, instead of departing from them so often and so capriciously, as it would seem? Why, for example, was the burnt-offering of seven bullocks and seven rams, prescribed by Ezekiel (xlv. 23–25) for each of the seven days of Passover, and of the Feast of Tabernacles, converted into two bullocks, one ram, and seven lambs daily at the Passover (Num. xxviii. 19, 24), and thirteen bullocks, two rams, and fourteen lambs on the first day of Tabernacles, to be repeated from day to day, with a gradually diminishing num-

ber of bullocks, to the end (xxix. 13 ff.)? We can understand how a Prophet, speaking in the name of God and presaging the Church of the future, could freely modify the established Mosaic ritual for the very purpose of intimating that the forms of the old Law were not immutable and would one day suffer change; but this recent hypothesis is quite incomprehensible, — that, after Ezekiel had with divine authority proclaimed a new and elaborate ritual, it should have been altered and added to and subtracted from by the priesthood in numberless particulars before it was set in operation.

4. It is not very clear that the time when the ceremonial had been for the present providentially abolished was the one for doing what, by the hypothesis, had never been done so long as the Temple stood and the priests were performing its daily service, viz., prepare a complete formulary for its worship. One would think that there were more practical and pressing needs of the exiles than this. But if Ezekiel did undertake to do it, it is strange that the larger part of his scheme is occupied with an utterly abortive, though most minute, description of a temple, which did not so differ from the plan of Solomon's as to further any important end. And, stranger still, the Levitical Law, which was meant to be an improvement upon Ezekiel, instead of giving the exiles intelligible directions for the rebuilding of their temple, substitutes an almost interminable account of the Tabernacle in the Wilderness, which is a pure fancy sketch of a structure that never existed.

5. The so-called Torah of Ezekiel was issued with his own name, as revealed to himself. There was no "legal fiction" in the case, and no pretence of being from Moses; which is an additional warrant for believing that any other law published at that time or subsequently, by competent authority, would not have appeared under an assumed name, but have frankly and honestly announced the authority from which it proceeded, and on which it rested its claim to be obeyed.

6. And we are still further puzzled to understand how the new ritual could have been gotten into operation under the circumstances. By the hypothesis, it was a totally new departure made under false pretences. Every one knew that it was not only not Mosaic, but was diametrically opposed to the Mosaic system. All the prejudices that clung to the ancient ritual were opposed to it. So were the class interests of the priests, who, it is alleged, were now degraded from their former prerogatives to the inferior rôle of Levites; and the attachments to local sanctuaries, which it is supposed were now summarily abolished. And when we remember the persistence with which open idolaters faced Jeremiah, and even carried their point in spite of his remonstrances (Jer. xliii. 2 ff.; xliv. 15 ff.), the opposition from these various quarters could not have been slight. The new Law could not have gained prevalence from the authority of Ezekiel, for it freely deviates from the Law which he had given. It ran directly counter to the instructions of Jeremiah, as these are interpreted to us by the

advocates of the new hypothesis, for "he knew no divine law of sacrifice under the First Temple" (p. 374); counter also to Isai. lxvi. 1–3, which, on the Professor's critical principles, was by a Prophet of the Captivity later even than Ezekiel, in which, upon the same method of interpretation, Jehovah repudiates all earthly sanctuaries and sacrificial rites. And yet, in spite of all these elements of a formidable opposition, the Levitical Law was no sooner brought forward by Ezra than it was at once accepted and submitted to as "the Law of Moses, which the Lord had commanded to Israel" (Neh. viii. 1, 14, x. 29), and that, too, as distinguished from post-Mosaic enactments (xii. 45).

But waiving these difficulties of a general nature, how is it with those particulars in the Torah of Ezekiel, which recent critics affirm must have preceded the Law of Leviticus? We quote from Prof. Robertson Smith (p. 374): —

"The first that strikes us is the degradation of the Levites. The ministers of the old Temple, he (Ezekiel) tells us, were uncircumcised foreigners,[1] whose presence was an insult to

[1] The allegation that "uncircumcised foreigners" were employed to "keep the ward of the Sanctuary" . . . "as long as Solomon's Temple stood" (p. 250) is based on an extraordinary series of *non sequiturs*. David's body-guard of Kerethim and Pelethim has been conjectured to be "Cretans and Philistines," on the basis of a doubtful etymology, which was not accepted by Gesenius, and has not been by the subsequent editors of his Lexicon. The mention of "Carians," either in II. Sam. xx. 23 or II. Kings, xi. 4, is much more doubtful and improbable still. The men "who were clad in foreign garb, and leaped over the threshold" (Zeph. i. 8, 9), has nothing in the world to do with "Philistines" or "foreign janissaries." So that the inference that these imag-

Jehovah's Sanctuary. Such men shall no more enter the House, but in their places shall come the Levites not of the House of Zadok, who are to be degraded from the priesthood because they officiated in old Israel before the idolatrous shrines (xliv. 5, *seq.*). This one point is sufficient to fix the date of the Levitical Law as later than Ezekiel. In all the earlier history, and in the Code of Deuteronomy, a Levite is a priest, or at least qualified to assume priestly functions; and even in Josiah's reformation the Levite priests of the high places received a modified priestly status at Jerusalem. Ezekiel knows that it has been so in the past; but he declares that it shall be otherwise in the future, as a punishment for the offence of ministering at the idolatrous altars. He knows nothing of an earlier Law, in which priests and Levites are already distinguished, in which the office of Levite is itself a high privilege."

The distinction of priests and Levites, though rarely alluded to in the pre-exilic history, since there was no occasion so to do,[1] is yet explicitly recognized in I. Sam. vi. 15; II. Sam. xv. 24; I. Kings, viii. 4.

inary foreign guards "are unquestionably identical with the uncircumcised foreigners whom Ezekiel found in the Temple" rests merely upon a series of positive but unfounded assertions. The unlawful presence of uncircumcised foreigners in the Temple is of a piece with the open practice of idolatrous rites within those sacred precincts (Ezek. viii. 3 ff.; II. Kings, xxi. 4 ff.). This shameless violation of law is no proof that the Law was not in existence. The Nethinim (Ezra viii. 20) and children of Solomon's servants (ii. 58) do not fall under the same condemnation (Neh. x. 28, 29). They were, no doubt, circumcised; and performed such menial services for the Levites as were permissible for proselyted foreigners (Josh. ix. 27).

[1] The distinction is not even made in Malachi (see ii. 4–8, iii. 3), though he could not, on any critical hypothesis, have been ignorant of its existence.

Upon the first return of the exiles under Zerubbabel, ninety years before the alleged date of the Levitical Law, we not only find priests and Levites sharply distinguished and separately enumerated, but distinctions are made among the Levites themselves, who are variously classed, as by hereditary descent, singers, porters, etc. (Ezra ii. 36 ff.; Neh. vii. 39 ff., xii. 1–9). Compare also the account of the first inhabitants of Jerusalem after the Exile (1. Chron. ix. 2 ff.). The same thing recurs upon the going up of Ezra, fourteen years before the supposed origin of the Levitical Law (Ezra vii. 7, 24, viii. 15 ff.). These distinctions cannot have been introduced by Ezekiel's Torah; they could not have arisen in the Exile, when there was no temple service and no occasion for singers and porters. They must, of necessity, have been transmitted from the period before the Exile, and represent the distribution of functions then made among those that were employed at the Sanctuary. Priests and Levites must, therefore, have had separate duties and formed distinct classes while Solomon's Temple still stood. But further, the subdivisions of the Levites above referred to are also unknown to the Levitical Law, which apportions them in quite a different manner, having no possible relation to post-exilic times, but only to the wandering in the Wilderness, viz., the functions which they severally performed in the transportation of the Tabernacle and its furniture (Num. iv.).

Again, that the Levitical Law of the priesthood was prior to Ezekiel, and not *vice versâ*, appears from the nature of the case. While the former limits the priesthood to the family of Aaron, Ezekiel goes still further, and restricts it for cause to the line of Zadok, one of his descendants.[1] While the Levitical Law does not define the sanctuary duties of the Levites, but leaves them, as they might naturally be left at the outset, to perform such services as the priest might require of them (Num. xviii. 2), long usage gradually assigned to them specific tasks, as the charge of the gates, slaying the sacrifices, boiling their flesh, etc. (II. Chron. xxiii. 4, xxx. 17, xxxv. 13); and this is what Ezekiel expects them to do (xliv. 11, xlvi. 24). Indeed, Ezekiel seems to make allusion to the Levitical Law in the very passage under discussion. He calls the employment of the uncircumcised foreigners in the Temple a breach of God's Covenant (xliv. 7). It was, therefore, in his eyes, the violation of a positive divine statute, which can only be Num. xviii. 4 where any "stranger," *i.e.*, non-Levite, is prohibited from doing the work assigned to Levites. And if Levite had always, prior to the time of Ezekiel, been synonymous with "priest," or at least denoted one who is "qualified to assume priestly functions," it is remarkable that

---

[1] It has, indeed, been denied that Zadok (I. Kings, ii. 35) was of the seed of Aaron. But such a groundless denial of what is explicitly settled by his genealogy (I. Chron. vi. 8, 53, xxiv. 3, xxvii. 17) is fitly characterized by Delitzsch as "manufacturing history." And how the Levitical regulation could, in that case, have been built upon that of Ezekiel, and the restriction of the priesthood to the family of Zadok could have led to its restriction to another family of quite different descent, becomes still more inexplicable.

he should employ it as he does without any modifying epithet (xlviii. 11–13), in contrast with priests, and in the sense of those who are disqualified from assuming priestly functions.

"A second point in Ezekiel's Law is a provision for stated and regular sacrifices." Nehemiah engages the people to "a voluntary charge of a third of a shekel for this purpose (Neh. x. 32)." "In Ex. xxx. 16 the service of the Tabernacle was defrayed by the fixed tribute of half a shekel." If this "refers to the continual sacrifices," it differed from Nehemiah's rate plainly enough, but it does not follow that "this law," which bears no evidence of being a permanently obligatory precept, "was still unknown to Nehemiah, and must be a late addition to the Pentateuch." And, on the other hand, if it does not refer to them, it is a rash and unwarranted conclusion on the part of the Professor that stated offerings were ordained with no provision for supplying them.

"A third point in Ezekiel's Law," and the last which Prof. W. R. Smith insists upon, "is the prominence given to the sin-offering and atoning ritual. The altar must be purged with sin-offerings for seven consecutive days before burnt sacrifices are acceptably offered on it (xliii. 18, *seq.*). The Levitical Law (Ex. xxix. 36, 37) prescribes a similar ceremony, but with more costly victims. At the dedication of Solomon's Temple, on the contrary (1. Kings, viii. 62), the altar is at once assumed to be fit for use, in accordance with Ex. xx. 24, and with all the early cases of altar-building outside the Pentateuch. But, besides this first expiatory ceremonial,

Ezekiel appoints two atoning services yearly, at the beginning of the first and the seventh month (xlv. 19, 20, LXX.), to purge the house. This is the first appearance, outside of the Levitical Code, of anything corresponding to the great Day of Atonement in the seventh month, and it is plain that the simple service in Ezekiel is still far short of that solemn ceremony. The Day of Atonement was also a fast day. Now, in Zech. vii. 5, viii. 19, the Fast of the Seventh Month is alluded to as one of the four fasts commemorating the destruction of Jerusalem, which had been practised for the last seventy years. The Fast of the Seventh Month was not yet united with the 'purging of the house,' ordained by Ezekiel. Even in the great convocation of Neh. viii.–x., where we have a record of proceedings from the first day of the seventh month onwards to the twenty-fourth, there is no mention of the Day of Expiation on the tenth, which thus appears as the very last stone in the ritual edifice."

Prof. Robertson Smith affirms that there were no expiatory rites for cleansing the altar of Solomon's Temple; but the sacred historian, in explicit terms, declares the very reverse. In the summary account of the transaction given in Kings, the order of the ceremonial is not particularly stated, except that the services were continued "seven days and seven days." This of itself suggests a distinction between these two periods, and implies that there was a week preliminary to the proper week of the annual feast; and the most obvious purpose of such a week is that of sacrificial purgation. This very natural presumption is confirmed by the express language of II. Chron. vii. 9: "they kept the dedication of the altar seven days, and the feast seven days."

The Day of Atonement, it is true, is not mentioned by Ezekiel, but his silence does not prove that he knew nothing of it. For he likewise makes no allusion to the Feast of Weeks, which belonged even to the first legislation (Ex. xxiii. 16, xxxiv. 22), and this though he speaks of Passover and Tabernacles (Ezek. xlv. 21, 25). He does not allude to the daily evening sacrifice (I. Kings, xviii. 29, 36; II. Kings, xvi. 15; see Ezek. xlvi. 13 ff.); nor to the high-priest (II. Kings, xii. 7, 10, xxii. 4, xxiii. 4); nor to the priestly dues enjoined in Deut. xviii. 3, (see xliv. 28 ff.). It is also true that no mention is made of its observance in the Old Testament history, nor in fact for a long time after. The earliest allusion[1] to it is by Josephus (Ant. xiv. 16, 4), who tells us that Herod took Jerusalem (B. C. 37) on the solemnity of the Fast, as Pompey had done twenty-seven years before. The Feast of Weeks is spoken of but once between Moses and the Exile (I. Kings, ix. 25; II. Chron. viii. 13). The Sabbatical Year is not mentioned until the period of the Maccabees (I. Macc. vi. 53). The Fast of the Seventh Month, alluded to by Zechariah, in commemoration of the murder of Gedaliah (II. Kings, xxv. 25), was entirely distinct from the Annual Humiliation for Sin. The Professor seems to think that the Day of Atonement was not instituted for some years after the Levitical Law was brought out by Ezra. This will involve him in fresh difficulties;

---

[1] It is perhaps referred to, though this is not certain, in Josephus, Ant. xiii. 10, 3, where the high-priest Hyrcanus is spoken of as alone in the Temple, offering incense.

for, as Delitzsch remarks, it will be necessary to exclude from Ezra's Law not only Lev. xvi., where the services of the day are described in detail, but also all the allusions to it elsewhere,—as Ex. xxx. 10, which speaks of one annual atonement; Lev. xxiii. 26–32, xxv. 9; Num. xviii. 7, which speaks of a priestly duty within the Veil; Num. xxix. 7–11; and all passages containing the name given to the lid of the Ark in consequence of the expiation effected there, viz., the Mercy-Seat; and it would be very extraordinary if the ritual of the Day of Atonement, in which the Mercy-seat occupies so conspicuous a place, dated from a time when the Ark and Mercy-seat had ceased to exist.

It is a significant fact also that Ezekiel's Torah was revealed to him (xl. 1) "in the beginning of the year, in the tenth day of the month." If the tenth of Tisri, the first of the civil year, be meant, this was the Day of Atonement, and likewise the day on which the trumpet was blown to usher in the Year of Jubilee. The combination of this day with the release of prisoners is clearly shown by Isai. lviii. 6; and that the Prophet was acquainted with the Law (Lev. xxv. 8–10) is shown by his allusion to its terms (Isai. lxi. 1 ff.). Ezekiel was acquainted with the Year of Jubilee, and speaks of it as well known, which consequently involves a knowledge of the Day of Atonement, with which it began.[1]

---

[1] We add some further particulars from Delitzsch's very thorough and satisfactory discussion of the Day of Atonement, considered in relation to this recent critical hypothesis, from which the above discus-

We have now completed our task. And as we lay down our pen, may we not say of this latest critical attempt to roll the Pentateuch off its old foundations, that it has not achieved success? It has enveloped Mount Blanc in a cloud of mist, and proclaimed that its giant cliffs had forever disappeared. But, lo! the mist blows away, and the everlasting hills are still in place.

sion of this point has been for the most part borrowed. The word צוּם, *to fast*, which is already found in the prophet Joel, is foreign to the law of the Day of Atonement; the standing phrase there is עִנָּה נֶפֶשׁ, but without using the post-exilic derivative תַּעֲנִית (Ezra, ix. 5). The post-exilic language and literature offer nothing for the explanation of עֲזָאזֵל; עִתִּי *opportune obvius* (Lev. xvi. 21) and אֶרֶץ גְּזֵרָה *terra obscissa* (ver. 22) are expressions found nowhere else, which, if they were post-exilic, might have been expected to reappear in post-biblical writings.

THE WORSHIP IN HIGH PLACES.

THE period covered by the Books of Samuel is so important in its bearing on the question of the prior existence of the Law of Moses as to require a fuller discussion than was possible within the narrow limits of an article in a quarterly review. The proof was there given that the Mosaic Tabernacle located at Shiloh was the one sole place of regular sacrificial worship, from the time when it was set up by Joshua until the capture of the Ark by the Philistines. It was resorted to by all Israel; the feasts of the LORD were annually observed there; its services were conducted by a priesthood descended from Aaron. So far as we have any means of ascertaining, the Mosaic ritual was strictly observed there, the contrary assumption being altogether gratuitous, since all the alleged departures from that ritual admit of ready reconciliation with the legal requirements. There is not, from Joshua to Samuel, a recorded instance of sacrifice elsewhere than at Shiloh which is not explicitly declared to have been offered either in the presence of the Ark, or in connection with an immediate manifestation of the presence of Jehovah or of the Angel of Jehovah. And no sacrifice was offered by any one not a descendant of Aaron, except when Jehovah or the Angel of Jehovah had appeared to him. The only exceptions are expressly characterized by the sacred historian as open and flagrant transgressions of known law, — as the idolatry at Ophrah (Judg. viii. 27), and that of the renegade Micah (xvii. 5), not to speak of the apostasy to Baal and Ashtoreth, which is reprobated and chastised from the beginning to the end. The Book of Judges does not contain a trace of sanctioned, or even tolerated, worship upon high places. The test applied to Israel was "to know whether they would hearken unto the commandments of the LORD, which He commanded their fathers by the hand of Moses" (iii. 4). The hypothesis of Prof. Robertson Smith would restrict these commandments to what he denominates "the first legislation." But until it can be shown that the remaining portions of the Mosaic Code were not enacted at the time when they claim to have been given, the reference must be understood to be to the entire Law of Moses, — a meaning which is further rendered necessary by the constant usage of this and of equivalent terms in the historical books of Scripture (II. Kings, xxiii. 3, 25; I. Kings, ii. 3, vi. 12, ix. 4, 6, xi. 33, 38; compare Deut. viii. 11, xii. 1).

We approach the life of Samuel, then, from this vantage ground afforded by the entire antecedent history. The unity of the Sanctuary was unbroken from Moses to Eli, unless by confessed idolaters.

And the accepted Code of the nation was the Law of Moses; and, so far as anything yet appears to the contrary, that Law in its entire extent. This was still the case in the early years of Samuel. The one Sanctuary was at Shiloh. It had its Aaronic priesthood. It was the place of commanded sacrifice (I. Sam. ii. 29). There Jehovah dwelt between the cherubim above the Ark of the Covenant (iv. 4). To it all Israel went to pay their worship (ii. 14, 29, iii. 20, 21). Thither the child Samuel was brought by his parents to appear before the LORD, and with the expectation that he would abide there forever (i. 22). But the fatal battle at Eben-ezer, in which the Ark was lost, suddenly changed the whole aspect of affairs. We never find Samuel, or the Tabernacle, or a priest, or a sacrifice in Shiloh again from that time forward. Why was this?

Whether the Philistines extended their ravages to Shiloh, as some have supposed, or not, the city was thenceforth regarded as deserted of God. The fact that He permitted the priests, who were entrusted with the care of the Ark, to be slain, and the Ark itself to be carried off by the enemy, was accepted as a practical declaration that the Most High had withdrawn His presence from the place, and that He no longer acknowledged it as His habitation. This result had been predicted to Eli as the inevitable consequence of the atrocious conduct of his sons (I. Sam. ii. 29 ff., iii. 11 ff.), and the corrupt priesthood reflected but too accurately the corruption of the people. The Psalmist thus interprets the event and its moral causes: "They tempted and provoked the Most High God and kept not His testimonies. . . . They provoked Him to anger with their high places, and moved Him to jealousy with their graven images. When God heard this, He was wroth and greatly abhorred Israel, so that He forsook the Tabernacle of Shiloh, the tent which He placed among men, and delivered His strength into captivity, and His glory into the enemy's hand" (Ps. lxxviii. 56–61). And the Prophet Jeremiah says (vii. 12): "Go ye now unto My place which was in Shiloh, where I set My name at the first, and see what I did to it for the wickedness of My people Israel." (See also xxvi. 6, 9). Since God was provoked by the sins of the people to abandon the Sanctuary which He had established in the midst of them, all the sacredness of Shiloh was gone. Samuel, therefore, leaves it for his paternal home in Ramah (I. Sam. vii. 17); and the Mosaic Tabernacle was transferred to Nob, which either was already, or now became, a city of priests (xxii. 19). This was not a different sanctuary, but the same Tabernacle removed to another place, as appears from the identity of the priestly family (xxii. 11; compare xiv. 3) and the mention of the shew-bread (xxi. 6; compare Ex. xxv. 30; Lev. xxiv. 8, 9).

The capture of the Ark signified the withdrawal of God's presence from Israel, but it brought no lasting triumph to the Philistines. It was the source of humiliation to their idol and of deadly plagues upon themselves, until, to escape further inflictions, they sent it back to the land of Israel, with offerings in reparation of their trespass. The joy of the men of Beth-shemesh (I. Sam. vi. 13) was based upon the premature assumption that Jehovah's gracious presence was to be forthwith restored to Israel. The ritual requirements of the Mosaic Law were strictly observed in its reception. The Levites took down the Ark, and burnt-offerings and sacrifices (*i.e.*, peace-offerings) were sacrificed before it, — significant of devotion and of restored fellowship with God. But the act of irreverent criminality that followed was swiftly and terribly punished by the death of seventy men of the town and fifty thousand of the people at large.[1] The inhabitants of Beth-shemesh were terrified in consequence, and the presence of the Ark became as intolerable to them as it had been to the Philistines. "Who is able to stand before Jehovah, this holy God? and to whom shall He go up from us?" This language, uttered in their consternation, betrayed that they were aware of the breach existing between Jehovah and themselves; aware, too, of the fact that in suffering the Ark to be removed from them they were consenting to the departure of Jehovah Himself.

The Ark, which contained Israel's most sacred treasure, Jehovah's Covenant with them, engraved on stone by his own finger, the Ark, which was

---

[1] This seems to be the simplest explanation of ver. 19, which has given a needless amount of trouble to commentators. The offence was probably not that of looking into but of looking at the Ark of the LORD, which none might see divested of its sacred coverings (Num. Iv. 5, 20.)

the symbol and seal of God's presence in the midst of His people, — which had hitherto been Israel's glory and defence, and which had made the Mosaic Tabernacle, in a strict and special sense, Jehovah's dwelling-place, — was now become an unwelcome visitant, suggestive only of danger and of displeasure. And it was pushed aside into the obscurity of a private house. It was not taken back to Shiloh, which God had deserted. No new sanctuary was provided for it; no enthusiastic welcome was accorded to it; no crowd of worshippers flocked to the spot to do homage to Him who dwelt between the cherubim. The only question was how to dispose of what was so fraught with peril to all who were in its vicinity. One man was found brave enough and loyal enough to open his house for its reception, and to set his son apart to guard it until such time as the breach should be healed.

Twenty years passed (1. Sam. vii. 2), and still Israel was without the Ark and without a sanctuary. Meanwhile the heavy pressure of Philistine supremacy at length roused in the people a sense of their need of His saving help, whom they had alienated. "All the house of Israel lamented after the LORD." At the instance of Samuel, they put away their strange gods and served the LORD only. Shiloh was a sanctuary no longer. The degenerate priesthood were false to their high office. Samuel, as God's accredited messenger and plenipotentiary, assumed himself the functions which they were unworthy to discharge. He summoned the people to Mizpeh, who fasted and poured out water before the LORD, in token of penitent humiliation. He offered a sucking lamb as a whole burnt-offering, in token of the thorough consecration of a new-born people unto God. He cried unto the LORD for Israel, and the LORD heard him, and granted them a decisive victory over their oppressors at Eben-ezer, — the very spot where they had previously suffered the overwhelming defeat in which the Ark was lost. Hence it appears why Mizpeh was selected as the place for this penitent assemblage; it was in order that God's power might be signally exerted on His people's behalf upon the scene of their former disaster and disgrace, thus rendering the fact conspicuous that it had not occurred through any weakening of His arm of might. (Compare Hos. i. 10). The sway of the Philistines was thus broken; and, though the struggle between them and Israel went fiercely forward for years to come, " the hand of the LORD was against the Philistines all the days of Samuel," and they never again regained their former power.[1] (Compare II. Kings vi. 23, 24.)

[1] Though not essential to our argument, it will lead to a clearer comprehension of the narrative to observe that I. Sam. vii. 13–17 is a summary view of the rest of Samuel's life, which is introduced here, not because it chronologically belongs before ch. viii., but because the writer here, as uniformly throughout the book, formally concludes one theme before proceeding to another. With this rapid survey of the judgeship and life of Samuel, which in point of time extends down to I. Sam. xxv. 1, he winds up what he has to say of it separately, and then passes to the reign of Saul, detailing in ch. viii. ff. the circumstances which led to his appointment as king. In like manner I. Sam. xiv. 47–52 brings to a close the first period of Saul's reign, his successful conduct of Israel's affairs and his victories over surrounding foes.

And now we should expect a grateful people to have made their submission afresh to Him who had wrought this glorious deliverance, and to have reposed their unwavering trust and confidence in Him as their divine and all-sufficient Helper. Thus the way might have been prepared for the Most High again to set up His dwelling-place in the midst of them. But, instead of this, the next thing that we hear (ch. viii.) is the demand of the people, "Make us a king to judge us, like all the nations." In this crisis of their affairs — though the LORD had just demonstrated His power and readiness to save a penitent and obedient people — they distrust His help. Their invisible Sovereign can no longer content them; they must have a king. This inopportune request, and the spirit in which it was made, were most distressing to Samuel and displeasing to God,

The writer then enters, in the next chapter, upon the narrative of Saul's trespass and rejection, thus preparing the way for the anointing of David to be king in his stead. So (II. Sam. viii. 15-18) the summary statements respecting David's reign and his principal officers conclude the account of the early portion of his reign, with its uninterrupted prosperity and success. The writer is about to enter upon the next period, which was marked by David's great sin, and the disturbances which followed in its train. Accordingly, after mentioning an incident (ch. ix) which was not only illustrative of David's character, but had a bearing on matters to be stated subsequently (xix. 24 ff.), he proceeds at once (ch. x.) with the occasion of the campaign against the children of Ammon, in the course of which David's crime against Uriah was committed. In like manner II. Sam. xx. 23-26 marks the termination of the next period of David's life, in which he has at length succeeded in suppressing all rebellion against his royal authority, and thus prepares the way for the supplementary and rather miscellaneous incidents that remain to be given.

who said to his aged Prophet (ver. 7), "They have not rejected thee, but they have rejected Me, that I should not reign over them." It was the purpose of God that the kingdom should be established in Israel. It was contemplated in the Mosaic Law itself, and provision made for its erection (Deut. xvii. 14). The language of this law is incorporated in the narrative of this transaction to an extent which plainly shows that it was in the mind of Samuel and the people at the time; at least it is so conceived and represented by the sacred historian. (See above, p. 65, note.) It would not have been wrong for them to ask for a king under circumstances and in a manner which did not imply a lack of reliance upon God, or a transfer of their confidence from Him to another. If they had desired a king in the spirit of Pss. xx. and xxi., Samuel would not have opposed it, nor would the LORD have been offended by it. It was their preferring a king above the LORD as their protector, and persisting in their wilful choice in spite of the remonstrances of the LORD'S Prophet and of the plainly expressed disapproval of the LORD Himself, which gave character to the whole proceeding; and this is the feature which is made prominent in the history.

The LORD did not refuse the people's request, as He would have done if the thing desired had been in itself sinful, and the appointment of a king had been at variance with the divine constitution of Israel. But He granted it in such a way as to teach them that while the kingdom, with God's presence and favor, might be a great blessing, it would be the reverse if erected and maintained in a spirit of insubordination to the divine will and authority. He gave them first in Saul a king without God, then in David a king after God's own heart. He chose Saul in strict correspondence with the ideal that the people had in mind, a man of goodly person, brave, energetic, and capable, who fought their battles valiantly, and was victorious over their foes (1 Sam. viii. 19, 20). Moreover he was a worshipper of Jehovah, and was not devoid of religious impulses and a certain measure of reverent homage. But he did not place Jehovah's service and his sovereignty paramount. He was not concerned for the restoration of the Sanctuary. His reign was not conducted on the true theocratic principle that Jehovah was the real Monarch of Israel and the king was but his vicegerent and deputy; and in his impetuous nature he more than once broke loose from the restraints of express divine commands.

With the people thus leaning on an arm of flesh, and the king in whom they trusted ruling in his self-sufficiency, of course the Ark must remain in Kirjath-jearim, in the house of Abinadab. The way was not prepared for the LORD to come back to his people (Isai. xl. 3). He had forsaken Shiloh; but there must be a different state of things, before He could properly choose a new sanctuary. This does not mean that He had utterly abandoned Israel for the time, and withdrawn from them every token of His favor; but He had put them under a course of discipline by giving them that for which they asked, a king to judge them instead of God, and He withdrew Himself to await the issue (Hos. v. 15). They were in the condition of Absalom, whose crime was so far condoned that he was permitted to return to his own house, but was forbidden to see the face of the king (II. Sam. xiv. 24.)

But Samuel did not at once abandon hope for the people and their king, nor desist from his endeavors to bring them to a better mind; and the LORD employed various gracious measures for the same end. Samuel anointed Saul, and gave him the kiss either of allegiance or of affection. The spirit of the LORD came upon him, and God gave him another heart. The LORD wrought deliverance by him from the Ammonites. And Samuel, in the most earnest and touching manner, entreated the people to "turn not aside from following the LORD, but to serve the LORD with all their heart." And yet Saul's repeated acts of disobedience obliged Samuel at last to give him up, and to say to him (I. Sam. xv. 26), "thou hast rejected the Word of the LORD, and the LORD hath rejected thee from being king over Israel;" and the strong language is used (ver. 35) that "the LORD repented that He had made Saul king over Israel." And the remainder of his life was filled up with a bitter and relentless persecution of David, who by divine direction had been anointed in his stead. It was a reign without God. Saul had apparently no desire to re-establish the Sanctuary of God, or to have the Ark brought forth from its obscure retreat. Neither the people nor the king returned unto the

LORD, and the LORD did not return unto them (Mal. iii. 7).

But David was no sooner established in his kingdom than he instituted measures to have the Ark brought to his capital. Recognizing the momentous significance of the act, he assembled "all the chosen men of Israel, thirty thousand" (II. Sam. vi. 1), and brought it up with solemn pomp and numerous sacrifices, abasing himself before the Ark in a manner that drew upon him the reproaches of his wife, but which he justified by the fact that "it was before the LORD" (ver. 21). Jehovah had returned to take up his abode amongst His people. That this was the point of view from which it was regarded by the sacred historian appears from the emphasis with which in his mention of the Ark, both as taken from Shiloh (I. Sam. iv. 4,) and as reinstated in Zion (II. Sam. vi. 2), he associates with it "the LORD of Hosts who dwelleth between the cherubim." It was not a consecrated vessel, it was God Himself, for whom this enthusiastic welcome was prepared, and who now fixed His residence on Zion with a magnificence that, to the eye of faith, equalled His former grand descent on Sinai (Ps. lxviii. 16 ff.).

The facts then are these. Jehovah dwelt between the cherubim, or sat enthroned above the cherubim, that were upon the Ark. Wherever the Ark went, Jehovah went. He left Shiloh, and came into the camp of Israel. Dagon, in his own temple, fell prostrate and was broken in pieces before Him. His hand was laid so heavily upon the Philistines as to compel them to send the Ark back to the land of Israel. The violation of its sacredness by the over-curious men of Beth-shemesh and by Uzzah was punished by sudden death. Jehovah went up from Beth-shemesh when the Ark was taken away. He came to Zion when the Ark was carried thither. The place of the Ark was the place of sacrifice, and, until the abandonment of Shiloh, was the only place of stated legitimate sacrifice. The Ark is in the history exactly what it is in the Levitical Law, with all the sacredness and the sanctions and the requirements governing its transportation and its custody.

Such was Israel's estimation of the Ark; and yet the Ark was suffered for more than a generation to lie unnoticed and apparently forgotten in the obscurity of a private house. No sacred tent was erected to receive it. No pilgrimages were made to it as always heretofore. No festivals were held in its neighborhood. No sacrifices were offered there. No responses were sought or given. No homage was paid. There were no attendant priests; there was no daily ceremonial. The historian plainly traces this to the terror which it inspired. Israel was afraid to come near to this symbol of Jehovah's presence, or to have it brought near to them. They were profoundly sensible of the disharmony that had arisen; and even though " they lamented after the LORD," they kept aloof.[1]

Samuel had been trained up from early childhood in the Temple at Shiloh, where the Ark of God was. He knew that that was the sole place of sacrifice for

[1] See p. 170.

all Israel. He knew the meaning and the sacredness of the Ark. And yet, from the time that the LORD abandoned Shiloh, Samuel forsook it too, and never returned. He knew the full significance of the capture of the Ark, and of the slaughter of its priestly attendants; and he set himself to heal the breach between Jehovah and His people. The promising symptoms of the penitent assemblage at Mizpeh were soon destroyed by the want of faith in Jehovah, which clamored for a king to save them from their enemies, in spite of the urgent entreaties of Samuel himself, and the disapproval of the LORD. The hope to which he still clung, that the people might yet prove faithful to the LORD after their request had been granted, and that Saul might reign as a true servant of Jehovah, was dimmed and dimmed by successive disappointments, until it was absolutely quenched by Saul's wilfulness and transgression. All that Samuel could do further was to anoint David in Saul's stead, and wait and pray for better times.

During all this period of sad degeneracy and earnest labors for Israel's reformation, Samuel prayed for the people, and pleaded with them, and led their worship. He sacrificed at Mizpeh, at Gilgal, at Ramah, at Bethel (possibly), and at Bethlehem, but never once at Kirjath-jearim. He never assembled the people at or near the house of Abinadab. He never took measures to have the Ark present at any assembly of the people, or upon any occasion of sacrifice. The LORD had not indicated His will to establish another sanctuary, where He might record His name, in place of

Shiloh which He had forsaken. Israel was not spiritually prepared for God's return to dwell among them (Josh. xxiv. 19). Matters were not ripe for the renewal of the interrupted covenant relations. Under these circumstances it was not regularity of ritual which was demanded but a genuine inward reformation.

Jehovah was not a mere tribal god or a national deity in any such sense as Dagon was of the Philistines, Chemosh of Moab, Moloch of Ammon, and Baal of the Canaanites. His service was not outward, formal, and mechanical. The fundamental demand of the covenant was "Ye shall be holy; for I the LORD your God am holy." The Old Testament is full of the most explicit assertions that, if this was disregarded, the covenant could not be maintained (Ex. xxxiii. 3; Deut. iv. 23–26; Amos, iii. 2, 3). Sacrifices and lustrations were no acceptable substitutes for piety of heart and life. The principle by which Samuel was actuated throughout is formulated by himself (1. Sam. xv. 22, 23), "To obey is better than sacrifice, and to hearken than the fat of rams; for rebellion is the sin of witchcraft, and stubbornness is iniquity and teraphim." The people must be brought back to God in penitent submission, before He can be brought back to them and own Himself once more their God. Samuel was, therefore, laboring for the re-establishment of the Sanctuary in the only way in which it could be effectually brought about, so as to be a divine reality and not an empty and unmeaning form.

It is further to be observed that Samuel was God's accredited messenger and representative, charged with the declaration of His will to Israel; and we have the right to assume that in what he did he was guided by immediate divine direction. So that when he offered sacrifices elsewhere than at Shiloh, from which God had withdrawn His presence, and when he assumed the functions of a priesthood which was unworthy to exercise them longer, this was not because every one was at liberty to usurp the priestly prerogative at will, as Saul found out to his cost, nor because sacrifices might be acceptably offered wherever any one chose to offer them, but because the Prophet was in all this only the instrument of the divine will. Doubtless Samuel might have said of each act and place of sacrifice as Elijah said of his sacrifice at Carmel (I. Kings, xviii. 36), "I am thy servant, and I have done all these things at thy word." This is in fact explicitly recorded of his sacrifice at Bethlehem (I. Sam. xvi. 2); compare xiii. 8, 13, where Samuel's appointment in relation to a sacrifice is called the LORD'S commandment.

The allegation that Samuel's conduct shows him to have been ignorant of the Levitical Law, or proves that this law was not then in existence, is therefore wholly without foundation. He acted upon those great underlying principles upon which the ritual law itself was based; and he acted under the immediate direction of Him by whom that law was given. He acted in Israel's defection precisely as the great lawgiver himself acted on the occasion of the transgression of the Golden Calf. (See above, p. 100.) Moses and Samuel are accordingly combined by Jeremiah xv. 1 and Ps. xcix, 6, neither the Prophet nor the Psalmist conceiving that there was any variance between the work of Samuel and the Law of Moses rightly understood. If Samuel's conduct can be justified notwithstanding his acquaintance with the Ark, which cannot be denied, it is equally capable of being reconciled and in the very same manner with his knowledge of the whole round of Mosaic institutions.

But when David removed the Ark from Kirjathjearim, why was it not at once restored to its place in the Mosaic Tabernacle, which was then at Gibeon in the neighborhood of Jerusalem? or if it was to be taken to Zion, why did he erect a new tent for it there, when the Tabernacle of Moses might so easily have been brought to Zion likewise? The reason is to be sought in the fact that a transition point had now been reached in the affairs of Israel. God's earthly kingdom was entering upon a fresh stage of its existence, and a change should be made in the royal residence to correspond with it. "David perceived that the LORD had established him king over Israel, and that He had exalted his kingdom for His people Israel's sake" (II. Sam. v. 12). The migratory period, properly represented by the Mosaic tent, was over. The unsettled state of things, which had lasted until the time of David, the struggle with yet unsubdued Canaanites, and the wars with the Philistines, who were lately dominant, had at length come to an end, and Israel had gained complete and undisturbed possession of the land which the LORD had given them. It was fit that God's dwelling-place in Israel should no longer be a movable tent, such as was constructed for the march through the desert, or was adapted to the troublous times which had witnessed and compelled its transportation from Shiloh to Nob, and from Nob to Gibeon. God had now given firm establishment to His people, and His abode among them ought henceforth to assume the character of a fixed and permanent habitation (I. Chron. xxiii. 25, 26). He had granted prosperity and rich abundance to the kingdom, and this should be reflected in the royal palace; "the house to be builded for the LORD must be exceeding magnifical, of fame and of glory throughout all countries" (I. Chron. xxii. 5).

Accordingly David did not replace the Ark in the Mosaic Tabernacle, inasmuch as this was not such a house as it was fitting for Jehovah to have thenceforth in Israel. He set it in a tent which he had pitched for its temporary accommodation (II. Sam. vi. 17). And the very next record in the history is his proposal to erect a temple (ch. vii). This project, which was carried into effect by Solomon, was the guiding idea of David's reign, who made extensive preparations for it by the treasures amassed in his various wars (II. Sam. viii. 11; I. Kings, vii. 51). Hence for the remainder of David's reign there were two heads of the priestly order (II. Sam. viii. 17, xv. 24–29, 35, xx. 25), instead of one as at every other period before and after. These represented two distinct lines of descent from Aaron: Zadok, who was of the family of Eleazar, ministered in the Mosaic Tabernacle at Gibeon; and Abiathar or his son Ahimelech, of the family of Ithamar, ministered before the Ark on Zion (I. Chron. xvi. 39, xxiv. 3). This duplication ceased with the defection and deposition of Abiathar (I. Kings, ii. 26, 27), which fixed the priesthood in the line of Phinehas, as had been predicted long before (Num. xxv. 11-13; I. Sam. ii. 30 ff.).

From the abandonment of Shiloh to the erection of the Temple of Solomon, the worship on high places was allowable (I. Kings, iii. 2), as it had not been before and was not afterwards. During this interval there was no "place which the LORD had chosen to put His name there," so that the law of the unity of the Sanctuary was necessarily in abeyance (Deut. xii. 5 ff.). But from the time of Solomon onward, high places are nowhere sanctioned, directly or by implication. The idolatrous high places built by Solomon for his foreign wives (I. Kings, xi. 7, 8; II. Kings, xxiii. 13) were in palpable violation of Jehovah's covenant; so were those that were frequented in the reign of Rehoboam and other ungodly kings (I. Kings, xiv. 22-24). The fact that "the high places were not removed," even under such pious kings as Asa (I. Kings, xv. 14), Jehoshaphat (xxii. 43), Joash (II. Kings, xii. 3), Amaziah (xiv. 4), Uzziah (xv. 4), and Jotham (ver. 35) is confessedly disapproved by the author of the Books of Kings (compare also I. Kings, xiii. 32, 33; II. Kings, xvii. 9, xxi. 3); and it implies no sanction on the part of these monarchs, but simply that they were not able to effect their extirpation, and perhaps were not as zealous in the matter as they should have been. That they did seek to remove them, and with a measure of success, is explicitly affirmed by the author of Chronicles (II. Chron. xiv. 3–5, xvii. 6); and this is not contradicted by anything in Kings. Some of these high places were dedicated to the worship of Jehovah (II. Kings, xviii. 22; Isai. xxxvi. 7; II. Chron. xxxiii. 17), and Levitical priests officiated at them (II. Kings, xxiii. 9); but this does not disprove the existence of the law forbidding them, any more than the corruptions of the Middle Ages would justify the assumption that the New Testament had not yet been written. And if the worship on high places was accounted legitimate until the reign of Hezekiah, how comes it to pass that there is not a trace of such a view in the Psalms or in the older Prophets? God is invoked and described as dwelling in Zion; no other habitation is ever alluded to, no other Sanctuary is ever mentioned with approval. The critics tell us that it is the character of the worship offered on the high places, and not the high places themselves, which the Prophets condemn. But the fact is that no mention is made in the entire body of the prophetical writings of a single high place where pure and acceptable worship was offered, or to which it was proper to resort. The people are never told that they may sacrifice on the high hills and under green trees, or at Bethel and Gilgal and Beersheba, if only they sacrifice to the LORD alone and in a proper manner. They are never told that

THE WORSHIP IN HIGH PLACES. 157

God will be pleased with the erection of numerous altars, provided the service upon them is rightly conducted.

It cannot be pretended that the Prophets of Judah look otherwise than with disfavor upon the worship on high places. This is acknowledged of Jeremiah (iii. 2, vii. 31, xvii. 1-3) and of all the Prophets after his time. (Compare Ezek. vi. 3, 6, xvi. 16, xx. 27-29.) It is equally plain in Joel (ii. 1, 15, 32, iii. 16, 17, 21), Obadiah (vers. 16, 17, 21), Micah, (i. 5, iv. 1, 2, 7), and Isaiah (not to repeat passages already cited, p. 119, xi. 9, xii. 6, xviii. 7, xxiv. 23, xxvii. 13, xxviii. 16, xxix. 1, 8, xxx. 29, xxxi. 4, 9).

But it is urged that the antithesis suggested by Hosea and Amos, who prophesied in the Northern Kingdom, is not between the worship on high places and worship at Jerusalem, but between high places and the true service of Jehovah, showing that it was not the unity of the Sanctuary but purity of worship which they had at heart. We not only freely admit but strenuously insist that purity is above unity and unity is for the sake of purity. This attitude of the Prophets, however, so far from conflicting with the Levitical and Deuteronomic codes, or showing that the Prophets were unacquainted with them and with their binding authority, is identical with the openly professed intent of these codes themselves (Lev. xvii. 3-7; Deut. xii. 2-5). It would not be strange if some leniency were shown to the pious among the Ten Tribes in this matter, and if irregularities were considered excusable in their case, which the exigencies of their situation rendered, if not unavoidable, yet extremely natural. Nevertheless even here there is not a word that directly or positively sanctions worship on any high place, or in any other than the one sole Sanctuary.

If a pure worship, freed from idolatrous adjuncts and from carnal enticements, was maintained in the Sanctuary on Mount Zion alone, then Hosea's appeal to his hearers to abandon Gilgal and Bethel, as incompatible with a true reverence for Jehovah (iv. 15, ix. 15), his affirmation that snares are laid on Mizpeh and a net spread upon Tabor (v. 1), his rebuke of multiplied altars (viii. 11, x. 1, xii. 11), and his denunciation of judgment on Bethel and its high places (x. 8, 15), are equivalent to so many exhortations to his hearers to frequent the one place of true worship, and must have been so understood by them. Then, too, when Amos opposes seeking Bethel and Dan and Gilgal and Beersheba to seeking the LORD (iv. 4, v. 4–6, viii. 14), or threatens desolation to the high places of Isaac and the sanctuaries of Israel (iii. 14, vii. 9), he is in effect recalling the transgressing people to the worship at Jerusalem. If, however, it be maintained that there were other sanctuaries than that on Zion where the worship was pure, and that Hosea and Amos had these in mind, we wait for the proof of an assertion which Hosea and Amos certainly do not make, which is directly counter to the testimony of other Prophets, which finds no confirmation in the expressed views of the sacred historians or in any known facts of the history, but is simply

THE WORSHIP IN HIGH PLACES. 159

assumed in the interest of a critical hypothesis. Moreover, Amos expressly affirms that Zion is Jehovah's Seat, from which He sends forth the utterances of His might (i. 2); and both he and Hosea range themselves in line with the Prophets of Judah by their recognition of the fact that the rightful sway over Israel belonged to David's Royal House (Hos. iii. 5, viii. 4; Amos, ix. 11).

We are now prepared to estimate the following paragraph from Prof. Robertson Smith (p. 235): "The earlier history relates scarcely one event of importance that was not transacted at a holy place. The local sanctuaries were the centres of all Hebrew life. How little of the history would remain if Shechem and Bethel, the two Mizpehs and Ophrah, Gilgal, Ramah and Gibeon, Hebron, Bethlehem and Beersheba, Kedesh and Mahanaim, Tabor and Carmel were blotted out of the pages of the Old Testament."

1. Of the fifteen places thus promiscuously thrown together, there are three, viz., Mizpeh (east of Jordan), Kedesh, and Mahanaim, in which there is no recorded instance of sacrifice in post-Mosaic times; and, in two of them, there is no mention of sacrifice at any time, whether before the age of Moses or after it. Mizpeh, where Jacob and Laban covenanted and offered sacrifice (Gen. xxxi. 49, 54), and Mahanaim, where the angels met Jacob (xxxii. 2), like other spots memorable in the lives of the Patriarchs, and like Bannockburn, Bunker Hill, and Gettysburg in more modern times, were hallowed by their associations, and were for that reason likely to be selected

for patriotic gatherings or for important uses. The children of Israel assembled at Mizpeh to oppose the Ammonites (Judg. x. 17); and if, as seems probable, it was the same as Ramoth-gilead (Josh. xiii. 26), it was one of the cities of refuge (xx. 8). Mahanaim was a Levitical city (xxi. 38), the capital of Ish-bosheth's kingdom (II. Sam. ii. 8), and the place to which David fled from Absalom (xvii. 24); and Cant. vi. 13 speaks somewhat obscurely of "the dance of Mahanaim." But there is nothing that implies that either was a sanctuary for worship. Jephthah is said (Judg. xi. 11) to have "uttered all his words before the LORD in Mizpeh." But so David and Jonathan made a covenant "before the LORD" in the wood where the former was hiding (I. Sam. xxiii. 18). David walked "before the LORD" in the whole of his pious life (I. Kings, iii. 6), as did Jotham (II. Chron. xxvii. 6) and Hezekiah (xxxi. 20). The foes of Asa were destroyed "before the LORD" in battle (II. Chron. xiv. 13). Manasseh humbled himself "before the LORD" in his captivity at Babylon (xxxiii. 12, 23). Nehemiah (i. 4) prayed "before the God of Heaven" in the capital of Persia.

The Professor tells us (p. 424) that Kedesh, which was a Levitical city and a city of refuge (Josh. xxi. 32), and where Barak marshalled his army against Sisera (Judg. iv. 10), "is proved by its very name" to have been a sanctuary; but he fails to inform us when or by whom this name was imposed and what gave occasion to its being called a consecrated place. The argument is as faulty as that (p. 323) from

"Deut. i. 1, and other similar passages, where the land east of the Jordan is said to be across Jordan, proving that the writer lived in Western Palestine;" as though Cisalpine Gaul and Transalpine Gaul changed names to the old Roman generals as often as they crossed the Alps. Or it may be classed with his inference that the use of *Negeb* for "south" and *sea* for "west" "proves quite unambiguously that the Pentateuch was written in Canaan;" and by parity of reasoning we may infer that *September* is the seventh month of the year, that *landlords* are always owners of real estate, and that *lunacy* is produced by the influence of the moon. There is no more familiar phenomenon in language than that words often retain their secondary senses, even when these have ceased to be in accord with their primary sense.

2. Three others in the above list of alleged Israelitish sanctuaries, viz., Shechem, Beersheba, and Tabor, were places of idolatrous worship only, so far as we know, in post-Mosaic times. Shechem contained a temple of Baal-berith (Judg. ix. 4, 27, 46). Amos uttered his warnings against the sinful worship of Beersheba (v. 5, viii. 14), and Hosea against the net spread upon Tabor (v. 1). But there is no intimation that any other style of worship was maintained in these places, or in any one of them. Shechem, by the oak of Moreh, was Abram's first abode in the Promised Land; there the LORD appeared to him and he builded an altar (Gen. xii. 6, 7). Jacob came back to Shechem on his return from Padan-aram, and

he erected an altar there (xxxiii. 18, 20); and all the strange gods and idolatrous emblems of his household were buried under the oak by the city (xxxv. 4). In memory of these facts Joshua assembled the people at Shechem (Josh. xxiv. 1) when he would urge them to put away their strange gods (vers. 14, 23), and he set up a monumental stone (ver. 26) under the old oak which still continued to stand—not "by," as the English Version has it, but as it is in the Hebrew—"in the sanctuary of the LORD." The very form of the expression shows us that the sanctuary here spoken of was not a building, and there is no intimation that sacrifices were offered there upon this or any subsequent occasion; it was simply a spot venerated from its ancient and sacred associations. The place gained new sacredness from these parting counsels of Joshua, and was hence selected for the coronation of Abimelech (Judges ix. 6) and of Rehoboam (I. Kings, xii. 1), and for the royal residence of Jeroboam (ver. 25). It was also one of the cities of refuge (Josh. xx. 7); but it is nowhere affirmed or implied that it was a sanctuary for the worship of Jehovah.

The LORD appeared to Isaac (Gen. xxvi. 23–25) and subsequently to Jacob (xlvi. 1.) in Beersheba, both of whom offered sacrifices there. It was also the scene of an interesting incident in the life of Abraham, who also worshipped there (xxi. 31, 33). This ancient sacredness no doubt contributed to its selection as one of the chief seats of idolatry in later times. The lofty summit of Tabor sufficiently accounts for its becoming a place of idolatrous sacrifice (Hos. iv. 13). The suggestion (p. 424) that it is "alluded to in Deut. xxxiii. 18, 19, as the Sanctuary" of Zebulun and Issachar, is wholly without foundation.

3. Six of the alleged sanctuaries are places where sacrifices were offered on some special occasion or during some brief period, but were not, so far as there is any record upon the subject, permanent places of sacrifice. We read of offerings in five of these places in the provisional period from Samuel to Solomon, and in that exclusively; they are Mizpeh (west of Jordan), Ramah, Gibeon, Hebron, and Bethlehem. The one offering spoken of at Mizpeh (1. Sam. vii. 5, 9) was by Samuel when the place of Israel's defeat was by divine help converted into one of victory (see above, p. 143). It is with allusion to this event that Mizpeh is said (1. Macc. iii. 46) to have been "a place of prayer aforetime for Israel." In 1. Sam. x. 17 this same spot was significantly selected for the gathering of the people "unto the LORD," when Samuel recited God's gracious acts of deliverance, which in their demand of a king they had so sinfully disregarded; but no mention is made of sacrifice. Nor was any sacrifice offered when the people were gathered "unto the LORD" in Mizpeh (Judg. xx. 1), to go up to battle against Benjamin. The reason why they met there was not the superior sacredness of the place, but its proximity to Gibeah where the crime had been committed. It was a convenient point for negotiations with Benjamin (ver. 12), or if need be for hostilities against them. When they desired to ask counsel of

God (vers. 18, 27), or to offer sacrifices (ver. 26, xxi. 4), they went for the purpose to Bethel, to which the Ark was temporarily brought from Shiloh for the occasion. Samuel judged Israel in Mizpeh from year to year (I. Sam. vii. 16); but he is nowhere said to have offered more than the one sacrifice there.

Ramah was another place of Samuel's judgment, and there he built an altar unto the LORD (ver. 17); this was the scene of the sacrifice spoken of, ix. 12. Gibeon was "the great high place" (I. Kings, iii. 4) in the early years of Solomon, because the Mosaic Tabernacle was there (II. Chron. i. 3, 13). Hebron, where Abraham dwelt and built an altar (Gen. xiii. 18), and where Jacob lived (xxxvii. 14), was a priestly city and a city of refuge (Josh. xxi. 13). David went thither by divine direction (II. Sam. ii. 1), and was anointed king over Judah (ver. 4), and subsequently king over Israel, after making a league there with the elders of the people "before the LORD" (v. 3); but the only thing recorded which implies a sacrificial service there, is Absalom's vow (xv. 7–9). Samuel by God's command offered a sacrifice in Bethlehem (I. Sam. xvi. 2 ff.); and David's family held a yearly sacrifice there (xx. 6). All the offerings now recited occur in the interval between God's forsaking Shiloh and the building of the Temple, which has been already sufficiently discussed. There is no hint of post-Mosaic sacrifices at any of these places before or after this term of the cessation of the divinely instituted Sanctuary.

Elijah, acting under express divine orders (I Kings,

xviii. 36), offered his sacrifice at Carmel, repairing for the purpose the previously existing altar of the LORD which had been broken down (ver. 30). This shows, as we learn further from xix. 14, that the pious in the apostate Kingdom of Israel, who were cut off from attendance at Jerusalem, preferred to sacrifice in an irregular manner rather than be precluded from offering to Jehovah altogether. This neither implies ignorance of the Mosaic Law, nor a wanton disregard of it. It is a breach of outward order for the sake of preserving God's worship from extinction. The forced construction of Mic. vii. 14, which makes it declare that God dwells in the midst of Carmel, and in which Baudissin[1] follows Hitzig, will probably commend itself to few. There is no reason to suppose that the Professor adopts it.

4. But three of the alleged sanctuaries remain, viz., Bethel, Ophrah, and Gilgal, in each of which sacrifices were offered upon special occasions only, and for assignable reasons; and each subsequently became a seat of idolatry. Gideon's present of a kid and unleavened cakes was converted into a sacrifice by the Angel of the LORD who appeared to him in Ophrah (Judg. vi. 20, 21), whereupon he built a memorial altar (ver. 24); afterwards by express divine command he threw down the altar of Baal, erected one to Jehovah in its stead, and offered a bullock upon it (vers. 25 ff.). An ephod, which he set up in Ophrah, was perverted to an idolatrous use (viii. 27). Bethel,

---

[1] Article "Höhendienst," p. 183, in Herzog und Plitt's Real-Encyclopædie.

where God appeared twice to Jacob (Gen. xxviii. 10 ff., xxxv. 9 ff.), was temporarily a place of sacrifice during the presence of the Ark (Judg. xx. 18, 26, 27); and, when the regular services of the Sanctuary were suspended in the time of Samuel, mention is made of men going up with their offerings to God to Bethel (1. Sam. x. 3). These sacred associations no doubt influenced Jeroboam in determining to set up one of his Golden Calves at Bethel (1. Kings, xii. 29).

Gilgal, which was Israel's first encampment in the Holy Land (Josh. iv. 19), and where they renewed their covenant with God by circumcision and the Passover after the long period of alienation and wandering in the Wilderness (v. 2 ff.), was selected by Samuel with a view to these old memories as one of his places of judgment (1. Sam. vii. 16), and particularly for the sacrifices by which the kingdom was inaugurated (x. 8, xi. 14, 15), as he sought to reclaim the people from their forgetfulness and rejection of the LORD. And it was here that Saul's repeated acts of disobedience (xiii. 9 ff., xv. 15 ff.) destroyed every hope that the ancient experience of Gilgal might be repeated, so long as he sat upon the throne. This consecrated spot was for that very reason chosen by idolaters for their worship (Judg. iii. 19,—where "quarries" of the English version should be "images,"—Hos. iv. 15, ix. 15, xii. 11; Amos, iv. 4).

We have now gone with some care through the entire list of what the Professor calls "local sanctuaries;" and the facts show that apart from idolatrous perversions, there was not a single sanctuary for permanent worship among them. Deduct the two or three instances, in the period of the Judges, in which Jehovah or the Angel of Jehovah appeared to men, and sacrifices were offered on the spot, — deduct further the sacrifices offered when Israel had no sanctuary, after God had withdrawn from Shiloh and before the Temple was built, or in the peculiar circumstances of the Ten Tribes in the lifetime of Elijah, — deduct these sacrifices which were due to special causes and were strictly limited to the occasion that called them forth, and there is not a particle of evidence that any one of these places was a sanctuary for the worship of Jehovah. This whole hypothesis of "local sanctuaries" rests on absolutely unsupported conjecture. With a total disregard of the considerations that rule in some exceptional case, the conclusion is at once drawn that it represents a permanent and habitual course of action. Each instance of special sacrifice is adduced as evidence of a new sanctuary. By a like process of argument, some future historian of the American Colonies may infer from the fact that the Continental Congress met at various places during the exigencies of the Revolutionary War, that Lancaster, York, Princeton, and Annapolis were all permanent capitals like Philadelphia, and that instead of one united body of representatives from all the colonies, there must have been several distinct bodies holding their sessions simultaneously and meeting continuously at these different points.

The question here recurs: Do the known facts respecting Israel's worship militate against the Mosaic origin of the Pentateuchal laws? The critics tell us that the law of the unity of the Sanctuary was constantly disobeyed until the time of Josiah, — that previous to his reign, both the ungodly and the godly portion of the people, both wicked and pious princes, act in a manner which shows that no such law was known to them or heeded by them. Josiah's vigorous reforms must accordingly mark the first serious attempt to introduce this law, and Deuteronomy must be dated from his reign, or shortly before it.

Now, what is the real state of the case? The Ark of the covenant and the Mosaic Tabernacle constituted the sole Sanctuary of Jehovah from the entrance into Canaan until the capture of the Ark by the Philistines. From that time until the Ark was taken to Zion it was simply lodged in a private house, and no sacrifices were offered before it; but Samuel and others sacrificed in different parts of the land. A time so evidently anomalous, however, supplies no criterion for a normal state of affairs. It cannot be inferred that there was no law restricting sacrificial worship to the Sanctuary, because this restriction was not observed when no sanctuary existed. Would any one think of arguing that Washington City was not the legally established seat of government in the United States, because the President and Congress were dislodged by the burning of the Capitol and other public buildings in 1814, — or that England is not by its constitution a hereditary monarchy, because Oliver Cromwell ruled as Protector?

From the time that the Ark was lodged in Solomon's Temple and the divine glory took manifest possession of it, this was Israel's exclusive Sanctuary. And the attempt to disprove this by urging the subsequent existence of high places, which the sacred historian condemns and which the Prophets with one voice disallow, is as though some one were to infer that no prohibitory law had ever been passed in Maine, because liquor continues to be sold in the State, and that, as is alleged, with the connivance of officers elected on the temperance ticket. There was but one Ark from the days of Moses to the Babylonish captivity, and Jehovah dwelt between its cherubim. This fact, which can neither be denied nor explained away, is the impregnable stronghold of our position.

And let it be remembered that the preceding argument has been conducted without the aid which we are entitled to draw from the Books of Chronicles. It is confessed by all that if their testimony is admitted into the case, the Mosaic origin of the institutions of the Pentateuch is unassailable.

ADDENDUM

To Page 149, Line 4 from bottom.

And in the very midst of the glad and triumphal transportation of the Ark to the city of David, the whole procceding was suddenly arrested by the manifestation of Jehovah's displeasure, in the death of Uzzah. David feared to take the Ark further, and it was once more deposited in a private house. There it remained for three months, until the blessing bestowed upon the house of Obed-edom, because of the Ark, gave assurance that the anger of the LORD was turned away, and His favor was again restored to His people.

KUENEN ON THE PROPHETS AND PROPHECY IN ISRAEL.

KUENEN ON THE PROPHETS AND PROPHECY IN ISRAEL.

THE recent work by Professor Kuenen, of the University of Leyden, entitled "The Prophets and Prophecy in Israel,"[1] is written from the standpoint of the most ultra criticism and of absolute anti-supernaturalism. The concurrent judgment of all past ages has found a surprising coincidence between the predictions of these Prophets and the facts of subsequent history. The defenders of revealed religion have esteemed this one of the firm bulwarks of their faith, and have ranked it among the convincing evidences of the divinity and inspiration of the Scriptures. They, to whom the Scriptures were not in any supernatural sense the Word of God, have confessed the potency of this argument by the extraordinary pains which they have taken to rid themselves of it by every expedient of criticism and exegesis. But withal they have not been, in Dr. Kuenen's opinion,

[1] "The Prophets and Prophecy in Israel." An Historical and Critical Enquiry, by Dr. A. Kuenen, Professor of Theology in the University of Leyden. Translated from the Dutch by the Rev. Adam Milroy, M.A., with an Introduction by J. Muir, Esq., D.C.L. London: Longmans, Green & Co. 1877. 8vo, pp. 593.

sufficiently thorough-going. "The supporters of the naturalistic hypothesis themselves," he says (p. 6), "do not maintain it in a thorough and consistent manner, but in their description of Israelitish prophecy introduced features which are borrowed from the traditional theory, or at least find there alone their proper place."

This weakness and inconsistency he proposes utterly to eschew. He would relieve the hypothesis of the purely human origin of the Bible from the burden by which it has hitherto been pressed. With this view, he denies the existence of any such correspondence between prophecy and the event as has been hitherto claimed by believers, and confessed to no small extent even by those who dispute its supernatural inspiration. He undertakes to point out in detail that a large proportion of the prophecies have never been fulfilled at all in any proper sense, and that the fulfilment of many more has been but partial. And he makes this the basis of his entire argument to discredit their divine origin. If it be true that the major part of these predictions have not been fulfilled, then they are certainly not from God, and the comparatively few instances in which they have been verified in fact must be otherwise accounted for. They may have been shrewd conjectures, or the prophecy may have wrought its own fulfilment by its influence on those to whom it was addressed, or the coincidence may be purely accidental. In the introduction John Muir, Esq., of Edinburgh, at whose solicitation the volume was prepared and to whom it is dedicated, thus expresses his confident persuasion of the cogency of the argument (p. xxxix): "The ample and satisfactory proofs which Professor Kuenen has adduced in support of his conclusions must, I think, produce a powerful effect on all candid inquirers who study them with care and attention, and tend to bring about in the minds of thoughtful men a great change of opinion in regard to the authority and the character of the Scriptures, whether of the Old or of the New Testaments."

We do not share this judgment. We have no idea that any serious revolution of opinion will result from this publication. We make no pretence to underestimate the learning and ability which it displays, nor the consummate art shown by Professor Kuenen in the presentation of his views. But we need not shrink from having the most searching test applied to secure foundations. The accomplishment of the predictions of the Prophets is not a question of recent origin or of uncertain issue. And the conviction which the Christian world has reached upon this subject is no mere prejudice blindly adopted, nor a hasty judgment formed after slight consideration and resting upon inadequate grounds, and liable consequently to be set aside by more thorough and searching inquiry. Every element that can possibly affect the settlement of this question has long since been brought forward and subjected to the most rigorous tests. The prophecies are before us. The facts of history are known at least in their main features. The correspondence is a palpable one, and no learned ingenuity can obliterate it. Every line in ancient authors that has any possible relation to this subject, near or remote, has long ago been adduced and diligently scanned. Buried monuments continue to be exhumed and are throwing welcome light on remaining obscurities, but these cannot revolutionize all history nor disturb well-known and well-attested facts. There is not a fact nor a historical testimony brought forward in this volume, as contravening or appearing to contravene what was foretold by the Prophets, that has not been elaborately discussed before in all its bearings and its full significance ascertained. It is not likely, consequently, that their fresh production now will occasion any great shock or be attended by important changes in well-established views. If there be anything in particular which can be called novel in Professor Kuenen's line of argument, it is the bravery with which he carries through what is known among logicians as the *petitio principii*, or begging the question, — covertly assuming the point at issue, and then working it out to an apparent demonstration. The prophecies are dealt with on the assumption that they are a merely human production; and then the conclusion that they are merely human necessarily follows.

The question at issue is indeed, as Professor Kuenen observes (p. 5), " closely connected with the deepest needs and the most important interests of mankind; and these have nothing to fear from the truth." We confess, however, that we see no good reason to indulge the hope, which he cherishes, that a speedy and decisive settlement can be reached which shall compel the assent of all parties. "It is," he says, "an historical problem. Every one knows the sources which must be consulted for its solution." Nevertheless his own volume forces the conviction upon us afresh that the time has not yet arrived for terminating the long controversy of ages. His own conclusions rest not on the historical data, but on the "dogmatic presuppositions" with which these have been approached, notwithstanding his repeated profession that he is wholly emancipated from such influences. Starting with the convictions that he has, he could arrive at no other result than he does; but they who entertain contrary convictions will not find it necessary to follow him. The recognition or the rejection of the divine and the supernatural is not a mere act of the intellect freely balancing intellectual considerations. There is an antecedent bias from each man's spiritual attitude. To him who is prepared to admit the reality of immediate communications from God to men upon rational evidence, the facts supply a convincing demonstration; while he to whom such communications are *a priori* inadmissible will either refuse to admit the facts or put some different interpretation upon them. It is this element of the will, entering into and influencing our judgments respecting divine and spiritual things, which gives them their moral character and makes every man morally responsible for his belief.

According to Dr. Kuenen's view, as stated by himself, "prophecy is one of the most important and remarkable phenomena in the history of religion, but just on that account a human phenomenon, proceeding from Israel, directed to Israel." It is from God in no other sense than as "from Him are all things." It is "a testimony not as out of heaven to us, but a testimony to men's need, and to Israel's peculiar destination to 'seek the Lord, if haply they might feel after Him and find Him,'"—a destination, by the way, which in the Scriptures is ascribed not to Israel, but to the Gentiles before Christ's coming. "A preparation for Christianity? Yes; but in another sense than that which tradition means by these words,—no prediction of facts in the life of Christ, but a preparation of the soil out of which Christianity was to spring, the prelude to the new religious creation which mankind owe to Jesus of Nazareth" (pp. 4, 5).

He seeks to conciliate favor for this view by calling it the historico-critical, or organic, as distinguished from the traditional. We cannot concede the propriety of this designation. The organic view of prophecy is not only entirely consistent with the supernatural conception of its origin and character, but is held as firmly by those who maintain its divinity and inspiration as by those who deny it. Its organic nature is dependent not on the question of its origin, but of its structure and relations. Prophecy grew directly out of the heart of the Israelitish people, took its shape from their necessities, was moulded by their changing circumstances age by age, and had its regular and consistent unfolding from first to last.

That all was nevertheless due to the immediate impulses of the Divine Spirit no more disturbs its human adaptations than the organic structure of a tree is damaged by the sunlight which produces it. It is the attempted elimination of the supernatural which is really at war with the organism of prophecy; for this deprives it of its necessary point of departure by first sweeping away the Mosaic revelation; it annihilates the vital force which gave it being, and, by the necessity under which it is of dislocating its several parts, shows them in a false juxtaposition, and sets aside the evidence of the genetic process through which it has passed.

And the naturalistic is so far from being the historico-critical method that it really sets at defiance a sound historical criticism, and bases itself on the wildest and most unsupported vagaries instead. We do not shut our eyes to the good service which critics, even of the most ultra type, have rendered to biblical studies by their investigations and discussions. They have ruthlessly run their ploughshare through what is venerable and sacred, yet they have, after all, aided in opening up the soil for cultivation, and have brought much that is valuable to the surface. And supernaturalists have not disdained to learn from their antagonists. Dr. Kuenen points to this with a triumphant air, and hastily infers (p. 7): " The dissolution of the traditional theory is already in rapid progess. It is with it as with a beleaguered fortress: it has not yet been abandoned or formally surrendered, but the enemy enters unopposed, by more than one breach, and some of its main bulwarks are either defended no longer or defended very feebly." This is altogether too fast and too sweeping when the only ground alleged for it is that broader views now prevail than those which limited " prophecy to prediction, the office of the Prophet to announcing the secrets of the future." The disproportionate prominence given by some early writers, and especially those engaged in the controversy with the Deists, to the apologetic use of prophecy, has been moderated by exalting other features of the Prophets' work in due measure. But this involves no abandonment of any important principle. The predictive quality of prophecy is affirmed as strongly as ever. It simply falls into its place in the general function of the Prophets as teachers sent from God. This is not to endanger the citadel, but to fortify the approaches and to extend and strengthen the outworks.

With much more reason it might be retorted that the positions of the antagonists of a supernatural revelation have been and are in constant flux. The whole field over which the battle has been waged is strewn with their spiked guns and abandoned intrenchments. Hypothesis has succeeded hypothesis, only to be in its turn discarded. The allegation of imposture and of unworthy motives, once so rife, is entirely given up. Dr. Kuenen is at great pains to show that he does not impugn the Prophets' integrity in any way. " The charges which, more than a hundred years ago, were here and there brought against the Prophets of Israel are all silenced. In high estimation of their aim and their work, all are agreed." In other matters, too, there is the utmost discordance. While on the one hand some are, as Mr. Muir concedes (p. xxvii.) concerning Professor Reuss, "more conservative and apologetic" than Dr. Kuenen, and Dr. Kuenen censures some of his party as not sufficiently thorough-going, he is himself, on the other hand, vehemently attacked by others as not sufficiently advanced in his positions. As to the real nature of prophecy, the age of the Prophets respectively, what are to be considered their genuine productions, and in what esteem they are to be held, there is no little variance in the critical camp.

Professor Kuenen proposes to settle the strife between the supernatural and the naturalistic view of prophecy by the single test of its fulfilment. To this we cheerfully assent. It is a test to which the sacred writers themselves appeal (Deut. xviii. 21, 22; Isai. xliii. 9-12; Jer. xxviii. 9); it is palpable, obvious, and easily applied. If these predictions have been fulfilled, they are from God; if not, they cannot be from him.

He divides (p. 25) the sources of our information respecting the predictions in the Old Testament into three classes, viz.: —

"1st. Writings of Prophets.

"2d. Historical accounts regarding what the Prophets have done and spoken.

"3d. Words of God addressed to historical personages, and incorporated in the narratives concerning them."

There is an undoubted propriety in giving precedence in this investigation to the prophetical books, in which the utterances of the Prophets are recorded by themselves; since the predictions scattered through the historical books come to us at second-hand, and are, moreover, much more limited in extent. In conceding this, however, we yield nothing to the disadvantage of the trustworthiness of the latter. The suspicions insinuated respecting their accuracy are altogether groundless; they may be and are as reliable as any other historical statements.

But have the books attributed to the Prophets really proceeded from them, and to what dates are they to be assigned? Here Dr. Kuenen finds it impossible to make out his case without availing himself of some modern critical conclusions at variance with the concurrent and accredited belief of ages, and at variance with statements contained in these books themselves, — conclusions which are largely based on an assumption of the very point at issue. A large part of the Book of Isaiah, every passage in which a knowledge of the Babylonish captivity is implied or is supposed to be implied, is denied to him and assigned to the period of the Exile; and this notwithstanding the independent testimony of the author of the Book of Kings (II. Kings, xx. 16–18), that this captivity was explicitly foretold by Isaiah; notwithstanding, too, the fact that it was also with like explicitness predicted by his contemporary Micah (iv. 10); and that the overthrow of Judah by distant and terrible foes is repeatedly declared in passages of Isaiah which even Dr. Kuenen confesses to be genuine, (*e. g.* v. 26–30) — as it had been in fact foreshown by Moses ages before (Lev. xxvi.; Deut. xxviii.) — an overthrow which he further affirms was not to be effected either by Syria (vii. 5–8) or by Assyria (x. 5–34). Jeremiah's prediction of Babylon's overthrow (chs. l., li.) is attributed to some nameless author of a later time, notwithstanding the express statement of its special title (l. 1), affirming it to be by Jeremiah, the circumstantial narrative at its close (li. 59–64), and the additional declaration that he did predict the fall and utter desolation of Babylon (xxv. 12, 13). The genuineness of the Book of Daniel is also denied, and it is declared to be the product of the period of the Maccabees. There are besides some other derangements of the true order, of minor consequence; Joel and Obadiah are put a century and a half later than they belong, while half of the Book of Zechariah is taken from him and referred to an earlier date with a motive which will appear hereafter.

It would divert us too much from our present purpose to undertake here the defence of those books, or parts of books, which Dr. Kuenen sets aside as not genuine. They have been abundantly vindicated by able critical scholars. We simply remark, in passing, that the allegation that these predictions were written after the event is equivalent to a confession of the accuracy of their fulfilment which cannot otherwise be evaded. But the question at issue can be settled by prophecies whose genuineness no one has yet ventured to dispute. After all that has been done in the way of attempted elimination, enough remain to establish unmistakably the divine origin of prophecy. If this can be first settled by what Dr. Kuenen himself confesses to be the genuine productions of the Prophets, he will no longer have the same motive to deny the genuineness of the rest, especially when it appears, as is in truth the case, that, even on his own critical hypotheses, these latter still afford evidence of divine prescience; for they contain predictions reaching beyond the date at which he alleges that they were written, and which have been manifestly fulfilled.

Dr. Kuenen groups what he calls the unfulfilled prophecies under three heads, as they severally relate to (1) the destiny of the heathen nations, (2) the judgments pronounced upon Israel, and (3) the expectations of the Prophets with regard to Israel's future. It will be convenient to follow him in this arrangement.

. The first instance adduced is this (p. 102): "The Prophets are unanimous in announcing the destruction of the cities of the Philistines." Whereupon he confesses: "It is true, indeed, that scarcely any traces remain of the very ancient glory of the five cities. They have shared in the same fate that has smitten the whole of Palestine. They have been laid desolate or have gradually decayed; after Jerusalem, indeed, but still like her, they too have fallen." This, however, he refuses to accept as the proper fulfilment of the predictions for two reasons. First, because "the judgment contemplated is plainly one that would be executed *soon*. When delayed for a long period it ceased to be a judgment, especially in such cases as we find in Amos (i. 6–8) and Ezekiel (xxv. 15–17), where a specific sin is mentioned as the reason of Jahveh's displeasure." But why the divine retribution forfeits its character if it does not occur soon is not very clear. There is something striking, no doubt, in a penalty that follows swiftly upon the heels of transgression. And yet most men would concede equal impressiveness to a doom which is sure to come, however long delayed. The length of the interval renders it all the more certain that God does not forget, and that even-handed justice will not fail eventually to strike its mark. And, in particular, that the Prophets, with whom we are now concerned, did not judge it essential that a recompense must be speedy appears both from their directly declaring the reverse (Hab. ii. 3), and from their undisturbed confidence when this very demand was made by presumptuous sinners of their own day (Isai. v. 19; Jer. xvii. 15; Amos, v. 18). This Dr. Kuenen seems here to have overlooked, though his memory is less treacherous in another place when he has an end to answer by it (p. 360): "The fulfilment of their predictions can be to themselves, to a certain extent, matter of indifference; that is to say, the fulfilment in this or that specific form at that specific time. It is to them a settled truth that Jahveh is righteous, and not less that at some period his righteousness shall be revealed in a dazzling and unmistakable manner; but *how* and *when* this revelation shall take place is a question of subordinate importance. . . . If it is not fulfilled now, then it will be fulfilled at a later time." If now, by Dr. Kuenen's own confession, the element of time enters so little into the Prophet's expectations, by what right can it be demanded that the prediction must be fulfilled speedily, or it is no fulfilment at all in the sense intended by the Prophet? This is surely unreasonable, unless he has himself specified some limit within which it must occur.

Is this done in the present instance? There is no pretence of it in Amos, Joel (iii. 4-8), Ezekiel, Zephaniah (ii. 4-7), or Zechariah (ix. 5-7); only Isaiah (xiv. 31) and Jeremiah (xlvii. 2) speak of a calamity to come upon Philistia from the north; and "whenever Isaiah and Jeremiah make mention of an enemy out of the north, they intimate, in no doubtful manner, that they are thinking, the former of the Assyrians, the latter of the Chaldeans." Well, did the Assyrians and Chaldeans bring the predicted distress upon Philistia? Assyrian monuments furnish abundant evidence on this point. Sargon took Hanun, King of Gaza, prisoner and led him away into Assyria.[1] The King of Ashdod made his submission to Sennacherib, while the King of Ashkelon with his whole family were carried captive to Assyria, and a vassal placed upon the throne in his stead; the princes of Ekron were slain and impaled, numbers of the people sold as slaves, and a king created subject to Assyria.[2] Esarhaddon and Assurbanipal include the kings of Gaza, Ashkelon, Ekron, and Ashdod in their

[1] Oppert, "Les Inscriptions Assyriennes des Sargonides," p. 36.
[2] Ibid., pp. 44, 45.

lists of tributary monarchs.[1] And as Nebuchadnezzar subdued Phenicia and Syria, and carried his arms into Egypt,[2] he must have overrun the whole Philistine region. So far, therefore, from these prophecies remaining unaccomplished, the very fulfilment that Dr. Kuenen asks for did take place. The Philistines were chastised by both Assyria and Babylon, and the judgment predicted, instead of ceasing with these preliminary fulfilments, went on until the region was reduced to the desolation that it now is.

But Dr. Kuenen's second objection is that "the punishment of the Philistines takes place, according to the Prophets, in the interest of Israel. It is against the people of Jahveh that they have transgressed; it is the people of Jahveh, therefore, that shall reap the fruits of their destruction, take possession of their territory, and incorporate the remnant of them with themselves. In other words, with the Prophets the lot of the Philistines forms a contrast to that of the Israelites. In the Prophecy of Isaiah, Zion, founded by Jahveh, and a safe refuge for the poor of his people, stands in opposition to Philistia, whose inhabitants perish by famine and sword. The same Prophet expects that the reunited tribes 'shall fly upon the shoulder of the Philistines toward the west,'—that is, shall extend their dominion in that direction and make the Philistines subject to them." We might point him to the fact that the Jews under Jonathan Maccabæus and Alexander Jannæus did

---

[1] Schrader, "Keilinschriften und Altes Testament," pp. 229, 230.
[2] Josephus against Apion, I. 19.

capture the Philistine cities, that the name Philistine thenceforward ceased out of history, and that the population of the region was subsequently absorbed into or supplanted by Jewish residents. But has not the ancient glory of Israel faded away as well as that of the Philistines? Instead of the contrast which prophecy leads us to anticipate, have they not alike fallen into decline and ruin? The answer to this question obviously involves the correctness of the prophetic expectations regarding Israel, and, to avoid needless repetition, must be reserved until the prophecies respecting Israel come regularly before us in the course of our inquiry. Meanwhile let it be noted here that all that the Prophets have said concerning the Philistines has been in the fullest and strictest sense accomplished. The only point which, for the reason stated, we leave unsettled at this stage of the discussion is, Do the fortunes of Israel stand in the required contrast to those of Philistia?

The next prophecies adduced are those against Tyre by Isaiah (xxiii.) and Ezekiel (xxvi–xxviii.). Of the latter Dr. Kuenen says (p. 107): "What he predicts for Tyre is nothing less than entire destruction. The many nations that march against her to battle 'shall destroy her walls and break down her towers.' Jahveh 'shall sweep away her dust — the layer of earth on which her houses and gardens were placed — and make her a bare rock.' Thus she shall become 'a place where men spread nets in the midst of the sea.' The multitude of nations that execute this judgment are led by Nebuchadnezzar, the king of kings. He shall lay siege to the city, and finally 'shall enter in through her gates as men enter into a conquered town.' Then plundering and devastation follow until Tyre has ceased to exist."

Now, Dr. Kuenen confesses that "Tyre capitulated" to Nebuchadnezzar at the end of his long siege of thirteen years, and "wholly or partially lost her independence." And that this was really the case is abundantly demonstrated in Movers' elaborate investigation of this point,[1] an author whom none can suspect of being biassed in his conclusions by a regard for the authority of the Prophet. He further admits, what is too palpable to be denied, that Tyre is at present "an insignificant fishing village." Every trait in the prophetic description has long since been matched by the event. But he complains that this desolation was not effected all at once; the fulfilment of the prophecy was not exhausted by the victory of Nebuchadnezzar. The city was not laid waste by him, nor its trade destroyed. It continued to be a powerful and wealthy merchant city even under the Persian dominion. All that the prophecy declares has come to pass. The correspondence between the word of the Prophet and the condition to which this mistress of the seas has been reduced is signal and undeniable. But this was not brought about by Nebuchadnezzar alone. It was not the issue of his single siege. It was not accomplished in one age, nor by the operation of any one cause. The city was weakened and humbled by Nebuchadnezzar. It was

[1] "Das Phœnizische Alterthum," i. 427-450.

still further humiliated by Alexander the Great. Other wars and struggles followed. Other causes conspired to dry up the sources of its prosperity. And because the desolation described by the Prophet was only fully reached after a long interval, and was the result of many combined influences, it is most strangely argued that this must not be regarded as the fulfilment of Ezekiel's prediction. One would think that the greater the lapse of time and the more complicated the causes at work, the more decisive and complete would be the evidence of a far-reaching foresight, and that it was no merely human calculation from limited and imperfect data. The proof of prophetic power is surely not diminished or destroyed because that is foretold which only He could know who sees the end from the beginning, and to whom a thousand years are as one day.

But, says Dr. Kuenen, "is it not clear as day that it [the prophecy of Ezekiel] announces the overthrow of the Phenicians as being *close at hand?*" The Prophet says no such thing. On the contrary, it is "clear as day" that such a limitation of the prophecy to what was "close at hand" is wholly gratuitous, and is a covert assumption of the very question at issue. If the announcement made by Ezekiel were only a shrewd conjecture from the existing political situation, the prophetic horizon would have to be narrowed accordingly, and nothing that was remote, or that was dependent upon causes not yet apparent, could be admitted to fall within its scope. And after the prophecy has thus been degraded to a merely human anticipation, it is comparatively easy to show that it has failed. Eliminate or refuse to recognize the stamp of its divinity, and its non-fulfilment naturally follows; for that is tacitly involved in the primary assumption. Only it is strange, on Dr. Kuenen's view of the case, if the prophecy in its true intent, as understood by Ezekiel and his hearers, was restricted to events "close at hand," that they could themselves have retained any confidence in it as a message from God; for it was falsified before it was even put on record. The siege of Tyre came to an end years before the Book of Ezekiel was issued, and Tyre still survived. Now, if no exactness of correspondence in the future between the event and the terms of the prediction could be a fulfilment of the latter in the sense put upon it by the Prophet and his contemporaries, how does it come to pass that it was not utterly discredited in their esteem and refused a place in this collection professing to be uttered under the immediate inspiration of God?

Dr. Kuenen himself, when he would convert prophecy into a vague presentiment, or a pious deduction from the moral government of God, admits that the time when Jehovah's righteousness should be revealed is, to the Prophets, "a question of subordinate importance" (p. 360). They were convinced that the haughty oppressors of His people would some time be laid low by His avenging arm, but it was not indispensable that this should be done immediately. "When their anticipations were not realized, they will have easily satisfied themselves with the thought that the fulfilment would doubtless occur at a later period. In truth it makes *a very essential difference* whether any event is estimated *in and on account of itself* or as *the form in which something else is revealed.* In the first case its non-realization is a bitter disappointment, and for him who announced it a painful humiliation; but this bitterness and this pain are not felt when recourse is at once had to the conviction: if it is not fulfilled now, then it will be fulfilled at a later time; the righteousness of Jahveh endures and *must* positively some time come to light."[1] Dr. Kuenen fancies that Ezekiel himself expected Nebuchadnezzar to accomplish all that he uttered in his prediction respecting Tyre. This is nowhere stated in the prediction itself. It is merely Dr. Kuenen's opinion. But suppose him to be correct; what then? We do not claim omniscience for the Prophet, but simply inspiration and unerring truth for his prediction. And even on the low view of prophecy entertained by Dr. Kuenen, the essential thing in the Prophet's mind was the vindication of God's righteous judgment; the time when this should take place was of little consequence. The fact, not the period of its manifestation, was what he regarded as absolutely certain. Whenever this manifestation should occur, it would be to him the fulfilment of his prediction. How can Dr. Kuenen, therefore, on his own principles, justify his assertion that the event must be "close at hand" in order to verify the

[1] The italics in the various quotations from Dr. Kuenen are invariably his own.

Prophet's anticipation? Much less can it be necessary to the accomplishment of that which is a direct revelation from the omniscient God himself. In fact, it looks somewhat like grasping both horns of a dilemma at once, when Dr. Kuenen, in his zeal to fasten human infirmity on the prophecies, affirms with one breath that a particular event " close at hand " must have been intended by them, so that nothing else can be a fulfilment of them, and with the next declares that the manifestation of Jehovah's righteousness is the one fixed conviction of the Prophets, irrespective of either time or mode.

But, says Dr. Kuenen, " Ezekiel himself declares that his expectations concerning the fate of Tyre were not realized " (Ezek. xxix. 18–20). " Son of man, Nebuchadrezzar King of Babylon caused his army to serve a great service against Tyre: every head was made bald, and every shoulder was peeled: yet had he no wages, nor his army, for Tyre, for the service that he had served against it; " whereupon the land of Egypt is promised him for his wages. Dr. Kuenen very naturally apprehends that this proof will be suspected of being so very strong as to be worth nothing (p. 110): " How by any possibility can Ezekiel come forward as a witness against the realization of his own prophecy?" The fact is that the sense put upon this passage is an utter perversion of its meaning. Nebuchadnezzar must have performed the work against Tyre which the LORD had assigned to him, or he would not have earned the wages which are here promised him and declared to be rightfully his.

The Prophet revokes nothing of his former prediction. He confesses to no failure or disappointed expectations. He makes no attempt to accommodate the expressions which he had previously used to an event which had turned out differently from his anticipations. He simply says, Nebuchadnezzar has done his work, which was an exceedingly toilsome one, and has thereby earned larger wages than the spoils of Tyre afforded him; he shall have Egypt in addition to make up full payment. There is nothing surely in this that looks as though Ezekiel regarded his prophecy against Tyre as having failed in so far as respects the work committed to Nebuchadnezzar, but the very reverse.

Nevertheless, says Dr. Kuenen, "this much is plain, that Nebuchadnezzar did not enter in through the gates of Tyre as men enter into a conquered city" (Ezek. xxvi. 10). How does he know? And "as little did his troops carry away the wealth of Tyre and plunder her merchandise" (ver. 12). Tyre was open seaward during the entire siege. The wealthiest citizens may have fled to distant colonies and taken their goods with them (Isai. xxiii. 6, 7, 12). The treasures of their sanctuaries may likewise have been temporarily removed for safe-keeping. And the terms of the capitulation, of which we know nothing, may have limited the amount that the conqueror should receive. It is very easy to understand how he could have "made a spoil of its riches," and yet not be adequately paid for his long and toilsome service.

In regard to Isaiah's prediction against Tyre (xxiii.),

Dr. Kuenen complains that its fulfilment is sometimes sought in the siege of that city by Shalmaneser, King of Assyria, and sometimes in that by Nebuchadnezzar; and he insists that a choice must be made between them. But what is there to hinder its embracing both? It is a declaration of God's work of judgment upon Tyre, to be executed partly by one instrument and partly by another, which in the actual unfoldings of history met its partial accomplishment in different periods successively, but is here gathered up into a single picture of its future destiny.

To the general prediction of its overthrow, the Prophet adds the specific statement (vers. 15–18) that Tyre shall be forgotten seventy years, after which her trade shall revive, and her gains, instead of being treasured up for her own advantage, shall be holiness to the Lord. Dr. Kuenen remarks that "facts like those announced here cannot pass away without leaving some traces." And they have not done so, even though he professes that he has not been able to find them. The term of her humiliation is at once explained by the declaration of Jeremiah (xxv. 11), that the land of Judah and all contiguous nations, among whom (ver. 22) Tyre is expressly included, should serve the King of Babylon seventy years. This is precisely the interval between the decisive victory gained by Nebuchadnezzar at Carchemish over Pharaoh-necho King of Egypt (Jer. xlvi. 2), which opened his way to Jerusalem and the neighboring kingdoms that had combined against him, and the conquest of Babylon by Cyrus. That Tyre continued after its siege by Nebuchadnezzar to be subject to Babylon, till the latter city itself was overthrown by Cyrus, is apparent from an extract which Josephus[1] has fortunately preserved for us from Tyre's own annals. This informs us that Hiram, who was reigning in Tyre when Cyrus became king of Persia, as well as his brother and predecessor, had been brought from Babylon to be placed upon the throne.

But what shall be said of the predicted conversion of this heathen city, with its wealth, to the service of the LORD? There has been an incipient fulfilment of this which should not be overlooked. Tyre had its Christian disciples in the days of the apostles (Acts, xxi. 3-6), and subsequently a flourishing church. It was the seat of a bishop; its cathedral was the most elegant structure in Phenicia; synods were held there. It had a Christian population down to the time of the Crusades, when it was erected into a Latin archbishopric under the patriarch of Jerusalem. One of the most noticeable among the ruins of ancient Tyre is that of a Christian church, which was originally a large and splendid structure. This, however, is but the budding of a fulfilment, and by no means all that the prophecy leads us to expect. The consideration of what further is involved in it can best be postponed to a subsequent part of this inquiry, when it shall be taken up again, together with the claim made by Dr. Kuenen (p. 110) that the punishment of Tyre, as of

---

[1] Against Apion, book i. § 21. A hint of Tyre's reduced condition at the close of the Exile may be found in the fact that Zidon is mentioned before it (Ezra iii. 7) instead of after it, which is the usual order.

the other neighbors of Israel, should precede the return of Israel to their native land on the ground of Ezek. xxviii. 24–26. We can only appreciate this correctly when the prophecies respecting Israel shall come before us.

The next prediction introduced is that of Jeremiah (xlix. 23–27) against Damascus, where the whole ground of cavil is based upon an ambiguous word in the English version, of which advantage is taken to put a sense upon it which the original will not at all admit. "How is the city of praise not left!" is thus paraphrased, "Why might not Damascus have remained?" and this affirmed to imply "its permanent desolation;" whereas the first glance at the Hebrew is sufficient to show that "left" in this place means not *permitted to remain*, but *forsaken*, and there is no intimation whatever that it should not survive or recover from the threatened blow. In the scanty accounts that we possess of this entire period, it is not surprising that the event referred to has passed without mention. Josephus (Ant. x. 11, 1) speaks of captive Syrians taken to Babylon at the outset of Nebuchadnezzar's reign; and the subsequent course of events makes it more than probable that this was again repeated.

Of Ammon and Moab it is predicted, as Dr. Kuenen states, that "the two nations shall both be driven away or extirpated, and their cities shall be laid waste." And he adds, "this fate has in fact overtaken them." But he objects (p. 114) that "they were still inhabited and flourishing up to the seventh century of the Christian era; " whereas " the Prophets do not expect (Isai. xi. 14, xxv. 10; Zeph. ii. 9, 10) that Moab and Ammon shall in the course of ages lose their national existence along with or even after Israel, but *that Israel shall be a witness of the destruction of their enemies, and shall reap the fruits of that destruction.*" "The prophecy that Israel shall appear as the inheritor of Moab and Ammon of itself absolutely forbids us to see the realization of what Zephaniah expected, in the ruin of those nations six centuries after the second destruction of Jerusalem." But the punishment was not altogether postponed to this late period. The entire region was subdued and ravaged by Nebuchadnezzar. Josephus (Ant. x. 9, 7) specially mentions the subjugation of Cœlesyria, Ammon, and Moab. That he purposed specially to attack the Ammonites we learn from Ezek. xxi. 20; and he had reasons for so doing, both in the combination into which they had entered against Chaldea (Jer. xxvii. 3), and in their harboring and perhaps instigating Ishmael the murderer of Gedaliah, whom the King of Babylon had made governor after the capture of Jerusalem (Jer. xl. 14, xli. 2, 15).

The relation of these lands to Israel when restored will be postponed until that subject is considered in connection with other nations.

For proof of the fulfilment of the predictions respecting the Edomites we need not go beyond that furnished in Dr. Kuenen's own pages, and which he vainly endeavors to set aside. In the time of Malachi, as i. 3, 4 expressly states, Esau's mountains and his heritage were lying waste. If this was effected, as there is every reason to believe, by Nebuchadnezzar in the expedition[1] five years after the destruction of Jerusalem, in which he subjected the Ammonites and Moabites and advanced into Egypt, then here we have the evidence that " nearly a century after the end of the captivity," when the Jews were restored and Jerusalem was rebuilt, Edom was still a desolation, and the prospect of recovery was as remote as ever. This certainly is not the "very opposite" of the representation in Joel iii. 19, 20, but precisely coincident with it. Obad. ver. 18 and Ezek. xxv. 14 found accomplishment in the spoliation of the Edomites by Judas Maccabæus, then by John Hyrcanus, "who completely subdued them about B.C. 130, compelled them to adopt the rite of circumcision, and incorporated them into the Jewish State;" then "by Simon, son of Gioras, the head of one of the factions. The nation of the Edomites is mentioned no more after the destruction of Jerusalem (A. D. 70): it was partly incorporated with the Jewish nation, partly blended with other Arabian tribes. Meanwhile their former capital, Sela, and a great part of their ancient territory had already, many centuries before, passed into other hands." It is now reduced to utter desolation. Its interval of wealth and flourishing trade, during which it is better known to us by its Greek name Petra, and when it was occupied by others than

---

[1] Josephus, Ant. x. 9, 7. This is not at variance with Ezek. xxxv., or xxxvi. 5, which were first uttered after the fall of Jerusalem (xxxiii. 21), nor with Isai. xxxiv., which was not written in the Exile, but long before it.

Edomites, does not prevent this region, first wrenched from the children of Esau, then wasted as at the present day, from bearing its striking testimony to the truth of the prophecies.

Ezekiel's prediction of the forty years' desolation of Egypt (xxix. 11–16) has long proved perplexing to interpreters, and is, we frankly admit, somewhat difficult to reconcile with Herodotus's statement (ii. 177) that the reign of Amasis, a considerable portion of which falls within this predicted term, " was the most prosperous time that Egypt ever saw." This is no new embarrassment raised by Dr. Kuenen, however; the whole matter had been thoroughly sifted, and everything possible to be said had been said about it, before he was born, and that without shaking the confidence of those veteran scholars in the divinity of the Prophet's word. In spite of Dr. Kuenen's confidence that the result which he has obtained " defies all reasonable contradiction and will in the end be generally received," we think it can be made to appear that he is over-hasty in his conclusions. From the time of the decisive battle of Carchemish, at all events, as Dr. Kuenen correctly states, Jeremiah predicted that Nebuchadnezzar would invade Egypt and subdue that country (Jer. xlvi. 13–28). This he still continued to affirm years afterwards, when Jerusalem had been destroyed, and Gedaliah murdered, and the wretched remnant of Jews fled, contrary to the Prophet's earnest remonstrance, to Egypt for protection (Jer. xliii. 8–13, xliv. 12–14); and the death of King Pharaoh-hophra, by the hands of his enemies, is made the sign of its fulfilment (xliv. 29, 30). Ezekiel repeats, with still more particularity, that Nebuchadnezzar shall invade the land of Egypt, and that it shall be desolated for forty years, and the Egyptians shall be scattered among the nations; but at the end of forty years they shall be regathered into their own land, though Egypt shall thenceforth be a base kingdom, and no more exalt itself above the nations nor be any more the confidence of the House of Israel.

Now, of all this Herodotus gives no account. He makes no mention of the subjugation of Egypt by Nebuchadnezzar. But it is to be borne in mind that Herodotus received his information from Egyptian priests, and they did not scruple, as he himself declares his belief more than once (iii. 2, 16), to falsify the truth of history in their own interest. Herodotus nowhere mentions Pharaoh-necho's defeat by Nebuchadnezzar at Carchemish, which put an end to Egyptian rule in Asia, and this though he speaks of that very expedition of Necho and his victory over Josiah at Megiddo. He nowhere speaks of Nebuchadnezzar at all, or of his coming into armed collision with Egypt. And yet the silence of Herodotus does not, even with Dr. Kuenen himself, discredit the battle of Carchemish, or call in question its decisive character. Still further, Herodotus never alludes to the conquest of Egypt by any king of Assyria; and the assertion of the capture of Thebes made by Nahum (iii. 8–10) was discredited by Dr. Kuenen and other similar critics, on the ground that no ancient historian mentions it, and the monuments existing in unbroken continuity make no allusion to it and leave no room for it. But an inscription of Assurbanipal was found in which he relates the fact, and the critics were obliged to retract. The records of the Assyrians are similarly oblivious of defeats suffered by themselves. Sennacherib records in full his annual successes, but makes no allusion to his disastrous overthrow, of which we know both from the sacred historians and from Herodotus, the Egyptian priests having no motive for silence in this instance.

The silence of Egyptian informants is, therefore, not conclusive of the non-concurrence of what was disastrous to Egypt or mortifying to its pride. Now, if Dr. Kuenen will but distinguish between what the Prophets actually say, and what he imputes to them as their meaning but which they do not say, we do not despair of convincing even himself that what the Jewish Prophets predict respecting Egypt is entirely consistent with what Herodotus relates of the corresponding period.

"Hophra," he says (p. 124), with a flourish of italics, as though the Prophet were contradicted point-blank by the testimony of the historian, "did *not* fall in the war against Nebuchadnezzar." Well, no Prophet said that he would. Jeremiah says (xliv. 30), speaking from the mouth of God: "Behold, I will give Pharaoh-hophra, King of Egypt, into the hand of his enemies, and into the hand of them that seek his life." Again (xlvi. 26), "I will deliver them," *i. e.*, Pharaoh and all them that trust in him, "into the hand of those that seek their lives, and into the hand of Nebuchadrezzar, King of Babylon, and into the hand of his servants." Now, what is the testimony of Herodotus? It is thus summed up in Dr. Kuenen's own words: "An insurrection broke out. Amasis, who was commissioned by the king to suppress it, placed himself at the head of the insurgents, defeated the mercenary forces, took Apries (Hophra) prisoner, and after some hesitation consented to his death." Is not the language of Jeremiah fulfilled to the letter? Pharaoh-hophra was delivered into the hand of them that sought his life.

But in his zeal to bring forth a contradiction where there is entire harmony, Dr. Kuenen holds the following most extraordinary language: "The narrative of Herodotus leaves no room for a temporary subjection of the Egyptians to the Chaldeans, or even for a successful invasion of their country by Nebuchadnezzar. How could Hophra have been able to undertake an expedition against Cyrene in 569 B. C. if in or after 570 B. C. he had been defeated by Nebuchadnezzar? For in this year, the twenty-seventh of Ezekiel's captivity, the conquest of Egypt by the Chaldeans had not yet, according to this Prophet himself (xxix. 17–21), taken place. Is it not absurd to suppose that it happened immediately thereafter, still in 570 B. C., and in the following year had been already forgotten." It is astonishing that Dr. Kuenen can either content himself or expect to blind his readers by so transparent a trick as this. He has made an absurd supposition, which no one dreams of entertaining, as though it were involved in the truth of the Prophet's prediction, but he has altogether evaded the simple and obvious explanation of the case which offers itself at once upon his own statement of the facts.

If Nebuchadnezzar had not yet invaded Egypt 570 B. C., and Hophra was involved in civil war 569 B. C., what more natural, or more in accordance with the usual policy of ambitious monarchs, than that these domestic disturbances had either been fomented for the purpose or were seized upon as the occasion of foreign interference? Thus Sir Gardner Wilkinson:[1] "We can readily imagine that the Assyrians, having extended their conquests to the extremity of Palestine, would, on the rumor of intestine commotions in Egypt, hasten to take advantage of the opportunity thus afforded them of attacking the country. . . . From a comparison of all these authorities, I conclude that the civil war between Apries and Amasis did not terminate in the single conflict at Momemphis, but lasted several years; and that either Amasis solicited the aid and intervention of Nebuchadnezzar, or this prince, availing himself of the disordered state of the country, of his own accord invaded it, deposed the rightful sovereign and placed Amasis on the throne, on condition of paying tribute to the Assyrians. The injury done to the land and cities of Egypt by this invasion, and the disgrace with which the Egyptians felt themselves overwhelmed

---

[1] "Manners and Customs of the Ancient Egyptians," vol. ii. pp. 177-179. See also notes to Rawlinson's Herodotus, ii. 177, and ch. viii. of Appendix to Book ii. pp. 322 ff.

after such an event, would justify the account given in the Bible of the fall of Egypt; and to witness many of their compatriots taken captive to Babylon, and to become tributary to an enemy whom they held in abhorrence, would be considered by the Egyptians the greatest calamity, as though they had forever lost their station in the scale of nations. And this last would satisfactorily account for the title of Melek, given to inferior or to tributary kings, being applied to Amasis in some of the hieroglyphic legends accompanying his name."

If this view of Wilkinson and others is correct, — and it is difficult to see what well-founded objection can be made to it, — then it is perfectly easy to reconcile the statement of Herodotus that Pharaoh-hophra was put to death by the Egyptians, to whom he was delivered over by Amasis, and that of Josephus that he was slain by Nebuchadnezzar. The Egyptians were the immediate actors, but it was at the instance of the King of Babylon.

Dr. Kuenen's attempt to discredit the authority of Josephus, who here expressly vouches for the fulfilment of the Prophet's predictions, will scarcely gain the approval of any who do not agree with him in his foregone conclusion. Josephus[1] expressly appeals to the authority of Berosus for the affirmation that Nebuchadnezzar " conquered *Egypt* and Syria and Phœnicia and Arabia, and exceeded in his exploits all that had reigned before him in Babylon and Chaldea." The charge that Berosus is " altogether

[1] "Against Apion," i. 19.

unhistorical" in speaking of Egypt as subject to the Chaldean empire prior to the time of Nebuchadnezzar, sounds strangely since the discovery of Assurbanipal's conquest of Egypt, which, on the fall and partition of the Assyrian empire, would come under the dominion of Babylon, or at least be claimed by it. And how could Nebuchadnezzar have exceeded all other monarchs of the great Asiatic empire in his exploits if he failed in his attempt upon Egypt, which others had subdued? The language of Megasthenes, that Nebuchadnezzar "subdued the greater part of Libya and Iberia," is doubtless an exaggeration; but upon what could such an exaggeration have been built if he never even penetrated into Africa?

The allegation that Josephus infers his facts from the predictions is utterly groundless and gratuitous. That he mentions[1] the predictions respecting the King of Babylon's conquest of Egypt, and adds "which things came to pass," implies, on the contrary, that he discriminates between the prophecy and its fulfilment, and had independent information of the latter. That he borrows freely from the historical statements of Jeremiah is no ground for the unworthy sneer that he has been "caught in the very act" of narrating as fact that for which he had no historical voucher. The circumstance to which Dr. Kuenen appeals (p. 128), that Josephus does not record "the forty years desolation of Egypt, and the subsequent partial restoration which Ezekiel mentions," shows that he does not simply and without

[1] "Antiquities of the Jews," x. 9, 7.

warrant convert prophecy into history, as is charged upon him. The attempt to involve Josephus in chronological conflict both with himself and with the Prophet Ezekiel is based upon the following passage from the section just now quoted: " On the fifth year after the destruction of Jerusalem, which was the twenty-third of the reign of Nebuchadnezzar, he made an expedition against Cœle-Syria, and when he had possessed himself of it, he made war against the Ammonites and Moabites; and when he had brought all those nations under subjection he fell upon Egypt in order to overthrow it, and he slew the king that then reigned and set up another, and he took those Jews that were there captives and led them away to Babylon." Upon this Dr. Kuenen comments as follows: "That the Chaldeans conquered Egypt in the year 581 B.C. is irreconcilable with the testimony of Ezekiel, from which it is evident that the conquest had not yet taken place in the year 570 B.C., and with the account of Josephus himself, that Nebuchadnezzar besieged Tyre for thirteen years — probably from 585 to 572 B.C.: the invasion of Egypt cannot surely be regarded as an episode of that siege!" This is merely the cavil of one who is determined to create difficulties at all hazards: it has no other foundation than the assumption, without one word in Josephus to justify it, that all the events grouped together in the paragraph above quoted occurred in one and the same year.

And now, after all the ado made about these prophecies respecting Egypt, and the confident assertion that nothing but "dogmatical reasons" can lead any to continue to defend them, the case stands thus: The silence of Herodotus respecting a conquest of Egypt by Nebuchadnezzar is no just reason for questioning the reality of its occurrence. The facts that he does state coincide perfectly with the assumption of such a conquest, and are moreover in entire harmony with the statements of Josephus, who positively avers it, and the correctness of whose narrative there is no sufficient reason for impugning; while it is both intrinsically probable and has the explicit warrant of Berosus, a native Babylonish historian. In fact, the entire history of the period and the whole life of Nebuchadnezzar are unintelligible without the invasion of Egypt, which was the natural sequence of the victory at Carchemish, and of the struggle for predominance in Western Asia between the great empires of the east and south (see II. Chron. xxxv. 21).

Nebuchadnezzar, too, had steadily followed up his victory by the siege of Jerusalem, by over-running the contiguous lands, Moab, Ammon, and the rest, and by the reduction of Tyre, which finally opened the way for this long-contemplated campaign. That this was the well-understood policy of the Babylonish monarch from the beginning is shadowed forth by constantly repeated predictions to this effect from Jeremiah and Ezekiel, as Dr. Kuenen must confess; for even upon his low views of prophecy they reveal the popular expectation and the convictions of shrewd thinkers and the drift of events. Vitringa suggests, not improbably, that it was the current expectation of an invasion of Egypt by Nebuchadnezzar that gave rise to the oracle reported by Herodotus (ii. 58), that Necho, in building the canal to the Red Sea, was "laboring for the barbarian." And the fact that Nebuchadnezzar was occupied during the later years of his life with his magnificent buildings and adorning Babylon, implies the success of his invasion, and that he had reached the summit of his ambition and terminated the long strife between the empires.

But what, it may still be said, is to be thought of Ezekiel's prediction of the forty years' desolation of Egypt? These forty years are plainly the residue of the seventy years' domination of Babylon foretold by Jeremiah (xxv. 11, 12), beginning with the battle of Carchemish, which broke the power of Egypt and established the empire of Babylon in the west, and ending with the capture of Babylon and subversion of the Chaldean empire by Cyrus. A trifle more than thirty of these predestined years had elapsed when Nebuchadnezzar ended his siege of Tyre, and now, the last obstacle removed, was prepared to strike the final blow which he had meditated from the outset, by pushing his conquests into the very heart of Egypt. Thus began that period of desolating war and humiliating subjection to a foreign yoke which was terminated only by Babylon's own fall, in round numbers forty years, historically reckoned perhaps thirty-six or thirty-seven years; though, if absolute precision to the very letter be demanded in the fulfilment, while in the absence of full historical data of the period it cannot be rigorously demonstrated, there will be little difficulty in assuming it. The beginning and the end of such a period of calamity cannot be sharply defined. Egypt was harassed by internal dissensions, and doubtless by incursions from the troops of Nebuchadnezzar before his invasion was made in force. And the power of Babylon in the remoter parts of the empire was not instantly dissipated upon the capture of the city.

The surprisingly strong language of the Prophet (xxix. 10, 11), "I will make the land of Egypt utterly waste and desolate: . . . no foot of man shall pass through it, nor foot of beast shall pass through it, neither shall it be inhabited forty years," admits of a twofold vindication. 1. These universal and sweeping expressions are necessarily limited by the nature of the case. It is a strong description of the desolation which would follow in the track of war, the consternation, pillage, massacre, which would so change the face of the peaceful and populous empire that it might be said to convert it into a desert. It is the natural language of hyperbole, which every one understands, and in which it would be contrary to sound interpretation and be a perversion of the real meaning of the writer to insist on the exact literality of the expressions; as much so as when the evangelist says (John xxi. 25) that if all the acts of Christ were to be written, the world itself could not contain the books. Compare Luke xix. 40. It might as well be insisted that the language of every metaphor is to be pressed in its most literal sense. This is not interpretation, but perversion.

2. Again, it is to be borne in mind that prophecy does not always exhaust itself in a single fulfilment. This is the case here. The Prophet Ezekiel, while speaking more immediately and directly of the judgment to be inflicted on Egypt by Nebuchadnezzar, nevertheless has as his more general theme God's whole work of judgment upon Egypt, by which its hitherto colossal power and greatness were to be broken, and it should cease to be the object of idolatrous trust to Israel (xxix. 16) that it then was and had long been. The first and preliminary stage in this process of degradation and humiliation was to be effected by Nebuchadnezzar: this was the initial yet decisive blow which presaged and involved all the rest. In describing it, consequently, the Prophet does not view it as an isolated act and apart from its connections, but places it in combination with all that properly appertains to it in the design of God, links it with its whole train of predestined sequences, and virtually gathers into one picture what God, in bringing this to pass, designed to effect. The purpose of God which sent Nebuchadnezzar into Egypt was not limited to that one act, but contemplated the reduction and humiliation of Egypt. This invasion was but the first step of a more comprehensive plan, the initiative and pledge of more to follow, an integral part of an indivisible whole as viewed in the divine mind and as here regarded by the Prophet. Nebuchadnezzar's invasion of Egypt, as the first member of a closely concatenated series, carried with it in the purpose of God all that was to come after, all that

Egypt was thenceforward to suffer from subsequent invasions and oppressions by Persians, Macedonians, Romans, Saracens, Mamelukes, and Turks. And the strength of the Prophet's expressions are graduated accordingly. While primarily spoken of Nebuchadnezzar, they have a residuary meaning that covers all that has since been developed from them. In like manner our LORD, in His memorable prophecy (Matt. xxiv.), in which He blends together the destruction of Jerusalem and the end of the world as constituent parts of one grand drama of divine judgment on transgression, adds, " Verily this generation shall not pass till all these things be fulfilled." The first stadium of accomplishment, the foretaste and assurance of the whole, was then to be completed in the destruction of the Jewish capital, though there is a residuary meaning in His words which shall not be fully exhausted until the final judgment.

Dr. Kuenen does not disguise the contempt with which he regards this mode of interpreting prophecy, as though it were arbitrary in the extreme. We shall not at this point of the discussion enter upon its defence and confirmation. If prophecy is, as it claims to be, a divine product, there is no reason why it should not thus take its shape from the divine purposes. Whether it does so in actual fact we shall inquire more particularly hereafter. We only remark at present that such a mode of interpretation, if feasible and proper, would satisfactorily explain the Prophet's language, and justify us in peremptorily and in the most decided terms reversing our author's confident conclusion (p. 128), "that the future of Egypt was concealed from Ezekiel, and that the reality did not even remotely correspond to his postulates."

Isaiah's prediction (xx. 4), "that the King of Assyria shall carry the inhabitants of Egypt and Ethiopia away ignominiously out of their land," was fulfilled to the letter, as is shown both by Nahum (iii. 8-10), and by an inscription of Assurbanipal,—testimonies which are adduced by Dr. Kuenen himself (p. 121), and which he vainly seeks to set aside by the quibble that Isaiah "expects" this to be done by Sargon, whereas it was effected by his great-grandson. The sufficient reply to which is, that the meaning of the prophecy is to be determined not by what Dr. Kuenen conceives to be the "most obvious supposition" of what Isaiah "expects," but by its own explicit declarations. It was an expedition of Sargon which gave occasion to the prophecy; the triumph over Egypt, however, is ascribed not to Sargon, but to "the King of Assyria." The assault made by Sargon was followed up by his successors until the words of the Prophet were amply verified.

It is no prejudice to the inspiration of Isaiah or of Micah if "the overthrow of the Assyrian empire is not predicted" by them. Such a prediction could not be expected from Micah, for his prophecy is limited exclusively to the fortunes of the people of God. Isaiah, on the other hand, does foretell Assyria's downfall, with prominent reference indeed to Sennacherib's disastrous defeat (x. 24-34, xvii. 12-14, xxx. 31 ff., xxxi. 8, 9), but in terms which may easily be understood as reaching much farther and implying a more complete destruction. But at any rate the Prophet is not omniscient. He has no predictive faculty by which he can survey the future at will. He knows barely what is revealed to him; of all else he is as ignorant as ordinary men. The fact that Isaiah depicts in the blissful future " a highway out of Egypt to Assyria " (xix. 23), and that Micah (v. 5, 6) describes the coming Redeemer as Isaiah's protector against Assyrian invasion, may or may not warrant Dr. Kuenen's inference that for aught they knew the Assyrian empire would last until Messiah's days. But in either case the language is as consistent with strict truth as in any of those numerous instances in which the Prophets set forth the future under figures borrowed from the present or the past. How can the unknown be more intelligibly and impressively represented than by emblems taken from what is known and familiar? Thus when Isaiah would express the thought that the Exiles of Israel shall be brought back to their own land under immediate and evident divine guidance and protection, he represents their return from the land of their oppressors as a fresh exodus out of Egypt, in which the miracle of the Red Sea shall be repeated (xi. 15), and water again brought for them from the rock (xlviii. 21). The particular forms in which this almighty intervention shall be exerted on their behalf are of small account compared with the essential fact itself. Thus, too, when Ezekiel would make Israel sensible that they were on a par with the worst offenders, and that their future restoration was wholly of God's unmerited mercy, he tells them that Sodom and her daughters shall likewise be restored to their former estate as well as they, and be associated with them in the closest intimacy and relationship (xvi. 53, 55, 61); not, of course, that there was to be a literal resurrection of the Cities of the Plain, destroyed by fire from Heaven, but that the same grace which rescues Israel will reach to Sodom's spiritual counterpart, and bring into restored communion with God, and into fellowship with his people, the most degraded heathen, the very dregs of the human race. (Compare Isai. i. 10; Rev. xi. 8.)

It may have been of little consequence to Isaiah or to Micah, or to their contemporaries, to have the political changes disclosed to them by which Assyria was to be superseded on the map of the world or erased from the roll of nations; but it was of vast moment to them to know that, whether the ancient Assyria should survive or whatever new Assyria might arise to take its place, the strife between the great empires of the world should hereafter give way to peaceful and amicable intercourse, and instead of their present animosity toward the people of God, they should be heartily united with Israel in the service of Jehovah. And should any future Assyria venture to molest Israel or disturb his peace, his Messiah would effectually protect him and avenge his cause.

Of Nahum's and Zephaniah's predictions of the total destruction of Nineveh, Dr. Kuenen well says, "History has set its seal on these anticipations." He claims, however, that there was "one respect in which their predictions were not confirmed by the issue. Nineveh was depopulated and became a desolation in a comparatively brief space, but still not all at once" (p. 131). But how this militates against the truth of the prediction does not appear; much less what there is to justify Dr. Kuenen in speaking as he does (p. 133) of "the opposition between the contents of the prophecy and the historical reality." A summary statement of an event occupying long periods of time and passing through various phases, which seizes on its main features or depicts it in its consummation, may be just as true and for some important purposes vastly more effective than an account which enters into every minute detail. Nahum vividly describes the assault upon Nineveh, its capture and its desolation. That this would all be finished at a stroke he does not say. The fact is revealed to him; the length of time that it would occupy, and the successive steps through which it would attain to full accomplishment, are not revealed. But the fulfilment is none the less accurate on that account, now that every item in the prediction has been verified; in fact, the longer the process the more far-seeing is he who can infallibly forecast its termination, and the clearer the evidence that it is no mere deduction of human sagacity.

To this view of the case Dr. Kuenen interposes two objections: 1. "It is judicial *punishments* which the Prophets announce. But the destiny of the heathen nations loses that character when slow decay takes the place of sudden destruction." Unless Dr. Kuenen is disposed to dispute the moral government of God altogether, and to deny the reality of divine retributions in this world, he must mean, not that punishment ceases to be such because tardily inflicted or slowly evolved, but that men are in this case in danger of not recognizing it as such, and of being diverted from considering it in its real nature as a judicial infliction, to what is merely subordinate and incidental. And this brings to light a prominent reason for that frequent peculiarity of prophetic representation which we are now considering and at which Dr. Kuenen takes such offence. The Prophet not only discloses but interprets the future. It is the finger of God in human events which he is particularly concerned to mark. Prophecy is not the random disclosure of the future for the sake of gratifying curiosity, exciting wonder, or even confirming a divine commission. This last is an incidental end of great value, but the Prophet is mainly and properly the inspired religious teacher and guide of the people. The purposes of God in the future, so far as these are revealed to him, supply lessons of warning and instruction. He is concerned with the future only as it manifests the grace or the justice of God; with coming calamities only as judicial inflictions, with coming good only as a fruit of the divine favor. The minutiæ of historical detail, if disclosed to him, would be nothing to his purpose; the intervals of time, the fluctuations and varying phases of events, the second causes concerned in their production, are all unessential to the end for which prophecy is communicated, viz., that of impressing moral and spiritual lessons on the minds of the people. In fact, they are not only of inferior consequence, but it would be disturbing and distracting to introduce them. The lesson of God's judgment on a guilty nation is made more impressive by presenting it in its unity, by gathering it all up into one summary, comprehensive view, which shall truthfully represent and faithfully depict it in the aggregate or in certain marked and salient features, and direct attention to the moral sequences and the design of God in the whole from first to last. And, if this is to be done, it is of course necessary to pass over slightly or altogether leave out of sight much that is purely accessory and contingent, and which would only serve to turn away the thoughts from the main point to be inculcated.

And this is important, not only for the immediate hearers of the Prophet, but for those as well who live when the events predicted come to pass, to give them the true key for the understanding of that which they behold. Dr. Kuenen says, "surely none of those who witnessed the decay of heathen nations could regard it, as the Prophet wished it to be regarded, as the execution of a sentence pronounced by Jahveh." But, instructed by the Prophet beforehand, men can do this: they can then trace in the slow evolutions of history what he has foreshown in his condensed picture and set in its true divine relations. This "deviation in details," therefore, "between the prediction and the historical fact," at which Dr. Kuenen cavils, results from the divine adaptation of prophecy to its proper end in the instruction and training of the people of God.

Dr. Kuenen's second objection, to the view that a neglect of the relations of time is consistent with the truth of prophecy, is that prophecy not infrequently does take cognizance of these relations. "Fixed dates are not wanting in the prophecies. The Prophets thus show that they perceive very well that dates are anything but indifferent. In a number of prophecies the cardinal thought itself stands or falls with the succession of events therein announced." This is certainly so. And we quite agree with Dr. Kuenen's' criticism upon those who speak of the "perspective" character of prophecy as if it were one of its invariable features, or of inner intuition as the fixed form of prophetical revelation, that they attribute to all prophecies what is applicable only to a portion of them. The phenomena of vision may be serviceable in illustrating that frequent peculiarity of prophetic representation, to which we have before adverted; but to resolve prophecy into vision and to determine its laws accordingly, is to enter the region of doubtful speculation. The Spirit of the LORD is limited to no one method in making His disclosures. The ends of His revelation are better answered sometimes, as we have seen, by excluding all reference to the lapse of time; at others definite dates are given, and the chronological order of events is distinctly indicated. And when the latter is the case, the fulfilment must of course conform to the statements of the prophecy in these particulars.

The special application which Dr. Kuenen proposes of this principle is the following: "Is the judgment upon one or other heathen nation promised to the people of Israel, and represented as the reparation of the wrongs which they had endured, then the possibility of such a prophecy being realized ceases from the moment that Israel loses its national existence, and thus can no longer reap the fruits of the destruction of its enemies" (p. 136). The fallacy of this is obvious. Israel sustained a twofold character: it was both a political and a religious body; it was a nation, with its affinities of race and its hereditary institutions; and it was the people of God, in covenant with Him, and embracing those who feared His name and obeyed His will. These two aspects, though historically blended in Israel, were not inseparable; and even while they were united they might be and they were mentally distinguished. Now, nothing can be plainer than that in their promises of future good the Prophets contemplate Israel, not as a nation, but as the people of God. It is their constant theme that the wicked must be purged out of Israel by divine judgments (Isai. i. 24 ff.) before the promised blessings can come, and that the holy seed alone shall be spared (Isai. vi. 13); though they were as numerous as the sand of the sea, only a remnant should return to the LORD and stay themselves on him (Isai. x. 20–22). It shall be well with the righteous; it shall be ill with the wicked (Isai. iii. 10, 11). "All the sinners of my people shall die by the sword" (Amos ix. 10). "There is no peace, saith the LORD, unto the wicked" (Isai. xlviii. 22). Their possession of the Temple that was called by the LORD'S name, and of the land which he had given them (Jer. vii. 14), and the promises made to their fathers (xi. 3 ff.), would not save them if disobedient and unfaithful. It was shown to Jeremiah (xxiv.) under the emblem of the good figs and the bad figs, and to Ezekiel in the vision of his eleventh chapter, that the wicked, however they might be outwardly connected with Israel, were no real part of it (Hos. i. 9), and they had no proper share in the blessings that were in reserve. But, on the other hand, the sons of the stranger that join themselves to the LORD shall share the privileges of His people (Isai. lvi. 3–8). Egypt and Assyria, when they too serve the LORD, shall occupy the same relation to Him as Israel (Isai. xix. 23–25). The merchandise of Tyre (Isai. xxiii. 18) shall, like everything in Jerusalem (Zech. xiv. 21), be holiness to the LORD. Of all the nations that have provoked divine judgments, the LORD declares (Jer. xii. 16), "If they will diligently learn the ways of My people, to swear by My name, the LORD liveth, then shall they be built in the midst of My people." "Many nations shall be joined to the LORD in that day, and shall be My people" (Zech. ii. 11). Egypt, Babylon, Philistia, Tyre, and Ethiopia are to be accounted as native-born in Zion (Ps. lxxxvii. 4).

On the basis of such statements, which abound upon every page of the prophetic writings, we are amply justified in affirming that the national existence of Israel was, to the Prophets, quite a distinct thing from the existence of Israel as the people of God. They clearly contemplated the possibility that the former might be overturned; they over and over again positively predict that it shall be; but the latter abides perpetual, unaffected by the ruins of the former. The national existence of Israel is no more. But the people of Jehovah, who worship and fear Him, who reverently receive and obey His Word through Moses and the Prophets, are more numerous than ever. They belong to every nation. They are found in every land. They are sprung from every race and family of mankind. These are the Israel of God in the true sense of the Prophets, who regard not natural lineage, but spiritual kinship.

So far, then, from the termination of Israel's "national existence" having set a limit to the fulfilment of the prophecies under consideration, the enlargement of the faithful remnant of Israel by the accession of believing Gentiles is supplying the required conditions and preparing the way for a fulfilment in a fuller and more adequate sense than ever. The fulfilment began in each case with the judgment inflicted upon these nations severally by Assyria or by Babylon before Israel's political existence was extinguished, and when they could behold the avenging of their cause by the providence of God, and to some extent reap the benefits of it before the captivity or after the return. But "the meek shall inherit the earth;" and the time is yet coming when these desolated seats of the ancient foes of God's people shall be occupied by those who truly fear His name.

These are the two talismans on whose magical virtue Dr. Kuenen relies to set aside what have been hitherto ranked among the most signal fulfilments of prophecy; and thus easily and effectually are they disenchanted. They cannot abide the test of a candid examination. It is not essential to the accomplishment of a prediction that it should take place speedily or all at once, when the prediction itself makes no such requirement. And the loss of Israel's national existence does not put an end to the possibility of fulfilling the judgments predicted on their foes. We accept without hesitation the view which he imputes to believers in prophecy (p. 135), that it is "fulfilled exactly and literally, or in another form and at another period, but still *always fulfilled;*" though we repel the latent sarcasm in his form of putting it, as though their only concern were to bring out a fulfilment by fair means or by foul. The truth is that an honest interpretation of prophecy, and comparison with the facts of history, uniformly carries with it the evidence of a fulfilment; and this is only to be escaped by some such method as that of Dr. Kuenen, imposing arbitrary conditions not authorized by the prediction, and refusing to admit a fulfilment, however obvious, unless these are complied with.

To the predictions of Isaiah and Jeremiah respecting Babylon, with the exception of some trivialities, the bare statement of which would be a sufficient refutation, he has nothing to object but "the lingering process of decay through which the mighty city passed" to its desolation so accurately foretold ages before.

Dr. Kuenen confesses that all which the Book of

Daniel contains respecting "Alexander the Great and his successors," and especially "the fortunes of Antiochus Epiphanes, and that prince's measures against the Israelitish religion," is strictly accurate. But then he alleges that the account of the latest years of Antiochus and all beyond that time is contradicted by the event; and its account of matters "before Alexander the Great is not only incomplete, but defective, and partly inaccurate." Hence he infers that this book cannot have been the genuine production of the Prophet Daniel, but must belong to a much later date. "The writer's ignorance of these facts is at once explained if we assume that he wrote in the age of Epiphanes, and that in the year 165 B. C. But how can that ignorance be made to agree with the supposition that he was enlightened by supernatural revelation with regard to all the preceding matters? Did that revelation begin to fail him at a certain point?" But how if no such ignorance exists except in Dr. Kuenen's imagination, or must we even say it, his misrepresentation? How, still further, if the book contains clear and unambiguous prophecies, which have been undeniably fulfilled, reaching far beyond the date when he himself alleges it to have been written? His argument against its genuineness and its inspiration then falls of itself; and the admission which he has made of its correctness in relation to events long after Daniel's time becomes a confession of a long series of predictions accurately accomplished.

This it is not difficult to show. The charge (p. 144,

note 7), that, whereas Antiochus died in Persia, it is predicted (Dan. xi. 40–45) that he should find his end in Palestine, is refuted by simply reading (ver. 45), " And he shall come to his end, and none shall help him ; " this was to be after he had planted " the tabernacle of his palace in the glorious holy mountain," but that it should be immediately after or in the same locality is neither said nor implied. An error is pretended in the 2300 days (viii. 14), and in the three and a half years (xii. 7), the 1290 and the 1335 days (vers. 11, 12); but their literal exactness is defended not only by believing interpreters as Hävernick, but even by others who, like Bertholdt and Lengerke, attach no more credit to prophecy than Dr. Kuenen himself. The statement that the writer of Daniel " knows only of four Persian kings " has no other foundation than the circumstance that he has occasion to speak of Xerxes (xi. 2) as the fourth after Cyrus (x. 1).

The assertion that " he is in error even with regard to the Babylonian kings, of whom the last is, according to him, Belshazzar, the son and, as it appears, the successor of Nebuchadnezzar," is a very extraordinary one in the present state of our knowledge on this subject. Until a comparatively recent time Belshazzar was a puzzle, and the charge that the author of the Book of Daniel had blundered here was freely made. No other writer of antiquity makes mention of such a prince. All who speak of the last king of Babylon call him Nabonned, or by some name so nearly approaching this in form as to be plainly identical.

According to Berosus, he was not of royal descent, but reached the throne by a successful conspiracy; and, instead of being put to death when Babylon was taken (Dan. v. 30), he was at that time at Borsippa, which he surrendered without a siege, and was in consequence generously treated by Cyrus, who made him Governor of Caramania, where he died. Xenophon, indeed, says that the king, whose name he does not give, but whom he styles " impious," was slain in the capture of Babylon. But it was the fashion to discredit Xenophon and Daniel, and to affirm that the native historian Berosus must be right. Thus the case stood until a few years since, when the whole matter was cleared up and Daniel thoroughly vindicated by the discovery of a cylinder [1] of Nabonned, King of Babylon, in which he makes repeated mention of his eldest son Belshazzar (Bel-sarussur). No doubt Nabonned had associated his son Belshazzar with himself in the sovereignty. When Nabonned was defeated by Cyrus and obliged to shut himself up in Borsippa, Belshazzar remained in Babylon and perished in the overthrow of the city. If we suppose Nabonned to have been married to a daughter of Nebuchadnezzar,[2] who would then be the queen of Dan. v. 10, Nebuchadnezzar could with as much propriety be called the

[1] Menant, "Babylone et la Chaldée," pp. 254 ff.
[2] This supposition is commended not only by its perfectly reconciling all the statements in the case, and by the analogy of Neriglissar (Nergal-sharezer), the successful conspirator against his brother-in-law Evil-Merodach, but likewise by the fact, attested by the Behistun inscription, that Nabonned had a son Nebuchadnezzar, who was twice personated by impostors in the reign of Darius Hystaspes.

father of Belshazzar (Dan. v. 2 ff.) as David is called
the father of King Josiah (II. Chron. xxxiv. 2, 3). If
now, as Dr. Kuenen would have us believe, the Book
of Daniel is the production, not of a contemporary and
an eye-witness, but of some nameless Jew of Palestine
nearly four centuries after the fall of Babylon, how
comes it to pass that it alone of all ancient writings
has preserved the name of Belshazzar and the memory
of his existence?

Another equally unfortunate thrust at the credibility
of Daniel is the charge that he " thrusts in the Median
monarchy between the Babylonian and the Persian."
His mention of the brief rule of Darius the Mede,
which is also certified by Xenophon, and has besides
such intrinsic probability under the circumstances, is
another instance of minute accuracy where other historians of the period have passed over in silence a
reign attended by no lasting consequences and eclipsed
by the greater glory of that of Cyrus. The idea of a
" Median monarchy," however, following the Babylonian, and distinct from the Persian, is not sanctioned
by Daniel, but foisted upon him by Dr. Kuenen for a
purpose of his own. In order to bring the contents
of the dream of Nebuchadnezzar (Dan. ii.) and of the
vision of the four beasts (vii.) into the period preceding the time which he has fixed for the composition of
the book, he maintains (p. 141) that "the four kingdoms are the Babylonian, the Median, the Persian,
and the Grecian (that of Alexander the Great and his
successors)." But that the Median and the Persian
are not two, but one and the same kingdom, appears

from the fact that the Medes and Persians are always united, both in this book and elsewhere. It was announced to Belshazzar (v. 28), "Thy kingdom is divided, and given to the Medes and Persians." Under Darius the Mede the law is that of the Medes and Persians (vi. 8, 12, 15). The ram with the two horns in the vision of ch. viii. represents (ver. 20) the kings of Media and Persia. So under Ahasuerus (Xerxes) it is Persia and Media (Esth. i. 3, 14, 18), the Persians and the Medes (i. 19). And in the Behistun inscription of Darius Hystaspes we find repeatedly the same combination, Persia and Media, the Persian and Median army. The same thing appears from the nature of the case. The Median was not overturned by the Persian kingdom, as the Babylonian by the Persian and the Persian by the Grecian; but there was simply a change in the reigning monarch by peaceful legitimate succession. The four heads of the third beast (vii. 6) indicate the fourfold division of the third monarchy, which was true of the Grecian kingdom (see viii. 8, 22), but inapplicable to the Persian.

If, now, the Medo-Persian is but one kingdom, the second, and the Grecian the third, then the fourth kingdom must be the Roman,—which best suits the description, and which is the interpretation that has been put upon it from the beginning. This delineation of the character and conquests of the Roman empire, the erection of Messiah's kingdom while it still lasted, its subsequent weakness and subdivision, and the arising of a great persecuting power out of it, are predictions which were manifestly fulfilled long after the time of Antiochus Epiphanes, and which require the assumption of a divine supernatural foresight, even though the book were written at as late a period as that to which Dr. Kuenen himself assigns it, — not to speak of the further prophecy of the seventy weeks (ix. 24-27), fulfilled in the ministry and vicarious death of Jesus Christ, at the predicted time, and the subsequent destruction of Jerusalem. Can such evidence of inspiration coexist with imposture? Can predictions such as these, the reality of which even the most advanced critical hypothesis fails to set aside, be joined in the same production with pretended predictions which are not really such, which are not genuine utterances of the Prophet from whom they claim to be, but falsely issued in his name after the events had come to pass? This prediction, that the Grecian empire would be succeeded by the Roman, further shows that Daniel did not expect the resurrection and final judgment to follow immediately after the deliverance from the persecutions of Antiochus Epiphanes, and thus corrects the false inferences drawn from the transition in xii. 1, 2. Moreover, if the Book of Daniel were a spurious production, first written and published 165 B.C., and contained the extravagant and fanatical expectations imputed to it by Dr. Kuenen respecting the miraculous death of Antiochus in Palestine, to be followed at once by the coming of the Messiah and the resurrection — expectations which were falsified by the event within two years — must it not have been discredited at once? How could it ever have gained credit as the genuine work of a true

Prophet of God, who lived nearly four centuries before? and especially how could it have attained such speedy and acknowledged influence that the Book of Maccabees, in recording the history of these times, adopts its very language and borrows its forms of expression?

In regard to the judgments predicted upon Israel, Dr. Kuenen is at great pains to represent the Prophets as at variance with one another and with the facts of the case; and the methods which he employs are as extraordinary as the results at which he arrives. He alleges that neither Hosea nor Amos "expect the destruction of the kingdom of Judah," though they clearly intimate that it shall be destroyed (Hos. i. 11, viii. 14; Amos ii. 5, ix. 11); and this is besides a subject foreign to their theme, in which silence cannot with any propriety be construed as a denial. Amos predicts the captivity of the ten tribes, but Dr. Kuenen cavils because he does not explicitly mention the Assyrians, nor state how long it would be before the Exile, and because he exhorts the people to repentance; from which the inference is drawn that he could not have foreseen that they would remain obdurate, and that the judgments which he threatens would really be inflicted. He endeavors to show that Hosea is vacillating and self-contradictory, and finally confesses that he "does not contradict himself, if we regard his intention more than the words he employs."

Micah iii. 12 predicts the destruction of Jerusalem, which was accomplished by the Chaldeans. Isaiah predicts that it shall be spared in the invasion of Sennacherib.[1] And this is gravely represented as a con-

---

[1] Of course Dr. Kuenen makes the most that he can out of the chronological difficulty which Assyrian scholars pretty unanimously agree to find in Isai. xxxvi. 1, and the parallel passage, II. Kings xviii. 13. While the testimony of the monuments confirms the statements of these chapters in the most remarkable manner, and even in minute particulars, it would appear that Sargon was still King of Assyria in Hezekiah's fourteenth year, and that the invasion of Sennacherib very probably did not take place till thirteen years later. "It is impossible," he says (p. 288), "to imagine that we have here an error of a copyist; but how then can a blunder so remarkable have originated with regard to such an important fact?" His solution is that an expedition of Sargon has been confounded with that of Sennacherib; and this mingling of two separate events, which awakens a suspicion of other inaccuracies, betrays a writer long posterior to the occurrences themselves. In his opinion this narrative was not written by Isaiah himself, but has been adopted into the volume of his prophecies from the books of Kings. Consequently, "*in its present form*," it "is about a hundred and fifty years later than the events which it records" (p. 287).

Refreshing as it is to find Dr. Kuenen thus playing the unaccustomed *rôle* of an assertor of the accuracy of the received text, we cannot help thinking that, if the conclusions of Assyriologists be correct in this instance, the readiest mode of reconciliation is to assume an error in the number, and to suppose that "fourteenth" has been wrongly substituted for "twenty-seventh." It would not be difficult to account for such a mistaken attempt at correction on the part of transcribers. Hezekiah's sickness (Isai. xxxviii. 5; compare II. Kings xviii. 2) occurred in the fourteenth year of his reign. Hastily assuming the order of narration to be the order of time, and inferring a closer chronological juxtaposition from the general expression "in those days" (Isai. xxxviii. 1) than the terms really require, transcribers may have judged that consistency demanded the number "fourteenth" in xxxvi. 1, and have made the requisite emendation. But now if xxxviii., xxxix. really precede xxxvi., xxxvii. by thirteen years — and that they are prior in order of time appears from xxxviii. 6 — then a convincing argument thence arises that these chapters are original in Isaiah and borrowed thence in Kings. This inversion of the chronological order is unac-

tradiction, though, to make it out, Micah's comment on his own words (iv. 10), "thou shalt go even to Babylon," must be eliminated from the text, and Isaiah's prediction of the Babylonish captivity (xxxix. 6) is oracularly pronounced to be spurious.

Isaiah predicts (vii. 7, 8) that within threescore and five years Ephraim shall be broken that it be not a people, and (ver. 16) that this process of extinction shall be begun by the desolation of the land of Ephraim before a child could reach that age at which it could know to refuse the evil and choose the good. To Dr. Kuenen's mind these passages contradict one another, though both are in exact accordance with the event, — the one fulfilled by Tiglath-pileser, the other by Esarhaddon. Of the latter he rids himself in the easiest manner possible by assuming an interpolation. Allow him to expunge what he pleases, and to put his own meaning on what he suffers to remain, and he need not find it difficult to prove or disprove anything he likes.

Isaiah further predicts (vii. 15, 16) that Judah should be relieved from the present invasion by Syria and Ephraim within three or four years; that butter and honey, the subsistence of a ravaged country, should

countable in Kings, while in Isaiah the whole structure of the book demands it. The entire preceding section of the book of Isaiah consists of prophecies relating to the Assyrian invasion, which is first completed by the narrative of its actual occurrence. Then the sickness of Hezekiah, followed by the King of Babylon's message and the prediction of the captivity in Babylon (xxxix. 5–7), begins a new section, containing prophecies relating to that event and the deliverance from it.

not be eaten beyond that time. Dr. Kuenen refers it to a subject with which it has nothing in the world to do, and makes it mean that the invasion by Assyria and Egypt spoken of in the subsequent verses of the chapter should occur within this brief interval. And then he triumphantly exclaims (p. 169) : "But it did not take place. In the reign of Ahaz, and also during the first half of the reign of Hezekiah, Judah continued to be exempt from an Assyrian invasion."

Jeremiah's prediction, steadfastly adhered to from the beginning to the end of his ministry, of the overthrow of Jerusalem and the exile of the people, was confessedly fulfilled. But Dr. Kuenen tries to break its force by alleging that other Prophets took a contrary view. Habakkuk's brief prophecy is wholly occupied with the judgment upon the Chaldeans; we cannot accordingly expect in it a statement of what shall befall Jerusalem, and yet even here see i. 5–10. Upon this book Dr. Kuenen makes the following most extraordinary comment: "In vain do we attempt to thrust in the fall of Jerusalem anywhere into his prophecies. Habakkuk has not even a faint presentiment of it; or rather he denies distinctly that such a catastrophe should be admitted into Jahveh's purposes." Joel of the preceding period, and Zechariah (xii.–xiv.) from the period after the Exile, are dislocated from their true position, affirmed on the most precarious critical grounds to be Jeremiah's contemporaries, their language applied to a matter of which they are not treating, and they are thus made to declare that, contrary to the allegations of Jeremiah, the land would not be invaded by the Chaldeans, or that the LORD would visibly interfere at the moment of the capture of the city. And to cap the climax, the false prophet Hananiah (Jer. xxviii.) is bolstered up by being placed in such company, and represented as declaring in the name of Jehovah, with as much right to be considered His messenger as Jeremiah, directly the opposite of what the latter asserted. And on this showing it is affirmed that we have here Prophet against Prophet!

As for "the predictions which have reference to the restoration of Israel," Dr. Kuenen affirms, and he italicizes his affirmation, "*not one of them has been realized.*" We admit, without a moment's hesitation, that if these predictions are to be understood solely in a national and local sense, they have never yet been accomplished in anything like their full extent of meaning. But this very fact creates a presumption against such a limitation. The judgments denounced against Israel and the nations have all been inflicted, as we have seen, notwithstanding Dr. Kuenen's contradiction. And it would be strange if in the promised blessings there is no correspondence whatever between the prediction and the reality; and this especially as there was in the return from the Babylonish captivity an incipient fulfilment of these promises in every particular, which, as Dr. Kuenen is himself forward to assure us, the subsequent Prophets recognized as "the beginning of the realization" of them (p. 194), and which they accepted as the pledge of their full and final accomplishment. There was a return from Exile though it was partial, not total; and there was no such vast multiplication of the people as had been promised. There was an end of the schism and of all hostility between Judah and Ephraim, though no complete union was effected of these two branches of the covenant people in one body. They were led by a prince of the House of David, but no son of David sat as king upon his father's throne; and Israel remained subject to the domination of the Gentiles instead of themselves ruling the world. There was not the full return of the people to God, nor the abundant tokens of His favor which were promised in the blissful future.

Considered as the first stage of accomplishment, the restoration from Babylon might well be reckoned, as was done by Zechariah and his compeers, as an earnest of more to come. But in itself it plainly fell far below the prophetic anticipations, and cannot be regarded as a complete and satisfactory fulfilment of what had been foretold in such glowing terms. And Dr. Kuenen is right in insisting that these predictions are no longer "capable of being realized," if this budding fulfilment has proved abortive, and after the lapse of two thousand years there has not only been no further progress towards fulfilment, but these imagined tokens of it have themselves been falsified and obliterated by the complete abolition of Israel's national existence and the long dispersion of ages. To urge as the only defence that can be made on behalf of these predictions, that whereas they "are not realized as yet," they "*shall be realized* some time" by "the return of the whole of Israel to their native country, and Israel's supremacy over the nations of the earth in the last days," is to "contradict the explanation of the old prophecies which is presented in the Old Testament itself" (pp. 186, 196).

But whatever may still remain to be developed in the future, and in whatever form, the past has not been unproductive. The promise given in the return from captivity has already been succeeded by large results. The remnant of Israel has become a vast multitude. The Son of David is seated upon His everlasting throne, and is extending His conquests among the nations; and the blessings of His reign are unfolding themselves in the experience of mankind. The hope of Israel is realized in Christ and the Gospel. All the prophetic anticipations of coming good for Israel and the world were linked with the great Redeemer and King who was to rise from David's line.

Strangely enough, Dr. Kuenen goes groping through the whole Old Testament, and absolutely professes his inability to find any prediction of a personal and individual Messiah there at all. "The word 'Messiah' is not used in the Old Testament *in any one instance*," he tells us in emphatic italics, "to denote a descendant of David who shall reign over Israel restored" (p. 202). The promise to our first parents (Gen. iii. 15) "has no connection" with this subject; "the serpent is — a serpent and nothing more" (p. 377). The promise to Abraham is not that all families of the earth shall be blessed in him or in his seed, but that "he shall be so prosperous, his posterity shall be so numerous and fortunate, that nothing better or higher can be imagined than the enjoyment of what he or his race possesses." The blessing pronounced upon Judah (Gen. xlix. 10) is not of the coming of Shiloh, but of the coming to Shiloh, "the common sanctuary."

Jeremiah "does not expect one single king of David's family, but an unbroken succession of Davidic kings" (p. 205). The same is the case with Ezekiel (p. 209). So, too, Micah and Zechariah (ix.–xi.): "The king whom they announce is described as one of the children of men, but therefore seems also of necessity to partake of mortality, the lot of them all." Probably in Zechariah i.–viii. " the man whose name is Branch " is " regarded also by him as the first of an unbroken succession of rulers like to him." " In Isaiah also he is no supernatural being." " 'Mighty God' (Isai. ix. 6), viewed in itself, might have afforded some ground for the conjecture that a supernatural ruler was present to the mind of the Prophet, and that the more because the same name is employed elsewhere to denote Jahveh (x. 21). But this conjecture is not confirmed: all the other features point to a king of human origin." " It is possible that Isaiah attributed an endless reign to the king himself whom he expected," but his meaning more probably is " that nothing shall interrupt the regular succession of the kings of his house."

In Isaiah xl.–lxvi. "the servant of Jehovah" is commonly understood by believing interpreters to denote the true people of God, including and culminating in the Messiah, who was to spring from the midst of them, and with whom they are here associated or identified in their mission, character, and destiny, in humiliation and in glory. This simple and obvious interpretation is demanded by the reference (lv. 3) to "the sure mercies of David;" it explains what Dr. Kuenen admits to be "undeniable, that the servant of Jahveh is sometimes described as if he were one individual;" it also explains how he can have a work to do for Israel as well as for the nations, and how his sufferings can be unmerited and vicarious; and it brings Isaiah into harmony with himself and with the other Prophets. But Dr. Kuenen prefers to find here a diversity between the Prophets: "The very remarkable phenomenon presents itself, that the expectations concerning the dynasty of David become disjoined from their proper object, and are transferred to the whole people" (p. 220). He actually adduces the apparent conflict between the death and burial of the Servant of Jehovah (Isai. liii. 8, 9), and his prolonging his days and enjoying a satisfying reward (vers. 10, 11), in proof that "the particulars which the Prophet mentions must be distributed among the different persons who together constitute the collective number." And he alleges that "what is communicated regarding the destiny of 'the servant' does not admit of being harmonized with the description of the scion of David given by Isaiah and Micah" (p. 223).

The Son of Man, who came with the clouds of Heaven (Dan. vii. 13), is in his view not the Messiah, but the Israelitish nation. And Daniel's prophecy of the 70 weeks (ix. 24 ff.) has nothing to do with a Messiah of the House of David. The author, who is assumed to have lived under Antiochus Epiphanes, is simply describing, under the veil of prophecy, what had already taken place. Jeremiah, xxv. 11, 12, xxix. 10, had assigned the term of seventy years to the desolations of Jerusalem, and this had been strictly fulfilled according to Ezra i. 1; II. Chron. xxxvi. 22. But this imaginary author is supposed to have thought otherwise, and accordingly to have conceived that Jeremiah must have meant, not ordinary, but sabbatical years, or weeks of years, and to have developed in vers. 24–27, his conception of that prophecy and his adjustment of it to what had taken place down to his own day. "The going forth of the commandment to restore and to build Jerusalem," which is (ver. 25) the starting-point of the 70 weeks, is alleged to be Jeremiah's prophecy already referred to, though this related to an entirely different matter from the building of Jerusalem, — viz., the period of Babylon's domination and of Israel's subjection and captivity. From this prophecy in the fourth year of Jehoiakim until "an anointed prince," who is not the Jewish Messiah, but Cyrus, is declared to be "seven weeks," or 49 years; though in actual fact, and according to the biblical reckoning, it was 70 years (a computation which is implied even in Dan. ix. 2), the discrepancy being laid to the account of ignorance in the writer. After 62 weeks more, or 434 years, "Messiah is cut off," not the Jewish Messiah, nor Cyrus as before, but the high-priest Onias. In reality Onias was murdered 365 years after the first of Cyrus, leaving an error of 69 years to be accounted for as the preceding. This is further aggravated in the present instance by the allegation made in a different connection, that the writer knew of no Persian king later than Xerxes, and that he imagined him to be the antagonist of Alexander. The deficit is thus swelled to 200 years, and it becomes necessary to assume that he assigned 362 years instead of 162 to the empire of Alexander and his Syrian successors preceding the death of Onias. And this enormous blunder is committed in a period with the details of whose history he shows such familiarity in ch. xi. that mainly on this ground the book is pronounced spurious and its date fixed during the persecutions of Antiochus! And all this to escape the plain reference of the prophecy to the advent of the Messiah. Can any one be so blind as he who is determined not to see?

Two things remain to be accounted for after this total abstraction from the Old Testament of the doctrine of the Messiah, and especially the disappearance in the latest Prophets of any expectation even of a revival of the dynasty of David. One is that prophecies which are so destitute of any reference to the Messiah should ever have given rise to the expectation of His coming. Another is that they all admit of such ready application to Jesus Christ.

Dr. Kuenen objects that to find in Christianity the fulfilment of the prophecies respecting Israel is to "spiritualize" them, and thus give them another than their real meaning. We reply, on the contrary, that with some diversity in outward form and incidental circumstances there is nevertheless the closest adherence to the essential meaning of the Prophets. The fact is, as Dr. Kuenen states it (p. 188), with the view, not of recommending, but of disparaging the current opinion on this subject: The prophecies of the Old Testament are "*more than fulfilled*, or in other words, the reality under the New Testament dispensation *far surpassed* the expectations under the Old."

The Prophets everywhere recognize and insist upon the distinction between the outward forms of the Old Testament and their inward spiritual meaning. Isaiah declares (i. 11–20) that it is not sacrifices and burnt-offerings, oblations and incense, treading God's courts, new moons and sabbaths, feasts and assemblies, that God requires, but purity of heart and life, and obedience to His will. When now He speaks (ii. 2–4) of the nations hereafter going up to the mountain of Jehovah, to the house of the God of Jacob, it is plain that the external act of pilgrimage to that locality does not exhaust his thought: it is in fact a very subordinate part of it. Its only value or meaning to him is as the legitimate mode of expressing his essential idea that these nations would pay their worship to the God of Israel, would be taught by him of his ways, and would walk in his paths. And if any other mode of doing this is equally legitimate and acceptable to the God of Israel, who will say that it does not as perfectly meet Isaiah's expectation and correspond to his thought? — especially as a figurative character is given to this whole representation by its opening words. Dr. Kuenen himself says (p. 247): "The Prophet may be understood to have meant figuratively what he says about the exaltation of Zion on the top of the mountains;" but he adds, "On the other hand, the pilgrimage to the Temple on Zion must be understood literally. . . . We should deprive the prophecy of its meaning and force if we attempted to explain it spiritually." There is nothing to justify this assertion, or the arbitrary line here drawn between what is figurative and what is literal, unless it be the positive air with which it is done.

The same Prophet, or, according to Dr. Kuenen's critical hypothesis, another Prophet in a later age, declares (Isai. lxvi. 1–3) that heaven is Jehovah's throne and the earth His footstool; man can build Him no fitting house; the offering of oxen and lambs and incense is a crime and an abomination to Him, except as joined with and expressing inward piety; He regards with favor only him that is humble and of a contrite spirit, and trembleth at His word. He then adds (ver. 23): "And it shall come to pass that from one new moon to another, and from one Sabbath to another, shall all flesh come to worship before Me, saith Jehovah." Apart from the physical impossibility of weekly and monthly pilgrimages from all parts of the earth, even if this be limited to lands then known; apart also from the fact that this is greatly in excess of the requirements of the Law, which enjoined pilgrimages to the Sanctuary but thrice in the year, at the annual feasts — is it not plain that the stress is laid upon worship before Jehovah? The sacred seasons and the central sanctuary are simply referred to as the authorized place and times of acceptable service. If the same authority which had hitherto required them should hereafter dispense with them, of what account would they be in the Prophet's eyes? It is to " worship in spirit and in truth " that his thought was directed, and not to worship in Jerusalem, except as the divinely prescribed place of a true and spiritual adoration.

Jehovah's worship, though for the time then present it had a local seat, was not, in the judgment of the Prophets, bound to any one place by an indissoluble tie. The worship of their father Abraham, who was the friend of God (Isai. xli. 8), was untrammelled by any fixed locality. The place for the Sanctuary was " the place that Jehovah should choose " (Deut. xii. 5). Jeremiah speaks of God's doing to Jerusalem as He had done to Shiloh, which He had abandoned (vii. 12–14, xxvi. 6). He looks forward to a time when the Ark of the Covenant should not be remembered nor missed (iii. 16), and God's new covenant should be written in the hearts of His people (xxxi. 31 ff.). Ezekiel in vision saw the glory of Jehovah forsake the Temple and the city (xi. 23), and God himself promised to be a Sanctuary to His exiled people in the countries where they shall come (ver. 16).

And yet when a Prophet who so clearly distinguishes between the shell and the kernel depicts the Temple and the service and the Holy Land of the future, Dr. Kuenen insists that this must all be literally understood because of its "copiousness and entering into minute details" (p. 240). And the life-diffusing stream from the Temple (Ezek. xlvii.), which forms a part of the same picture, was in the intention of the Prophet "an actual stream," because the description is "so exact and detailed" (p. 234), though the corresponding streams spoken of by Joel (iii. 18) and Zechariah (xiv. 8) are admitted to be figurative. We are prepared to hear him say next, for a like reason, that the cherubim so minutely described (Ezek. i.) were actually existing beings, wheels and eyes and all; and the eagles of chapter xvii. were literal eagles; and the women of chapter xxiii. literal women; and when the restoration of Sodom and her daughters is promised (xvi. 53-61), the Prophet expected the buried city of Sodom to be brought up from the bottom of the Dead Sea and restored to its former condition. He could still silence all objections by the same plea that he uses now (p. 242): "What we should almost designate as fantastic is evidently in complete accordance with his [Ezekiel's] ideals."

Dr. Kuenen himself points out (p. 191) the close connection between the ideas of the return of Israel to Canaan and their conversion to God. A return to Palestine without conversion to God would not be what was in the Prophet's mind and heart. And it is only as Palestine was Jehovah's land that returning to it had any religious significance. A return to God and the enjoyment of his favor and blessing is the essential thought, and Canaan is but the outward form in which that favor was for the time concentrated.

Moreover, descent from the Patriarchs is not with the Prophets the constituent principle of the people of God. Participation in the blessings promised to Israel is not determined by lineage or by nationality, but by inward character and spiritual relationship. "Ye are not My people," said Hosea (i. 9), speaking in the name of Jehovah to the ungodly Israelites, "and I will not be your God." The Prophets with one voice denounce the judgments of God upon the sinners in Israel. The wicked mass must be purged away; they have neither part nor lot in the good things to come; it is only the pure remnant that are left for whom the promises are made. Ezekiel (xi. 15) was instructed to recognize "the whole house of Israel" in the exiles, to the disregard of the degenerate inhabitants of Jerusalem, who were abandoned of God and given over to destruction. And, on the other hand, the stranger that hath joined himself to Jehovah need not fear separation from the LORD'S people (Isai. lvi. 3). And when (Isai. xix. 25) "Jehovah of Hosts shall bless, saying, Blessed be Egypt My people, and Assyria the work of My hands, and Israel mine inheritance," what has become of national distinctions?[1] How can even Dr. Kuenen, with any consistency, refuse to recognize in Christianity the universal worship of Jehovah predicted by the Prophets, when he imputes to Malachi such an excess of liberalism that when he speaks (Mal. i. 11) of the incense offered to Jehovah's name in every place, "he is thinking of the

[1] See the passages of like tenor quoted above, pp. 220 f., and numerous others in the books of the Prophets.

zeal and sincerity with which the nations served their gods; he, convinced of the unity of Jahveh, regards their worship as being properly destined and intended for the one true God."

We have not adduced the authority of the New Testament, which is abundantly and decisively given upon this point, because this has no weight with Dr. Kuenen. We have interpreted the meaning of the Prophets in this matter by their own utterances. And, themselves being judges, no bar is interposed to the recognition of the fulfilment of their prophecies by the changes which have taken place in the outward forms of worship, or in its local seat, or in national relations. The Prophets may not have been aware of the changes which Messiah's coming would introduce. There were wise reasons why the temporary nature of the Old Testament institutions should not be prematurely disclosed. But while the temporary form in which their ideas were clothed has been stripped away, the ideas abide in their unchanging reality and truth. All that was essential in the Prophets' own estimation, and much more and better than they hoped or knew, has been accomplished in Christ and the Gospel.

We have now examined *seriatim* every prediction classed by Dr. Kuenen among the "unfulfilled prophecies," whether relating to the Gentiles or to Israel. We believe that no objection, great or small, that he has brought against them has escaped attention. And we are willing to submit it to the candid reader whether he has made out a case in any one instance.

Upon this flimsy basis rests the entire argument

contained in the volume which we are examining, everything else being subsidiary and supplemental. The remainder, though offering abundant and very inviting matter for comment, must be despatched in a very few sentences. Dr. Kuenen seeks to rid himself of the prophecies, which he confesses to have been fulfilled, in three several ways.

1st. By appealing to the non-fulfilment of others, which he claims to have established, — with what justice we have already seen.

2d. By the legerdemain of modern criticism, which peremptorily waives aside any witness that it is not convenient to hear, and which is ever ready to suspect the genuineness or the accuracy of the text upon grounds which, in their last analysis, cover an assumption of the very point to be proved, — viz., that prophecy is impossible.

3d. By the gratuitous and unfounded allegation of bad faith on the part of the Prophets themselves. He distinctly charges Jeremiah and Ezekiel in particular with having modified their predictions after the event, so as to make it appear that they had minutely and accurately foretold what they never had foretold at all. Thus he says, in regard to the latter Prophet (pp. 328–330): "The passages of Ezekiel explained above contain *no real predictions*. Whatever he may have *spoken* to his fellow-exiles in the years preceding the destruction of Jerusalem, he has *written* the prophecies which we now possess *after that catastrophe*, without troubling himself in the least about literal reproduction of his oral preaching." "Though it may be impossible to reconcile such a method of procedure with our notions of literary good faith, yet it was not uncommon in ancient times, and specifically in Israel." " They are not real predictions, but historical reminiscences in a prophetical form, *vaticinia post eventum*." He would accordingly have us suppose that these Prophets falsely claim in their writings to have uttered time after time the most astonishing predictions, which met in every case a literal and precise fulfilment; and yet their auditors, who must have known the falsity of this claim, at once accepted these writings and handed them down as true prophecies received by inspiration from the mouth of God. We confess that we are of Dr. Kuenen's own opinion with regard to this expedient of his (p. 328): " Many will at once be inclined to reject it as a subterfuge, by the help of which I try to escape from the dogmatical conclusions to which the literally-fulfilled prophecies of Ezekiel ought to have led." And how does this assertion, that Jeremiah and Ezekiel altered and retouched their predictions to make them correspond with the event, comport with what he maintains elsewhere, that both these Prophets have included among their writings predictions (*e. g.*, respecting Tyre and Egypt) which had been glaringly and notoriously falsified in their own day, and that Ezekiel admits it without being in the least disturbed thereby (p. 110)?

The accounts given of the Prophets in the historical books are swept away in the most summary and relentless manner. He admits (p. 401) that the predictions of " the Prophets of the historical books extend far beyond their political horizon, are characterized by definiteness and accuracy, enter into the more minute particulars, and are all, without distinction, strictly fulfilled." But the narratives containing them are in his esteem utterly untrustworthy. "They are, *in the first place*, a reflection and striking representation of the religious belief of their authors, and only *in the second place* are they testimonies regarding the historical reality. This reality is *nowhere* to be found perfectly pure and unmixed in these narratives, in so far as they are anything more than dry chronicles; it is *always*, though in a greater or less degree, colored by the subjective conviction of the narrator." "*The representation given of the Prophets and prophecy in the historical narratives of the Old Testament* is no testimony regarding, but is itself *one of the fruits of the real Israelitish prophecy*" (p. 436). "While the prophetical historians sketched the past of Israel, they not only felt themselves compelled to labor for the religious education of Israel, but they thought themselves also justified in making their description of Israel's fortunes subordinate and subservient to that object. The considerations which would restrain *us* from treating history in such a manner, or would impede *us* in doing so, had for them no existence" (p. 443). In other words, Israelitish history is a pious fraud, concocted by the Prophets from first to last, and this in spite of the exalted respect which he professes for their character and work! — and nothing whatever in it is to be credited but just what the critics tell us may be credited. Here is in a nutshell the principle and the method of all Dr. Kuenen's critical processes and results. He blows his subjective soap-bubble to whatever size he may fancy, and dances it before his readers in its variegated beauty and apparent solidity and readiness to burst.

It does not embarrass Dr. Kuenen in the slightest degree that the New Testament throughout "ascribes divine foreknowledge to the Israelitish Prophets." He very naïvely says (p. 448): "Its judgment concerning the origin and nature of the prophetical expectations, and concerning their relation to the historical reality, may be regarded as *diametrically opposed* to ours." His elaborate attempt to show that the New Testament writers are guilty of inaccuracies and mistakes in quoting from the Old Testament, and that they misunderstand and misinterpret it, merely proves what was superfluously clear beforehand, that their conception of its meaning and spirit is radically different from his. Its chief value consists in the practical demonstration which it affords, that they who reject the inspiration and authority of the Old Testament, or any part of it, must by inevitable logical necessity reject likewise that of the New.

Dr. Kuenen sees in prophecy simply a deduction from the Prophets' own religious convictions. Jehovah's purposes are inferred by them from their thorough persuasion of His inflexible righteousness and His sovereign choice of Israel to be His people on the one hand, and the judgment which they entertain of Israel's existing moral state or the character and conduct of Gentile nations on the other. Hence "the prophetical prediction of the future" is, as he states it (p. 359), the necessarily incorrect conclusion drawn from premises which themselves were only half correct." This naturalistic hypothesis falls with the failure to prove the non-accomplishment of the predictions of the Prophets. If, as is really the case, what they have foretold has unerringly come to pass, prophecy is thereby shown to be the word, not of him who knows not what a day may bring forth, but of Him who "declareth the end from the beginning." It is the word, not of man, but of God. And it is plainly futile to attempt to account for it on natural principles—as, for example, that Jeremiah's strong faith wrought upon the exiles, and their faith wrought upon Cyrus, who by a lucky chance appeared just at the right time and became the conqueror of Babylon (p. 315), and thus brought about the return from captivity after seventy years; or Isaiah by his faith persuaded Hezekiah and his people to persevere in their resistance to Sennacherib until fortunately the plague swept off his army (p. 298). On this principle such a chapter of accidents would be required to save the credit of the Prophets as would involve that very supernatural intervention that the hypothesis was invented to escape; and that, too, in a form far more incredible than the simple faith of ages, that "prophecy came not in old time by the will of man; but holy men of God spake as they were moved by the Holy Ghost."

DR. ROBERTSON SMITH ON THE PROPHETS OF ISRAEL.

DR. W. ROBERTSON SMITH ON THE PROPHETS OF ISRAEL.[1]

WE have read this second volume of Dr. Robertson Smith with disappointment and pain. The announcement of a fresh course of lectures from his vigorous and graphic pen, in which the Prophets of Israel were to be treated in relation to their own times, naturally awakened high expectations. It would have been unreasonable to demand in all his productions an equal measure of the literary charm that attached in such an extraordinary degree to "The Old Testament in the Jewish Church;" in which even unprofessional readers found the dry details of technical discussion invested with the interest of an exciting story, as they were led by a connected argument through the mazes of Biblical criticism, from the state of the text to the age of the Pentateuch. And it need occasion no surprise that his conclusions respecting the Prophets cannot be accepted by those who have been constrained to dissent from his views previously ex-

[1] The Prophets of Israel, and their Place in History to the close of the eighth century B. C. Eight Lectures by W. Robertson Smith, LL. D. Edinburgh, 1882.

pressed. But we confess that we were not prepared for the extremely low estimate here put upon the religion of Israel and the teaching of the Prophets.

With the devout spirit that breathed in the former work there seemed to be joined a high appreciation of the Old Testament revelation and of Old Testament saints, and particularly the Prophets as the advocates of a spiritual in opposition to a ritual or materialistic worship. And with this the critical conclusions respecting Deuteronomy and the Levitical law were not necessarily inconsistent. Though it was alleged that the Pentateuchal Law did not proceed directly from Moses, it was held to be the work of other servants of God, and to have been given to Israel in successive portions at later periods of time. The date was altered but the contents remained the same, and there was no apparent disposition to underrate their meaning or value. This might seem rather to be enhanced by the assumption that such laws were insupposable in the infancy of the nation and at the outset of God's dealings with Israel, and that they must mark subsequent epochs in the divinely guided history. The Prophets, however, suffer much more severely at his hands. They are with some exceptions allowed to stand each in his own proper date, but the contents of their teaching are evaporated in the crucible of the new hypothesis until an almost impalpable residuum of religious truth is all that is left; and even this was inaccurately conceived by the Prophets, who are, moreover, irreconcilably at variance with one another in their statements of it. And this is commended to us as the revelation of God through the Prophets.

We admit without hesitation that we can no more determine *a priori* what a revelation from God must contain as a whole, or in any of its parts, than we can prescribe how the world should be made. The Most High must always act worthily of Himself and suitably to the end which He has in view. But we learn what He judged it fit to do by ascertaining what, in actual fact, He has done. It is by the direct study of the Scriptures themselves, and of each separate portion of them by itself, — in the declarations there made and the phenomena exhibited, — not by *a priori* reasonings, that we are to discover in what sense the Scriptures are the Word of God and what revelations He has therein made to us. And in interpreting Scripture we must not make it square with our notions of what it ought to be, but simply inquire what it actually is. There must, we insist, be a thoroughly unbiassed and candid interpretation of its facts and contents. If force must not be put upon it to bring forth spiritual mysteries which it does not contain, or to find in its earlier sections disclosures which were reserved for a later time, neither must it, on the other hand, be pared down to the level of what some philosophical theory of religious development may be willing to allow.

The human element in Scripture, of which we hear so much at the present time, is not to be discarded or explained away. It has its importance and value for the proper understanding and due appreciation of the sacred volume. But neither is the divine character of Scripture to be depreciated or set aside. No theory of inspiration or of non-inspiration can be accepted, as the final truth upon this subject, which cannot abide the most searching examination in the light of all the facts bearing on the case. Any investigations which enter more deeply into this question or elicit any fresh data for its determination are to be welcomed. Every advance made toward a correct appreciation of any of the factors which have contributed to the formation of the Bible, or any of its books, is a positive gain, whatever may have been the motive or immediate aim of those by whom it is brought out. And particularly it is a hopeful sign if increased attention is directed to the persons of the Prophets and the times in which they lived, the conceptions which then prevailed, the ordinary life of the people, the questions which agitated men's minds, the emergencies which called for prophetic interference, and what was from time to time attempted or accomplished by it. Assuredly we shall decline no aid in these matters even from Wellhausen, Kuenen, or Duhm, especially as their views are interpreted for us in the lucid periods of Dr. Robertson Smith or modified into more acceptable forms by his independent reflections.

We have no quarrel with our author for the extent to which he is disposed to trace the personality of the Prophets in their several messages. This does not conflict in the slightest degree with the common doctrine of inspiration. The entire person of the Prophet was God's organ in making known His will. His native endowments, the experiences of his life, all that contributed to form his character, to determine or deepen his convictions, to shape his style of thought or action, in fine to make him what he was, was a part of his providential training for his work. The more thoroughly we know him as a man, the better we can appreciate his adaptation as a Prophet to his own age and to his own countrymen. The vexed question respecting Hosea's marriage, which has been a fruitful source of disputation from the days of Jerome, may never be settled to universal satisfaction. But there is certainly much that is attractive in the idea (pp. 178 ff.) that the Prophet was first taught the lesson by a bitter domestic experience, which he subsequently labored to impress upon the transgressing people, and that the yearnings of his own affectionate heart, toward one who had so basely wronged him, led him up to his conception of the persistent love of God to idolatrous Israel, and gave him a clearer insight into His providential dealings with His people. And we have in the book of Habakkuk a remarkably clear instance of the wrestling conflict of which revelations were born: the inward struggle with great moral problems that clamored for solution, the mental process by which the strife was calmed and assured conviction attained,— and distinguished from this, and additional to it, the divine communication for which the mind was antecedently prepared.

Dr. Robertson Smith expresses his dissent (p. 9) from the views of those who

"maintain that there was no specific difference between the growth of divine truth in Israel and the growth of truth among other nations. The Prophets who were the organs of God's teaching in Israel appear to them to stand on the same line with the other great teachers of mankind, who were also searchers after truth and received it as a gift from God. . . The practical point, in all controversy as to the distinctive character of the revelation of God to Israel, regards the place of Scripture as the permanent rule of faith and the sufficient and unfailing guide in all our religious life. When we say that God dealt with Israel in the way of special revelation, and crowned His dealings by personally manifesting all His grace and truth in Christ Jesus the incarnate Word, we mean that the Bible contains within itself a perfect picture of God's gracious relations with man, and that we have no need to go outside of the Bible history to learn anything of God and His saving will towards us, — that the whole growth of the true religion up to its perfect fulness is set before us in the record of God's dealings with Israel, culminating in the manifestion of Jesus Christ. There can be no question that Jesus Himself held this view, and we cannot depart from it without making Him an imperfect teacher and an imperfect Saviour. Yet history has not taught us that there is anything in true religion to add to the New Testament. We still stand in the nineteenth century where He stood in the first; or rather He stands as high above us as He did above his disciples — the perfect Master, the Supreme Head of the fellowship of all true religion" (pp. 10, 11).

The imperfect knowledge of God reached by Gentile nations, the lack of any solid and continuous pro-

gress in religious things among them, and the decay
of their noblest religions, as contrasted with the steady
progress in the knowledge of God given to Israel,
until it "merged in the perfect religion of Christ which
still satisfies the deepest spiritual needs of mankind,"
is urged in proof that the revelation of the Old and
New Testaments may fairly claim to be the revelation
of God to men in a special and absolute sense
(p. 14). "It is not necessary," he adds, " to encum-
ber the argument by comparing the way in which
individual divine communications were given to Israel,
with the way in which the highest thinkers of other
nations came to grasp something of spiritual truth;"
that is, as we understand him, it is undesirable to
raise the question whether Hebrew Prophets ascertained the truth in any such way as made them authoritative teachers of the will of God, and exempted
them from errors in its communication.[1]

[1] On page 82 the Doctor draws a distinction between prophets
and uninspired preachers, which might seem, at first sight, to be identical with the commonly received doctrine on this subject. "Jehovah
did not first give a complete theoretical knowledge of Himself and
then raise up prophets to enforce the application of the theoretical
scheme in particular circumstances. That would not have required
a prophet; it would have been no more than is still done by uninspired preachers. The place of the prophet is in a religious crisis,
where the ordinary interpretation of acknowledged principles breaks
down, where it is necessary to go back, not to received doctrine, but
to Jehovah Himself. The word of Jehovah, through the prophet,
is properly a declaration of what Jehovah, as the personal King of
Israel, commands in this particular crisis; and it is spoken with authority, not as an inference from previous revelation, but as the direct
expression of the character and will of a personal God, who has
made Himself personally audible in the prophet's soul." A careful

Now this may, in the connection, simply refer to the place that the supernatural claims of the Prophets should hold in an apologetical argument. In endeavoring to force conviction on unbelievers, it might not be wise to bring the supernatural evidences of our religion to the front, and engage in a disputation upon inspiration and infallibility in the first instance. As he says (p. 16): "The miraculous circumstances of its promulgation need not be used as the first proof of its truth, but must rather be regarded as the inseparable accompaniments of a revelation which bears the historical stamp of reality." There is unquestionably reason and sound sense is this. If the measureless superiority of the religion of the Bible over any Gentile system be first established by palpable and undeniable considerations, it may be hoped that the minds of opposers will thus be better prepared to admit the evidence of its supernatural origin. It is as the accompaniment and the attestation of revealed truth, and not as isolated prodigies, that miracles are convincing.

But when we consider the whole drift of the Lectures which are thus prefaced, we think that no injus-

inspection of these words, however, shows with what care they have been selected. God may "make Himself personally audible in the prophet's soul" simply as He does in the divine illumination enjoyed by all truly pious men. Their devout intercourse with God leads to an intimate acquaintance with His character, and an instinctive apprehension of what His will must be in any given case. And thus the thought will not be excluded that, along with "the word of Jehovah through the prophet," there may be uttered much that savors of human weakness and error. And that this is his real meaning appears from the entire tenor of the volume.

tice is done the distinguished lecturer by surmising that he meant more than appears upon the surface. If he can suggest no other reason for the sacredness of Sinai than (p. 34), "The storm that broke on the mountains of Sinai, and rolled across the desert in fertilizing showers, made the godhead of Jehovah real," and if the teachings of the Prophets were such as he *in extenso* represents them to be, we cannot help suspecting that his distrust of the supernatural facts of the Bible contributed to his reluctance to lay too much stress upon them.

And when he proposes (p. 16) to place the defenders of revelation on such vantage-ground that they "need no longer be afraid to allow free discussion of the details of its history," — that "they can afford to meet every candid inquirer on the fair field of history, and to form their judgment on the actual course of revelation by the ordinary methods of historical investigation," — the implication seems to be that a fair application of the ordinary methods of historical investigation would seriously alter the views commonly entertained respecting the actual course of revelation; and this it is the object of the volume before us to establish in regard to the Prophets.

It informs us, for instance, that the prophet Elijah was indifferent to the worship of the golden calves (p. 109). It seems that Hosea was the first to discover that there was anything wrong in this form of idolatry.

"There is no feature in Hosea's prophecy which distinguishes him from earlier Prophets so sharply as his attitude to the golden calves, the local symbols of Jehovah adored in the Northern sanctuaries. Elijah and Elisha had no quarrel with the traditional worship of their nation. Even Amos never speaks in condemnation of the calves" (p. 175). . . . "The revolution inaugurated by Elijah and Elisha appealed to the conservatism of the nation. It was followed therefore by no attempt to remodel the traditional forms of Jehovah's worship, which continued essentially as they had been since the time of the Judges.[1] The golden calves remained undis-

---

[1] In the connection this can have no other meaning than that the sanctuary of the golden calf at Dan was identical with the idolatrous shrine founded there by the Danites (Judg. xviii. 30, 31). But the duration of the latter is expressly limited to "the time that the house of God was in Shiloh;" this expired with the capture of the Ark by the Philistines. This expression defines the phrase in ver. 30, "the day of the captivity of the land," which can, therefore, only refer to the overthrow which Israel then experienced, and which is spoken of in similar terms (Ps. lxxviii. 61 ff.). And if the narrative received its present form before the Assyrian Exile, which there is no good reason to question, the Philistine domination is the only event to which it can naturally be referred. There is, besides, no intimation that Micah's graven image (Judg. xvii. 3) was in the form of a calf. There is no mention of calf-worship in Israel in the period of the Judges, or thenceforward until the time of Jeroboam, and there are no known facts from which its existence can be inferred. The establishment of the idolatrous worship at Bethel and Dan is explicitly referred to Jeroboam and the circumstances of its institution narrated in detail, 1. Kings xii. 28, 29. These point (ver. 2) to Egypt as its source, which was likewise the case in the only previous instance of it in the whole history of the people — namely, the trespass of Aaron in the Wilderness (Ex. xxxii. 4). The allegation (p. 38) that "in many places a priesthood, claiming kinship with Moses, administered the sacred oracle as his successors," is a very broad statement considering its narrow basis of fact. If the conjecture be correct that *literæ suspensæ* form no part of the text, then "Manasseh" (Judg. xviii. 30) should read "Moses," and there would be proof of "a priesthood claiming kinship with Moses," in *one* idolatrous sanctuary.

turbed, though they were plainly out of place in the worship of a Deity who had so markedly separated Himself from the gods of the nations" (p. 96).

Such statements cannot be characterized otherwise than as an atrocious misrepresentation. If there is any one thing of which Jehovah expresses His utter abhorrence everywhere throughout the Scriptures, it is the practice of idolatry in whatever form; and that a true prophet of the LORD, jealous as Elijah was for His name and worship in a time of widespread apostasy, and to whose divine commission such signal attestations were given by the LORD Himself, could possibly have been "indifferent" to what was so grossly dishonoring to God, or, as it is mildly put in the passage above cited, "plainly out of place" in His worship, is absolutely beyond belief. The earlier Prophets were precisely of the same mind with Hosea in respect to the golden calves. Ahijah of Shiloh, in the tribe of Ephraim, who had foreshown to Jeroboam his elevation to the throne (I. Kings xi. 29 ff.), denounced his sin in the strongest terms (xiv. 9). So did the man of God who came from Judah to prophesy against Jeroboam's altar (xiii. 2), and whose words were reaffirmed even by the lying prophet of Bethel (ver. 32). And Jehu, the son of Hanani, uttered a like message of denunciation to Baasha for walking in the way of Jeroboam (xvi. 1, 2). Jehoshaphat's distrust of the four hundred prophets who professed to declare to Ahab the will of the LORD, and his insisting on a prophet of Jehovah besides, shows what he thought of the worship of the calves;

and when Micaiah was summoned, he distinctly charged his antagonists with speaking under the influence of a lying spirit (I. Kings xxii).[1]

Unless therefore Dr. Robertson Smith is prepared to deny with Kuenen that any dependence is to be put upon predictions recorded in the historical books, the Prophets did lift up their voice against the worship of the calves from the very beginning. And even though these particular narratives be discredited the fact remains; for such stories could not have arisen, and gained credence, unless they correctly represented the known attitude of the LORD'S true Prophets.

We are told (p. 109) that the histories of Elijah and Elisha, as " every one can see," are ancient and distinct documents, which represent an earlier belief than the Books of Kings in which they have been incorporated.[2] It is nevertheless plain that the author of Kings, who never lets slip an opportunity to express his detestation of the worship of the calves, could not have suspected Elijah or Elisha of complicity with it, or he would not have failed to enter his dissent (II. Kings xvii. 13). If the reformation

[1] According to Wellhausen (p. 251 of his edition of Bleek's Einleitung) this account, as well as that in II. Kings iii., originated in the kingdom of Samaria. We may consequently presume that it is not colored to the prejudice of the national worship of the Ten Tribes.

[2] And p. 116: "The story of Elijah and Elisha clearly took shape in the Northern Kingdom; it is told by a narrator, who is full of personal interest in the affairs of Ephraim, and has no idea of criticising Elijah's work, as the Judæan editor criticises the whole history of the North, by constant reference to the schismatical character of the Northern sanctuaries."

undertaken by Elijah aimed at nothing more than was accomplished by Jehu, it would have been spoken of in similar terms (II. Kings x. 28, 29). These Lectures, however, assert that Elijah's zeal was not directed against the golden calves, which were recognized symbols of Jehovah, but simply against the service of Baal; though " in building and endowing a temple for his wife, Ahab did no more than Solomon had done without exciting much opposition on the part of his people." Perhaps the Doctor forgets that on this very account Solomon was threatened with the loss of his kingdom (I. Kings xi. 33), and the danger was sufficiently formidable to lead him to seek the life of Jeroboam (ver. 40). Ahab, it seems, had no idea that he was breaking the first commandment. "Even if we are to suppose that practical religious questions were expressly referred to the words of this precept, it would not have been difficult to interpret them in a sense that meant only that no other God should have the pre-eminence over Israel's king." If this be so, we do not see why a like latitude of interpretation might not have been applied to Deut. xii. 5, and "the place which the LORD shall choose" have been understood to mean any place whatever where divine worship was established. Jeroboam may not have thought himself guilty of any infraction of this law, nor any other adherent of the alleged "local sanctuaries." What then becomes of the argument for the non-existence of Deuteronomy, drawn from the neglect of this fundamental statute? It was simply set aside by a mistaken exegesis.

Elijah's austere opposition to "the god of a friendly state" was an advance upon all previous practice.

"Hitherto all Israel's interest in Jehovah had had practical reference to His contests with the gods of hostile nations, and it was one thing to worship deities who were felt to be Jehovah's rivals and foes, and quite another thing to allow some recognition to the deity of an allied race. But Elijah saw deeper into the true character of the God of Israel. Where He was worshipped no other god could be acknowledged in any sense. This was a proposition of tremendous practical issues. It really involved the political isolation of the nation; for, as things then stood, it was impossible to have friendship and alliance with other peoples if their gods were proscribed in Israel's land. It is not strange that Ahab, as a politician, fought with all his might against such a view; for it contained more than the germ of that antagonism between Israel and all the rest of mankind which made the Jews appear to the Roman historian as the enemies of the human race, and brought upon them an unbroken succession of political misfortunes, and the ultimate loss of all place among the nations" (p. 80). "From the point of view of national politics, the fall of Ahab was a step in the downfall of Israel. . . . In this respect, the work of Elijah foreshadows that of the Prophets of Judah, who in like manner had no small part in breaking up the political life of the kingdom" (p. 78).

From all this it may be inferred that Ahab was a more sagacious statesman, even if he was not a better man, than Elijah; and, while religion might have suffered, the political prosperity of Israel and of Judah would have been greater if Elijah and the Prophets had not interfered as they did. It was not without reason, then, that Ahab accosted the Tishbite as the Troubler of Israel (I. Kings xviii. 17). This libel upon the Prophets, and apology for impious transgressors and persecutors, which is continued *ad nauseam,* overlooks the cardinal fact that virtue and piety, and the blessing of Jehovah, are the true foundations of national welfare. It was the loss of these, far more than the want of foreign alliances or even the encroachments of the great empires, which led to Israel's downfall.

Elijah's ministry was exercised in a great crisis. The idolatrous worship of Jehovah established by Jeroboam was not enough for Ahab; he openly introduced the worship of Baal, and sought to make it the religion of the state (I. Kings xvi. 31–33). It may be true that he did not intend to give up the service of Jehovah (p. 48) as this was represented by the golden calves; but the LORD'S altars were thrown down, and His true Prophets slain with the sword (xix. 14), or forced to hide themselves in caves (xviii. 13). In this state of things, when the alternative was between Jehovah and Baal, rather than between the pure and the corrupted service of Jehovah, it need not surprise us if the golden calves are not more directly and pointedly alluded to. If some one were to place in our hands a plea for the Christian religion, issued when Atheism and ungodliness were rampant in the French Revolution, would it ever enter our minds to charge its author with "indifference" to the various corruptions which have defaced Christianity, because these were not discussed in the pamphlet? Elijah shows plainly enough where he stood, and to what he would recall the people. He never said or did anything which can be tortured into approval of the golden calves. He never sacrificed before them himself, nor urged others to do so. His one great sacrifice, designed to demonstrate to the people of the Ten Tribes the deity of Jehovah, was offered, not at Bethel[1] nor at Dan, but at Carmel. (See above, p. 164.) He addressed Jehovah as "the God of Abraham, Isaac, and of Israel" (1. Kings xviii. 36). Now we are told (p. 117) that the narratives of the Patriarchs, as we possess them, are for the most part, gathered about the "Northern sanctuaries," and were there constantly rehearsed. They must therefore correctly represent the ideas which Elijah and his countrymen had of their ancestors, and of the great object of their worship. From them we learn that Jehovah was to the Patriarchs "the Most High God, the possessor of heaven and earth" (Gen. xiv. 22, xxiv. 3), the almighty (xvii. 1) and everlasting God (xxi. 33), who has all nature under His control (xlix. 25), whose dwelling is in heaven (xix. 24, xxviii. 12, 13), who, when He manifested

---

[1] We subjoin here some characteristic specimens of Wellhausen's fairness in statement. He speaks (Bleek's Einleitung, p. 246) of Elijah as fleeing for his life "to the ancient sanctuary of Beersheba, in southern Judah, which was much frequented likewise by Israel," because he left his servant at that most southern point of the country, on his way to Sinai (1. Kings xix. 3 ff.). Again (p. 245), " he was nourished by a widow, in the very land of Baal, thus showing not the least hatred to heathenism in itself." How far he sanctioned heathenism by that visit appears from xvii. 12, 14, 24.

Himself on earth, appeared in human form (xviii. 1, 2, xxxii. 24, 30), and who was worshipped without any idolatrous symbols (xxxv. 2; comp. xxxi. 19, 30).

Jehovah was to Elijah not only supreme but exclusive in his godhead (I. Kings xviii. 21, 24). It is not merely that "there was no room for two. gods in the land" (p. 76). Elijah makes no such limitation; to his mind there could be but one God in existence. Such a conception of God does not consist with image-worship, which is, moreover, confirmed by his ridicule of the senselessness and vanity of idolatry (ver. 27). The twelve stones of the altar (ver. 31) show that he did not recognize the rightfulness of the schism, nor, consequently, of the apostasy to the worship of the calves, which was one of its direst fruits. But he utters his mind in a more direct and positive manner, when he declares to Ahab, in the name of Jehovah, "I will make thine house like the house of Jeroboam, the son of Nebat, and like the house of Baasha, the son of Ahijah." The whole passage (xxi. 21-24) is a manifest repetition of the language of preceding Prophets (xiv. 10, 11, xvi. 2-4), and the reference to the crime of the golden calves is unmistakable. They are classed along with serving Baal, as similarly offensive to Jehovah, and incurring a similar doom. It is confessed in these Lectures (p. 99) that Hosea ii. 5, 8, 13 means by Baalim "the local manifestations of Jehovah under the form of the golden calves." Ahijah expressly calls them "other gods" (I. Kings xiv. 9). We are accordingly justified in assuming, that, when Elijah charges both Ahab and his father's house (xviii. 18) with having "forsaken the commandments of the LORD and followed Baalim," he combines Ahab's service of Baal and Omri's service of the golden calves (xvi. 25, 26) under a common name.[1] The image worship nominally paid to Jehovah is an offence of like character with the open and declared worship of Baal, and finds in this its culmination. To the Prophet these are different grades of the same criminality, and, in standing up for Jehovah against Baal, he sets the pure worship of the one true God against them both alike.

In answer to Elijah's complaint against Israel the LORD directs him among other things (I. Kings xix. 15) to anoint Hazael to be king over Syria, that his sword may inflict deserved punishment. Elisha subsequently fulfils this commission (II. Kings viii. 12, 13) and Hazael executes the appointed vengeance, but not until the reigns of Jehu and Jehoahaz (x. 32, xiii. 3, 22), after the worship of Baal had been abolished and that of the calves re-established. Elijah therefore foretells a penalty to be inflicted on the worshippers of the golden calves; and this is in direct response to his arraignment of Israel for having forsaken the covenant of Jehovah. This conclusion cannot be evaded even by the desperate expedient of assuming a *vaticinium ex eventu;* for the narrative, which puts this

---

[1] This is still the case if "thou," in this verse, is restricted to Ahab alone; for his father's house, which worshipped the calves, is involved with him in "forsaking the commandments of the LORD."

prophecy in the mouth of Elijah, is not from the fault-finding "Judæan editor" but "clearly took shape in the Northern Kingdom" (p. 116). It is correctly conceived therefore in the spirit of Elijah. And we are at liberty to conclude that it would have been quite in character for him to regard Hazael's invasion of Israel as a proper penalty for their forsaking Jehovah's covenant, though their adoration was paid not to Baal but to the golden calves.

The significance of Elijah's journey of forty days and forty nights unto Horeb, the Mount of God (I. Kings xix. 8), is acknowledged in the Lectures (p. 83).

"It is highly characteristic, for his whole standing, that in the greatest danger of his life, when the victory of Jehovah on Mount Carmel seemed to be all in vain, he retired to the desert of Sinai, to the ancient mountain of God. It was the God of the Exodus to whom he appealed, the ancient King of Israel in the journeyings through the Wilderness." "The God whom he declared to Israel was the God of Moses."

It might be supposed from this that some satisfactory statement was about to be made respecting the conception of Jehovah, which this transaction involved. And we experience something like the sensation of suddenly dropping down from the sublime to the trivial, when we find that all this prelude has no further meaning than that Elijah, as a native of Gilead, had a proclivity for "the old nomadic life of the age of Moses," and was akin to the Nazarites, whose "vow to abstain from wine . . . was undoubtedly a religious protest against Canaanite civilization in favor of the simple life of ancient times."

We press the question, however: What notions were entertained of the God of Moses, whom Elijah by this significant action so plainly declares to be his God likewise? A few quotations will show us the point of view from which this question is regarded by Dr. Robertson Smith. He tells us (p. 70) that the difference between Jehovah and other gods

> "was not defined once for all in a theological dogma, but made itself felt in the attitude which Jehovah actually took up towards Israel in historical dealings with His nation."

> "The current ideas of the Hebrews about unseen things were mainly the common stock of the Semitic peoples, and nothing is more certain than that neither Moses nor Samuel gave Israel any new system of metaphysical theology. In matters of thought as well as of practice, the new revelation of Jehovah's power and love, given through Moses, or rather given in actual saving deeds of Jehovah which Moses taught the people to understand, involved no sudden and absolute break with the past, or with the traditions of the past common to Israel with kindred nations. Its epoch-making importance lay in quite another direction — in the introduction into Israel's historical life of a new personal factor — of Jehovah Himself as the God of Israel's salvation. . . . It was from this personal experience of Jehovah's character, read in the actual history of His dealings with His people, that the great teachers of Israel learned, but learned by slow degrees, to lay down general propositions about divine things. To suppose that the Old Testament history began with a full scheme of doctrine, which the history only served to illustrate and enforce, is to invert the most general

law of God's dealings with man, whether in the way of nature or of grace" (p. 58). "General propositions about divine things are not the basis but the outcome of such personal knowledge of Jehovah, just as in ordinary human life a general view of a man's character must be formed by observation of his attitude and action in a variety of special circumstances" (p. 82).

There is much in all this that is true and vastly important. Only God's revelation is arbitrarily limited to His manifestation of Himself in history, which men are to interpret with more or less divine assistance; while His direct and positive communications in matters of faith and duty are altogether overlooked. The principles above stated are applied to the age of Moses with the following result,—all preceding revelations made to the Patriarchs being peremptorily set aside:—

"It would seem that the memory of the God of the Hebrew fathers was little more than a dormant tradition [1] when Moses

---

[1] And yet the Doctor admits but a few lines before that he has no certainty on this point: "It is not easy to say how far the remembrance of this God was a living power among the Hebrews." But then "historical investigation" has made sad havoc of the patriarchal narratives, many of which, we are told (p. 166), "there are the very strongest reasons for regarding as allegories of historical events subsequent to the settlement of the Hebrews in Canaan." So without further hesitation he sets them down as on the same level with their heathen neighbors of the same ancestral stock. "The Semitic nomads have many superstitions, but little religion." "Among the Israelites, as among the Arabs of the desert, whatever there was of habitual religious practice was probably connected with tribal or family superstitions, such as the use of teraphim, a kind of household idols which long continued to keep their place in Hebrew homes." No doubt idolatry was practised to some extent by Israelites in Egypt (Josh. xxiv.

began his work" (p. 33). When Jehovah delivered them from the oppression of Egypt, "the new circumstances of Israel . . . created a multitude of new questions. On these Moses had to decide, and he sought the decision from Jehovah, whose Ark now led the march of Israel" (p. 36). From these solitary facts the lecturer deduces (p. 40) "the essential difference between Jehovah and the Baalim, which had to be preserved amidst all changes of circumstances if Jehovah was still to maintain his individuality. In the first place . . . Jehovah represented a principle of national unity, while the worship of the Baalim was split into a multitude of local cults without national significance."[1] Further, "Je-

14; Ezek. xx. 7, 8, xxiii. 3); but it is an incredible assumption that there was no true piety surviving among them, and that all correct knowledge of God had been obliterated or lost. And as to the connection of the teraphim with Hebrew homes, the evidence is scanty and exceptional. Rachel stole her father's teraphim, but without Jacob's privity (Gen. xxxi. 19, 32); and he required his household to put away everything of the kind (xxxv. 2). Michal, Saul's daughter, had teraphim in her house (1. Sam. xix. 16); but in what esteem they were held appears from Samuel's classing teraphim with witchcraft and rebellion (xv. 23); and in every remaining passage in which teraphim are spoken of, they are associated with open and confessed idolatry. Possibly there may be a few persons in Scotland who have a superstitious belief in witches; but what would be thought of a man who should gravely adduce this as a fact reflecting the general religious condition of that country, or as indicating the amount of religious knowledge possessed by the people?

[1] If this be so we submit that, upon the Doctor's own showing, it is naturally to be expected that Moses would issue just such a command as that in Deut. xii. 5. Later events may have interfered with its strict observance. But if "the religion of Jehovah . . . lost the best part of its original meaning when divorced from the idea of national unity" (p. 47), it would have been an unaccountable oversight in Moses not to have enjoined the perpetuation of that unity of the Sanctuary which was so essential, and which it is confessed was maintained in the Wilderness and during the Conquest.

hovah represented to Israel two of the greatest blessings that any people can enjoy. . . . The first of these was *liberty*, for it was Jehovah that brought Israel forth from the house of bondage; the second was *law, justice*, and the *moral order* of society, for from the days of Moses the mouth of Jehovah was the one fountain of judgment. So in the Ten Words, the fundamental document of the religion of the Old Testament, the claim of Jehovah to the exclusive worship of Israel is based on the deliverance that made Israel a free people, and issues in the great laws of social morality."

But if the Ten Words are Mosaic, and may be taken into the account in estimating the knowledge of God which was then possessed, they imply a conception of Him vastly beyond the meagre and purely political ideas suggested in these Lectures. Dr. Robertson Smith does not tell us just what he thinks of the Ten Words. From the manner in which they are here referred to, it might be taken for granted that he ascribed them to the period of the Exodus.[1] But the

---

[1] "The Old Testament in the Jewish Church" (p. 331) seems to impute the writing of the Ten Words to Moses, and (p. 334) plainly fixes them in the life of the great legislator. The Doctor there says: "The events of Sinai, and the establishment of the covenant on the basis of the Ten Words, did not cut short this kind of Torah," *i. e.* Moses' judging "his contemporaries by bringing individual hard cases before Jehovah for decision." This can only be reconciled with what he represents to be the Mosaic idea of God by assuming that the Ten Words of Moses were very different from the Ten Commandments as we now possess them. But of this he gives us no hint.

And there are other cases in which we are left in some uncertainty as to the Doctor's precise meaning. Thus in the volume before us (p. 34) he speaks of Jehovah as having "wrought the great deliverance at the Red Sea;" and he finds in the Exodus "a marvellous display of Jehovah's saving strength . . . when the proud waters rolled

contents of the first table are strangely overlooked. And he seems quite oblivious of any connection between Mount Sinai and the giving of the Ten Commandments. God's "kingly seat on earth" he tells us (p. 34) was by "an ancient tradition placed on Mount Sinai, which still appears in the Song of Deborah as the place from which the divine majesty goes forth in thunder-storm and rain to bring victory to Israel;" and (p. 43) "in the Song of Deborah, Je-

between the Hebrews and the shattered power of the Egyptians." We would never have dreamed that this could mean less than the miraculous interference which this transaction has always denoted to the great mass of the readers of Scripture, were it not that in the very same connection the LORD's descent upon Sinai is frittered away to a thunder-storm; and in all the discussion about Elijah the supernatural events in his life are not once alluded to. The Doctor is ordinarily so frank in the statement of his views, even the most startling, that we can imagine no motive for concealment here, much less for the employment of misleading phrases. Perhaps we do him injustice by the suggestion, but this unwonted reticence inclines us to suspect some remaining hesitation in his own mind respecting the ultimate issue of "historical investigation" into these matters, and a disinclination to drift altogether away from long-cherished traditional opinions until the last strand of the cable is parted.

Wellhausen, however, has no hesitation on this point. We quote from his article "Israel," in the *Encyclopædia Britannica*, (vol. xiii. p. 397), in which he says of Moses and the Exodus: "It was not through any merit of his that the undertaking (of which he was the soul) prospered as it did; his design was aided in a wholly unlooked-for way, by a marvellous occurrence quite beyond his control, and which no sagacity could possibly have foreseen. One whom the wind and sea obeyed had given him His aid. Behind him stood One higher than he, whose spirit wrought in him and whose arm wrought for him. . . . It was Jehovah. Alike what was done by the deliberate purpose of Moses and what was done without any human contrivance by nature and by accident came to be regarded in one great totality as the doing of Jehovah for Israel."

hovah has not yet a fixed seat in the land of Canaan, but goes forth from Sinai to help His people in their distress." It might with precisely the same propriety be inferred from Hab. iii. 3, that Jehovah had not a fixed seat in Canaan down to the time of Habakkuk, but still came forth from the desert for the succor of His people. All the sacredness of Sinai is in consequence of the revelations which Jehovah there made of Himself to Moses (Ex. iii. 2) and to Israel. No trace is to be found of any prior hallowing of the place, or of its being hallowed for any other reason. In the narrative of the first of the divine manifestations granted there, Horeb is called "the mountain of God" (Ex. iii. 1; comp. iv. 27) by anticipation; just as Eben-ezer is spoken of (1. Sam. iv. 1) before it received that name (vii. 12), or as we might say that the Indians wandered along the Hudson or over Mount Washington before America was visited by Europeans.

Every allusion to Sinai or to Horeb in the Old Testament is linked with the marvellous occurrences recorded at length in Ex. xix., xx., and is a fresh confirmation of their truth. The Song of Deborah celebrates the victory over Sisera by Him who once met Israel at Sinai with cloud and tempest, while the earth trembled and the mountain shook (Judg. v. 4, 5; comp. Ps. lxviii. 8, 17). The blessing of Moses (Deut. xxxiii.) — though its genuineness is denied in the face of the positive declaration in ver. 1, corroborated as this is by internal evidence — yet "shows us better," we are told (p. 118), "than any other part of Scripture how thoughtful and godly men of the Northern Kingdom understood the religion of Jehovah." Confessedly, then, it shows us the belief entertained by Elijah that God revealed Himself to Israel at Sinai, in brilliant splendor, and there gave them His Law through the instrumentality of Moses (vers. 2 – 5 ; comp. Hab. iii. 3, 4 ; Neh, ix. 13 ; Mal. iv. 4.) And the Prophet's visit to Horeb was not merely to some traditional seat of the godhead, but to the place where Jehovah gave His Law to Israel in awful magnificence, and where He established that covenant with them which the children of Israel had now so basely forsaken.

Now of this Law — that in actual fact and in the belief of Elijah (which is the point of especial consequence to us just now) was given at Sinai — the Decalogue must undoubtedly have been a part. It is the Ten Commandments which are said to have been spoken by the mouth of God amid the grand displays which betokened His presence on the mountain. And the Ark, which is admitted to be as old as the time of Moses[1] (pp. 36, 43), contained the

---

[1] Even Wellhausen owns (article " Israel," *Encyclopædia Britannica*, vol. xiii. p. 398) that " Jehovah's chief, perhaps in the time of Moses His only, sanctuary was with the so-called Ark of the Covenant." So Kuenen (" Religion of Israel," vol. i. p. 289) : " Scarcely any tradition of Hebrew antiquity is better guaranteed than that which derives the Ark of Jahveh from the lawgiver himself." The atrocious manner in which the latter critic is capable of perverting history may be illustrated by his utterly baseless substitution of an image of the Deity, or a fetich, for the tables of the law (p. 233) : " Was the Ark empty, or did it contain a stone — Jahveh's real abode, of which the Ark was only the repository. This we do not know, although the latter

tables of stone on which the Ten Words were written (Ex. xxxiv. 28, xl. 20; Deut. x. 4, 5; 1. Kings viii. 9, 21), and was hence called the Ark of the Testimony (Ex. xxv. 21, 22) and the Ark of the Covenant (Judg. xx. 27). The existence of this Ark is a palpable evidence, which cannot be set aside, of the antiquity of the commandments inscribed on these tables. If anything whatever is known of the Mosaic age, it is certainly known that the Ten Commandments were given then. There is nothing more surely accredited than this, whether by historical testimony or by monumental evidence.

Wellhausen, however, is keen-sighted enough to perceive that if the antiquity of the Ten Commandments is allowed, his whole critical hypothesis is undermined. "If," he says (article "Israel" p. 399), " the legislation of the Pentateuch cease as a whole to be regarded as an authentic source for our knowledge of what Mosaism was, it becomes a somewhat precarious matter to make any exception in favor of the Decalogue." He accordingly urges the four following arguments against its authenticity.[1]

opinion, in connection with the later accounts of the Pentateuch, appears to us to possess great probability."

[1] Kuenen, on the other hand, admits the authenticity of "the Ten Words as a whole," but saves himself by arbitrarily rejecting as much of each individual commandment as he sees fit. "The tradition which ascribes them to Moses is worthy of respect on account of its undisputed antiquity. Nevertheless, if it were contradicted by the contents and form of the Words we should have to reject it. But this is not the case. Therefore we accept it. Reserving our right to subject each separate commandment to special criticism, and, if necessary, to deny its Mosaic origin, we acknowledge it as a fact that Moses, in the name

"(1) According to Ex. xxxiv. the commandments which stood upon the two tables were quite different."

The ingenious conceit was first suggested by Goethe, that the laws of Ex. xxxiv. are the Ten Commandments according to a different tradition from that followed in Ex. xx. and Deut. v. It rests upon the assumption that the last clause in ver. 28 records the fulfilment of the direction given ver. 27 to Moses to write the words which precede, and which are alleged to be just ten laws, and hence identical with the commandments written upon the tables.[1] Its falsity appears from ver. 1, which shows that Jehovah, and not Moses,[2] wrote upon the tables, and that He wrote not the words now spoken but those that were in the first tables, which Moses had broken. This is a plain allusion to the preceding narrative (Ex. xxxii. 19) of the sin of the golden calf and the consequent rupture of the covenant so lately formed between Jehovah and Israel, which is further implied in the second pair of tables (xxxiv. 4), in the divine mercy and forgiveness emphasized in vers. 6, 7, in Moses' supplication (ver.

---

of Jahveh, prescribed to the Israelitish tribes *such a law* as is contained in the Ten Words." "Religion of Israel," vol. i. p. 285.

[1] In identifying the words which Moses is here directed to write with the Ten Commandments ("The Old Testament in the Jewish Church," p. 331) Dr. Robertson Smith appears to give his sanction to the extraordinary hypothesis now under consideration. But he does not openly avow it. See above, p. 52.

[2] The change of subject in ver. 28 cannot occasion the slightest embarrassment. It is of constant occurrence in Hebrew construction, where it would be readily understood by the reader or hearer. Comp. Gen. xxiv. 32; II. Sam. xi. 13.

9), and in Jehovah's engaging to make the desired covenant (ver. 10). The words vers. 11–26, according to the tenor of which God proposes to make this covenant, and which Moses is told to write, are taken substantially and in part *verbatim* from "the words of the LORD" which Moses wrote at the original ratification of the covenant (xxiii. 12 ff.). The selection is made with definite reference to the great crime just committed. As they had offended in the matter of worship, the injunction is repeated of the service to be paid to Jehovah and to Him exclusively. They had forfeited all claim upon His promise to expel the the Canaanites; accordingly this is repeated likewise. While Moses was to rewrite this portion of the original engagement, which had been particularly infringed, thus impliedly giving fresh sanction to the whole as the representative of the people on whose behalf he had been interceding, the LORD once more engraved in stone the same Ten Words which he had uttered from Sinai in the audience of the people, thus re-enacting on His part His imperishable covenant.[1]

---

[1] While the entire narrative in Ex. xix.–xxxiv. is continuous and consistent and intimately related in all its parts, Wellhausen ("Jahrbücher für Deutsche Theologie," pp. 564 ff.) discovers in it three entirely distinct and divergent accounts of the Sinaitic legislation. He assigns to the first, or Elohistic account, xix. 3–19, xx. 1–20, xxiv. 12–14, xxxi. 18, xxxii., xxxiii. 1–11; Num. x. 33. According to this writer the covenant was ratified and the people pledged obedience before the Law was given (Ex. xix. 3–8). In majestic grandeur God proclaims the Ten Commandments, which completes the Sinaitic legislation proper. The terrified people ask that Moses may speak to them instead of God. Moses is accordingly summoned into the mountain to receive the Decalogue written by God on tables of stone, and to spend

And while the critics, who claim that a variant version of the Decalogue is to be found in Ex. xxxiv, forty days in intimate converse with God. This is not that He may give him specific commands to report to the people as in xxi.–xxiii., of which this writer knows nothing, but that Moses may be so filled with divine wisdom as to be fitted to be God's oracle to the people ever after. Then follows the affair of the golden calf, whereupon Moses breaks the tables of the law, and the LORD refuses to suffer the transgressing people to remain longer near His sacred seat on Sinai. They had previously had no other idea than that they should remain there forever (the last clause of xxxiii. 1 and the first clause of ver. 3 are reckoned interpolations). The people are distressed by the unwelcome intelligence that they must leave the holy mountain. The LORD is, however, so far mollified by the people's penitence that He gives them for their guidance the Tabernacle, and, though it is not in the present text, the Ark likewise, containing the broken tables of the law. The people then begin their march from Sinai.

To the Jehovistic account he assigns xix. 20–25, xx. 21, 24–26, xxi.–xxiii., xxiv. 3–8, xxxiii. 1. In this God speaks nothing directly, but Moses goes alone to the mountain and receives from God His words and judgments, which he records, and the covenant is solemnly ratified. This completes the purpose for which they had come to Sinai; and without any extraordinary event requiring it they leave for Canaan.

The third account, which differs materially from both the preceding, is found in Ex. xxxiv. The first verse of this chapter is corrected by omitting all after the words "tables of stone." This, as well as the words "like unto the first" (ver. 4), has been inserted for the sake of linking this narrative with the preceding. Such manifest allusions to previous portions of the record used to be regarded as proofs of continuity in the history, if not of identity of authorship. But the critics have changed all that. They are now unhesitatingly traced to some editor intent upon "harmonizing" discrepant or independent narratives, and are summarily ejected from the text. In vers. 6–9 the reference to the transgression of the people "betrays the hand of the harmonist," again a conclusive argument of interpolation, which is here fortified by the carping criticisms that "the LORD passed by" (ver. 6) is inconsistent with "the LORD stood" (ver. 5), that ver. 10 is not an exact response to the petition in ver. 9, and that these verses mistake the meaning of ver. 5, where it is really Moses

are unanimous in affirming that this chapter contains just ten commandments, they are not altogether who proclaimed the name of the LORD. This allegation, for the sake of creating a fresh inconsistency wherever that is possible, is an effectual estoppel against all objection to assuming a like change of subject in ver. 28, where consistency requires it. Verses 10-13 are traced in great part to the same interpolaters, vers. 12, 13 being particularly obnoxious as squinting towards the unity of the sanctuary in the sense of the book of Deuteronomy. The Decalogue (vers. 14-26) "in its present expanded form only shows obscurely the decenary number, which once certainly was plainly to be recognized." Then the account of the ratification of the covenant by Moses as the representative of Israel, which the chapter must once have contained, has been omitted, as well as the conclusion following ver. 28, "for vers. 29-35 are not the continuation of what precedes."

With the chapter thus purged of all objectionable matter, and of all that he is pleased to consider spurious, Wellhausen has no difficulty in making of it a distinct tradition of the original promulgation of the Law, with its "two tables, Ten Words, and forty days. Only the tables are written not by God but by Moses, and . . . they contain what Jehovah spake to Moses, not to the people." There is also this marked contrast between Ex. xx. and Ex. xxxiv.: "in the former the commandments are almost all moral; in the latter they are exclusively ritual."

All this is wonderfully ingenious; and as a piece of literary jugglery it shows amazing dexterity and is vastly entertaining. But if seriously proposed as sober exposition and "historical investigation" it is to the last degree preposterous and absurd. It simply shows what ingenuity of a high order can effect by skilfully piecing together disjointed paragraphs, and how the entire sense of a chapter can be transformed by throwing out or putting in clauses and paragraphs at the will of the critic.

We do not object to the critics pursuing their investigations into the question of the Jehovist and the Elohist, and all the rest to any extent they please, if they will but use their common sense in the process. We consider the problem, in its perplexity and hopelessness, very much like that of squaring the circle. And while it is a matter of literary interest, we believe it to be void of all significance in determining either the age or interpretation of the Pentateuch. Nevertheless, we shall be thankful for all the facts that can be developed

agreed where the first of the commandments begins nor how the division is to be made.[1] From the diver-
respecting peculiarities of style, seeming repetitions, and the like. And if it can be shown that more than one writer had a hand in the production of the Pentateuch, very well. We are prepared to accept any conclusion upon this point that is strictly deducible from the facts, fully and fairly brought out and candidly considered.

But the operation in which the critics are engaged is a very difficult and delicate one, in which not only ripe scholarship but a sound judgment, clear head, and freedom from bias and pet theories are very essential; in which the chances of error are very great and multiply with every forward step, while each new complexity in the theory burdens instead of strengthening it; in which the evidence relied upon is largely recondite, commonly ambiguous, often conflicting, and frequently factitious. Certainly the case does not warrant the positive tone so frequently assumed, as though the critics were omniscient or infallible; nor does it justify the reckless manner in which a favorite theory is often driven through in the face of adverse facts and at all hazards, — the accredited text and obvious interpretation and established history and revealed truth, all made to give way before it, as though the critic's theory alone were certain, and everything must be squared to correspond with it.

[1] The schemes severally proposed by Hitzig ("Ostern und Pfingsten," 1838, p. 42), Bertheau ("Die sieben Gruppen Mosaischer Gesetze," p. 92), Ewald ("Geschichte des Israel," 2d edit. vol. ii. p. 217), Kayser ("Vorexilische Buch," p. 58), and Wellhausen ("Die Composition des Hexateuchs," p. 554, in "Jahrbücher für Deutsche Theologie" for 1876) are as follows, viz.: —

	Hitzig. vers.	Bertheau. vers.	Ewald. vers.	Kayser. vers.	Wellhausen. vers.
1	12–16	18	12–16	11–16	14–16
2	17	19, 20	17	17	17
3	18	21	18	18	18
4	19, 20	22 a	19, 20 a	19, 20	19, 20
5	21	22 b	20 b	21	21
6	22	23, 24	21	22	23, 24
7	23, 24	25 a	22	23, 24	25 a
8	25	25 b	23, 24	25	25 b
9	26 a	26 a	25	26 a	26 a
10	26 b	26 b	26	26 b	26 b

sity which exists among them it is plain that they could equally well have made out any other number that was desired, from seven to thirteen. And if it could be certainly established that there are just ten laws, it would not follow that, in the intent of the writer, they formed the original Decalogue. It has at least been quite plausibly maintained that the decenary structure prevails in several series of Mosaic laws, which are thus framed in imitation of the fundamental law of the system.

The commandments written upon tables of stone and preserved in the Ark are consequently not recorded in Ex. xxxiv. but, as has been universally believed from the beginning, in Ex. xx. and Deut. v. These two are manifestly copies of one and the same Decalogue, the textual discrepancies being purely verbal and without the slightest effect upon the sense except in the reason annexed to the fourth commandment. Exodus no doubt preserves the exact official transcript, and Deuteronomy its substantial repetition and enforcement by Moses in his address to the people. It is of no consequence, however, so far as our present argument is concerned, which of these is held to be the primitive form, or whether the attempt is made to elicit a text superior to either by the comparison of both.

Wellhausen throws out ver. 22 altogether, and corrects ver. 25*b* into accordance with xxiii. 18. Bertheau adheres to the common opinion in regard to the Decalogue, but maintains the decenary division of these laws, and generally of the Mosaic statutes in the three middle books of the Pentateuch. Ewald finds five successive decalogues in Leviticus vii. and vi.; (Authorized Version vi. 8–vii. 33).

Wellhausen's second objection to the authenticity of the Decalogue is (we quote again from the article "Israel"):—

"(2.) The prohibition of images was during the older period quite unknown; Moses himself is said to have made a brazen serpent which down to Hezekiah's time continued to be worshipped at Jerusalem as an image of Jehovah."

The second commandment occasions endless perplexity to this most recent school of critics. How ineffectually Kuenen struggles to rid himself of it appears from the following passage in his "Religion of Israel" (vol. i. p. 287).

"Moses' attitude towards the worship of images is a very disputed point. The second of the Ten Words forbids it without reserve, but is strongly suspected to have been remoulded and enlarged. Its great length of itself alone gives rise to this presumption. If it embraced nothing more than the words 'Thou shalt have none other gods before My face,'[1] we should not think of calling it incomplete; the rest is superfluous and is therefore suspected. Besides this, it has been remarked that the words 'thou shalt not make unto

---

[1] Kuenen reckons the preface to the ten commandments as the first of the Ten Words. The first and second commandments he throws together as the Second Word, which he would then condense by abolishing the second commandment entirely, or at least cutting out that portion of it which is distinctive and refers to the worship of images. And this arbitrary suppression of one of the fundamental requirements of the Decalogue is all the ground for doubt that he can extract from the Ten Words themselves. Dr. Oort, who is heartily in sympathy with Kuenen and his school, lops all that he possibly can from the commandments, reducing the second to the bald injunction, "make no image of a God" ("The Bible for Learners," p. 18). But even then the prohibition of image-worship remains.

thee any graven image, or any likeness of anything that is in heaven above or on the earth beneath or in the waters under the earth' — sever the connection between the preceding and the following sentences, and that after these words have been removed, nothing remains but the prohibition to serve other gods. Thus the Ten Words themselves alone give abundant ground for throwing doubt upon the Mosaic origin of the warning against images. But history also seems distinctly to bear witness against it. The worship of Jahveh under the form of a bull was very general in Israel in later times; and in the kingdom of Ephraim, during the two and a half centuries of its existence, it was the religion of the state. Is it likely then that Moses expressly declared himself opposed to it? According to a narrative in the book of Judges, a grandson of Moses, Jonathan ben Gershom, served as a priest at Dan in a temple in which a graven image of Jahveh was placed: would the commandment of the law-giver have been broken in this way by the members of his own family? Again, the author of the books of Kings informs us that Hezekiah 'broke in pieces the brazen serpent which Moses had made, for unto those days the Israelites had burned incense in honor of that serpent, and it was called *Nehushtan*' (i. e. brass-god); surely this implies that Moses was not so averse to images as the Peutateuch represents him to have been."

Dr. Kuenen might have pushed his argument much further. Professedly Christian states grant divorces for very insufficient reasons: is it likely that this can be prohibited in the New Testament? The Roman Catholic Church forbids its priests to marry, and commands its adherents to abstain from meats on Fridays and other special seasons: would it do this, if I. Tim.

iv. 3 were in its canon of faith? The Lord Jesus Christ instituted the eucharist, the bread of which is held up to adoration in every celebration of the mass: would even Dr. Kuenen dare to hold Him responsible for this perversion? And yet this is all that he has to say against the Mosaic origin of the second conmandment; and this is taken back by himself in the very next paragraph. He owns that the story of the brazen serpent, as every rational man must see at a glance, "signifies very little." "If it proves anything it proves only this, that the people knew nothing of a Mosaic prohibition so absolute as that which appears in the Decalogue." Will he say the same of the more modern worshippers of saintly relics? He adds: "The same applies to the other two facts to which we referred above. . . . The *existence* of the bull-worship is no sufficient argument against the supposition that Moses forbade any image of Jahveh. But the fact that this form of Jahveh-worship *continued to exist undisturbed* is very difficult to reconcile with that supposition." It "continued to exist undisturbed," only as other crimes which are perpetrated in the face of the known statute. It was not sanctioned or approved by the Prophets or other good men. It was openly denounced and censured, and the people punished for it by being given into the power of their enemies. Dr. Kuenen proceeds:

"There is one fact of which we may not lose sight in this investigation. From the Mosaic times downward there always existed in Israel a worship of Jahveh without an image. Scarcely any tradition of Hebrew antiquity is better guaranteed than that which derives the *Ark of Jahveh* from the Law-giver himself. . . . If Moses believed this (viz. that the Ark was the abode of Jahveh) and accordingly offered the common sacrifices before the Ark, then he himself certainly did not erect an image of Jahveh, much less ordained the use of one."

His conclusion is that while Moses opposed the use of Jahveh-images indirectly, the prohibition of them " was not decreed by him but at a much later period, although it was done in conformity with his spirit; " a conclusion which must be accepted, if at all, upon his sole *ipse-dixit*.

Dr. Dillmann[1] gives the following compact statement of the case.

" It cannot with good reason be maintained that such a prohibition, involving the idea of the impossibility of making any representation of God, as well as His invisibility and spirituality, is too advanced for Moses' time and his stage of knowledge, and therefore cannot have been given by him, but must have been first introduced into the Decalogue at a much later date. Apart from Ex. xxxii., where the narrative attributes to Moses a clear perception of the unlawfulness of an image of Jehovah, it is certain in the first place that in the traditions of their fathers a cultus without images is ascribed to the Patriarchs; and secondly, that in the post-Mosaic period it was a recognized principle, at least at the central Sanctuary of the entire people and at the Temple of Solomon, that no representation was to be made of Jehovah.[2]

---

[1] " Die Bücher Exodus und Leviticus," pp. 208, 209.

[2] As a specimen of the fairness of Wellhausen's statements, compare his remark, article " Israel," p. 406 : " Images of the Deity were exhibited in all three places [Jerusalem, Bethel, and Dan], and indeed in every place where a house of God was found."

The worship of an image of Jehovah at Sinai (Ex. xxxii.), in the time of the Judges, and in the kingdom of the Ten Tribes, does not prove that the prohibition of images was unknown, bnt only that it was very difficult to secure its proper recognition by the mass of the people, especially of the Northern Tribes, who were more Canaanitishly disposed. Or rather, it was for centuries an object of contention between the stricter and the more lax party, — the latter holding that it forbade only the images of false gods, the former that it likewise forbade any image of Jehovah. Prophets such as Amos and Hosea, who contended against the images of the calves at Bethel and at Dan, never announce the principle that no representation can be made of Jehovah as anything new, but simply presuppose it as known. However far we go back in the post-Mosaic history, we find it already existing, at least as practically carried into effect at the central Sanctuary; from whom then can it have proceeded but from the legislator, Moses himself?"

Dr. Robertson Smith does not explicitly deny the antiquity of the Decalogue, nor the right of the second commandment to a place in it, but he more than once expresses himself in a manner that appears to lead in that direction.

"The principle of the second commandment, that Jehovah is not to be worshipped by images, which is often appealed to as containing the most characteristic peculiarity of Mosaism, cannot, in the light of history, be viewed as having had so fundamental a place in the religion of early Israel" (p. 63). "If the prophecy of Hosea stood alone it would be reasonable to think that this attack on the images of the popular religion was simply based on the second commandment. But when we contrast it with the absolute silence of earlier Prophets we can hardly accept this explanation as adequate" (p. 176). "Hosea does not condemn the worship of the calves because idols are forbidden by the Law; he excludes the calves from the sphere of true religion because the worship which they receive has no affinity to the true attitude of Israel to Jehovah" (p. 177).

How he can say that "Amos never speaks of the golden calves as the sin of the Northern sanctuaries" (p. 140) is unaccountable, since this Prophet expressly groups together as objects of the divine judgment, "they that swear by the sin of Samaria, and say, Thy god, O Dan, liveth, and, The manner of Beersheba liveth" (Am. viii. 14). The god of Dan can be nothing but the Golden Calf; and the sin of Samaria is the same thing, for they that swear by it say "By the life of thy god, O Dan." It is called the sin of Samaria as the object of idolatrous worship to both the capital and the kingdom; in like manner Hosea calls it the Calf of Samaria (Hos. viii. 5, 6; comp. also Deut. ix. 21). The Doctor, in disregard of the connection, thinks that Amos alludes rather to the Ashera in Samaria (II. Kings xiii. 6). But why, upon his principles, Amos should inveigh against this, even if it were still there in his time, is not so clear; for we are told[1] that this is one of "the old marks of a sanctuary . . . which had been used by the Patriarchs and continued to exist in sanctuaries of Jehovah down to the eighth century," and the prohibition of which in Deuteronomy "is one of the clearest proofs" that this book is posterior to Hosea,

[1] "The Old Testament in the Jewish Church," p. 353.

Isaiah, and Micah. The terms, in which Amos, with distinct allusion to the second commandment (Ex. xx. 4), expresses his contempt and abhorrence of the objects of Israel's idolatrous worship, "which ye made to yourselves" (v. 26), equally cover the golden calves, and include them in the same category of man-made divinities. (Comp. Hos. viii. 6.) He also very plainly declares that Jehovah was not to be found at Bethel (v. 5), which cannot be interpreted differently from the precisely similar language of Hosea iv. 15; that to worship at Bethel was to transgress (Am. iv. 4); that its altars were specially obnoxious to the divine judgment (iii. 14), while Zion and Jerusalem was Jehovah's earthly abode (i. 2). When these passages are viewed in connection with those first cited, it is plain that the idolatry of the calves is prominent in his thoughts in these denunciations.

Elisha's attitude to the golden calves is shown by the message which he sent to Jehu (II. Kings ix. 9), in which he repeated the very words of Elijah (I. Kings xxi. 22; see above, p. 271). When Jehoram, who had "put away the image of Baal that his father Ahab had made" and adhered simply to the worship of the calves (II. Kings iii. 2, 3), sought the aid of Elisha in perilous circumstances, the Prophet's response was: "What have I to do with thee? Get thee to the Prophets of thy father, and to the Prophets of thy mother... As the LORD of hosts liveth, before whom I stand, were it not that I regard the presence of Jehoshaphat king of Judah, I would not look toward thee nor see thee"[1] (vers. 13, 14). It is also a significant fact that it was children of Bethel that mocked Elisha, and upon whom he pronounced his fatal curse (ii. 23, 24). In that seat of image-worship the children had caught the bitter feelings of their elders towards the aged Prophet of the LORD. It is further a suggestive circumstance that it is precisely in the kingdom of the Ten Tribes that the Prophets assume such unwonted prominence, and that such full and striking narratives are given of their labors as these of Elijah, Elisha, and the Sons of the Prophets under their superintendence. Whether the record is accepted as true, or dismissed as legendary, it nevertheless shows, in contrast with the dearth of like stories in Judah, that either in the plan of God or in the general sense of the people there was a peculiarity in the state of affairs in Ephraim which did not exist in Judah, and which demanded a measure of Prophetic interference and activity in the one, that was not requisite in the other.

The way in which the worship of the calves was regarded by other and earlier Prophets has been shown already (see above, p. 265); so that all objection to the prior existence of the second commandment on that score is fully set aside.

Wellhausen's third objection to the authenticity of the Decalogue is: —

---

[1] And this though the king, both in his exclamation (ver. 10) and in his appeal to the Prophet (ver. 13), confessed his belief in the supreme government of Jehovah. "The LORD hath called these three kings together, to deliver them into the hand of Moab."

"(3) The essentially and necessarily national character of the older phases of the religion of Jehovah completely disappears in the quite universal code of morals which is given in the Decalogue as the fundamental law of Israel; but the entire series of religious personalities throughout the period of the Judges and the Kings — from Deborah, who praised Jael's treacherous act of murder, to David, who caused his prisoners of war to be sawn asunder and burnt — make it very difficult to believe that the religion of Israel was from the outset one of a specifically moral character. The true spirit of the old religion may be gathered much more truly from Judg. v. than from Ex. xx."

Dr. Robertson Smith has relieved us from the necessity of replying to this objection. In opposition to both Wellhausen and Duhm he affirms in the most positive manner that the religion of Israel was moral from the beginning, and that its specific character was determined by the exalted nature of Jehovah himself; by which he means the living, acting personality of the Most High, and not barely the conceptions formed of Him by His worshippers.

"The real difference between the religion of Jehovah and the religion of the nations . . . lies in the personal character of Jehovah, and in the relations, corresponding to His character, which He seeks to maintain with His people. Properly speaking, the heathen deities have no personal character . . . in the sense of a fixed and independent habit of will. The attributes ascribed to them were a mere reflex of the attributes of their worshippers. . . . The god always remained on the same ethical level with his people. . . . Not so Jehovah. . . . He had a will and purpose of His own, — a purpose rising above the current ideas of His worshippers, and a will directed with steady consistency to a moral aim. . . . All His dealings with Israel were directed to lead the people on to higher things than their natural character inclined towards. To know Jehovah and to serve Him aright involved a moral effort " (pp. 66, 67). "When we speak of Jehovah as displaying a consistent character in His sovereignty over Israel, we necessarily imply that Israel's religion is a moral religion, that Jehovah is a God of righteousness, whose dealings with His people follow an ethical standard " (p. 71).

And the difficulty which Wellhausen deduces from the low moral standard and conduct of certain Old Testament worthies is dealt with in the following manner: —

" The fundamental superiority of the Hebrew religion does not lie in the particular system of social morality that it enforces, but in the more absolute and self-consistent righteousness of the Divine Judge. . . . There are many things in the social order of the Hebrews, such as polygamy, blood-revenge, slavery, the treatment of enemies, which do not correspond with the highest ideal morality, but belong to an imperfect social state, or, as the gospel puts it, were tolerated for the hardness of the people's hearts. But, with all this, the religion of Jehovah put morality on a far sounder basis than any other religion did, because in it the righteousness of Jehovah as a God enforcing the known laws of morality was conceived as absolute, and as showing itself absolute, not in a future state, but upon earth. . . . There was no ground to ascribe to Him less than absolute sovereignty and absolute righteousness. If the masses lost sight of those great qualities, and assimilated His nature to that of the Canaanite deities, the Prophets were justified in reminding them that Jehovah was

Israel's God before they knew the Baalim, and that He had then showed Himself a God far different from these " (pp. 73, 74).

Wellhausen's fourth and last objection is:—

" (4.) It is extremely doubtful whether the actual monotheism which is undoubtedly presupposed in the universal moral precepts of the Decalogue could have formed the foundation of a national religion. It was first developed out of the national religion at the downfall of the nation, and thereupon kept its hold upon the people in an artificial manner by means of the idea of a covenant formed by the God of the universe with, in the first instance, Israel alone."

No further reply seems necessary to an allegation so purely subjective, than that Professor Wellhausen's opinion is no law to other persons.

If, then, anything whatever is certainly known of the Mosaic age, it is indubitably established that the Mosaic Ark contained tables of stone on which were engraved the Ten Commandments. These were treasured in the most sacred apartment of the Sanctuary. They formed the basis of the covenant between Jehovah and Israel. They were the fundamental law of the commonwealth of Israel, by which all further enactments were regulated, and to which they were supplementary. They were believed to have emanated directly and even verbally from Jehovah Himself, and to have been by Him recorded in stone to indicate their perpetual, binding force. This sacred Ark, with its precious contents, was safely guarded until the time of Solomon, when it was transferred to the Temple (I. Kings viii. 6–9, 21 ; II. Chron. v. 7–10, vi. 11,

41). It is still spoken of in the time of Jeremiah (iii. 16), and the covenant on stone, which it contained, was only to be superseded by the law written on the heart (xxxi. 32, 33; see also II. Chron. xxxv. 3). Under these circumstances it is impossible that these commandments should not have been carefully and accurately preserved and transmitted. The positive statements in the Pentateuch itself that Moses wrote certain laws, Dr. Robertson Smith[1] seeks to limit to the Decalogue, but in so doing acknowledges that there is definite and explicit testimony that he did at least write it. Two copies of these commandments exist, attached to different codes of laws, and, with unimportant variations, are identical throughout. If monumental and historical evidence is of any worth, these are the very commandments delivered to Moses. And this conclusion is not to be set aside by conjectures of the critics, which have not even the pretence of any evidence to support them.[2]

These things being so, some important consequences follow. The sacredness of Horeb to Elijah sprang from the giving of the Ten Commandments on its

[1] "The Old Testament in the Jewish Church," p. 331.
[2] Such assertions as these of Wellhausen cannot be dignified by the name of proofs, unless his word is to be taken in lieu of evidence: "Some passages of the Decalogue have a Deuteronomic tinge, e. g., 'thy stranger that is within thy gates' (Ex. xx. 10), 'out of the house of bondage' (ver. 2), and the whole of ver. 6." How does he know but that, on the other hand, Deuteronomy received its tinge from the Decalogue? "The reason for the law of the Sabbath in ver. 11 first came from the last *redacteur* of the Pentateuch." "Jahrbücher für Deutsche Theologie," xxi. p. 558.

summit; and his recognition of the God of Horeb is in diametrical opposition to the worship of the calves.

But there are also two other deductions which have a much wider reach. First, Moses had a far more exalted conception of Jehovah than is allowed to him in these Lectures. The God of the Ten Commandments is a being of whom no image or representation can be made; the Creator of heaven and earth and sea, and all that in them is; the exclusive object of Israel's worship; a God of truth, punishing iniquity, and who lays His demands upon the affections and not merely upon the outward conduct, expecting the love of His worshippers, and forbidding them to covet the possessions of others. The religion of Israel began on this high plane, so far as divine revelation and requirements are concerned. And the Prophets, instead of evolving a spiritual religion from mere political ethics, or something lower still, simply recalled the people to this ancient standard, and enforced upon their contemporaries what had already been taught by Moses.

Secondly, the Decalogue affords palpable instances of laws well known, and of the highest authority, which were flagrantly disregarded. Every apostasy to Baal and Ashtoreth in the period of the Judges was in open violation of the first commandment. It was, as Dr. Robertson Smith concedes, a falling away to the service of the gods of their enemies, which endangered the very existence of the religion of Jehovah. It was a departure from the fundamental Law of Israel, even on the low ground assumed by the critics themselves that Jehovah was but a national deity like Chemosh or Milcom. And if Ahab could persuade himself that worshipping the God of a friendly state was no violation of this commandment, this is but a fresh illustration of the point in question. The second commandment was broken by Aaron at the very foot of Sinai, by the idolater Micah and the renegade Danites, and by the Ten Tribes which followed Jeroboam in the worship of the calves. If there could be these notorious violations of covenant laws, cut in stone and deposited in the Ark, what becomes of the argument that the non-existence of a statute may be inferred from the persistent disregard of it?

These two principles, thus established, completely overturn this recent critical hypothesis from its foundations, and demolish its reconstructed history of Israel's religion. The Ark of the Covenant is an invincible argument of its utter falsity.

Dr. Robertson Smith undertakes (p. 109) to divide the histories of the Old Testament into distinct groups and to assign to each a separate legal standard according to the period in which it was written.

"The latest history in the books of Chronicles presupposes the whole Pentateuch; the main thread of the books of Kings accepts the standard of the book of Deuteronomy, but knows nothing of the Levitical legislation; and older narratives now incorporated in the Kings—as, for example, the histories of Elijah and Elisha, which every one can see to be ancient and distinct documents—know nothing of the Deuteronomic law of the one altar, and, like Elijah himself, are indifferent even to the worship of the golden calves. These older narratives, with the greater part of the books of Samuel and Judges, accept as fitting and normal a stamp of worship closely modelled on the religion of the Patriarchs as it is depicted in Genesis, or based on the ancient law of Ex. xx. 24, where Jehovah promises to meet with His people and bless them at the altars of earth or unhewn stone which stand in all corners of the land, on every spot where Jehovah has set a memorial of His name."

The style of worship regarded as normal in Judges and Samuel has been sufficiently considered in preceding parts of this volume, and their distinct recognition of the law of one altar has been pointed out (pp. 87 ff., pp. 137 ff.). We have also seen that the histories of Elijah and Elisha are not indifferent to the worship of the golden calves; and they would not have been modelled on the religion of the Patriarchs if they were. In the entire lives of these two Prophets there is but one recorded act of sacrifice, the miraculous test of Jehovah's godhead at Carmel. If a sweeping conclusion is to be drawn from this single fact, it would certainly be as natural to infer that they chose to abstain from sacrifice on ordinary occasions, inasmuch as they were debarred from the central Sanctuary, as that they actually did sacrifice in various parts of the land, though this is nowhere intimated in the narrative.

It is plainly, however, a venturesome affirmation, that Deuteronomy was unknown, or even the Levitical Law, when these narratives were framed. Elijah's first word to the idolatrous king, "There shall be no rain" (I. Kings xvii. 1), is in precise conformity with the threatening, Deut. xi. 16, 17. The material for sacrifice and its manipulation (xviii. 23, 33), accords with the requirements of the Law, even to the use of its technical terms (Lev. i. 6–8, ix. 16); its time was fixed by that of the daily meat-offering (xviii. 29, 36), which was presented both evening and morning (II. Kings iii. 20), agreeably to Ex. xxix. 38–41; its consumption by fire from the LORD (xviii. 24, 38) has its counterpart in Lev. ix. 24. Indeed, almost all the miracles in these narratives bear a striking resemblance to those of the Pentateuch; e. g. the supernatural supply of food (xvii. 6, xix. 6; comp. Ex. xvi. 12) and of water (II. Kings iii. 17; comp. Num. xx. 8); necessary things made to last for an indefinite period (I. Kings xvii. 14; comp. Deut. xxix. 5); fire to consume the Prophet's adversaries (II. Kings i. 10, 12; comp. Num. xi. 1, xvi. 35); the LORD'S "taking" him to heaven (ii. 3 ff.; comp. Gen. v. 24); dividing the Jordan (ii. 8, 14; comp. Ex. xiv. 21; Josh. iv. 23); healing the waters (ii. 21; comp. Ex. xv; 25); the promise of a son to the Shunemite (iv. 16; comp. Gen. xviii. 10); the infliction of leprosy on Gehazi (v. 27; comp. Num. xii. 10 [1]); the healing of Naaman (v. 10; comp. Num. xii. 13; Lev. xiv. 7, 8); guarded by angels (vi. 17; comp. Gen. xxxii. 1, 2); smiting with blindness (vi. 18; comp. Gen. xix. 11). Even if it should be charged

---

[1] "Leprous as snow" occurs only in these passages and in Ex. iv. 6. And in some other instances here adduced the identity of characteristic expressions adds force to the similarity of the incidents.

that these are legends and not real occurrences, such stories could only have originated among a people familiar with the narratives of the Pentateuch. The slaughter of the priests of Baal (I. Kings xviii. 40) was in obedience to Deut. xiii. 9, xvii. 5. Elijah's visit to Horeb implies all that made this mountain sacred at the time of the Exodus, and his fast of forty days and forty nights (xix. 8) has its parallel in Ex. xxxiv. 28. The law concerning one devoted to utter destruction (xx. 42) is found Lev. xxvii. 29. Naboth's refusal to part with his vineyard (xxi. 3) is based on Lev. xxv. 23; comp. Num. xxxvi. 8, 9. The forms of law were observed in the judicial murder of Naboth (xxi. 10). The accusation was based on Ex. xxii. 28, which Dr. Robertson Smith considers ancient; but the two witnesses are in conformity with Num. xxxv. 30, Deut. xvii. 6, 7, xix. 15; and the mode of inflicting the sentence with Deut. xiii. 10, xvii. 5. Micaiah (xxii. 17) adopts the language of Moses (Num. xxvii. 17), and ver. 28 declares his readiness to abide by the test given of a true prophet (Deut. xviii. 22). The double portion, which Elisha asks (II. Kings ii. 9), was the legal inheritance of a first-born son (Deut. xxi. 17). The infliction upon the children at Bethel (ver. 24) is in accordance with Lev. xxvi. 22. Persons were made servants for debt (iv. 1; comp. Lev. xxv. 39, 40). The Sabbath and new-moon were observed (iv. 23; see Lev. xxiii. 3; Num. xxviii. 11), and presentation was made of the first-fruits (iv. 42[1]; see Num. xviii. 12, 13;

---

[1] The word translated "full ears of corn" occurs nowhere else in this sense, outside of the Levitical Law (Lev. ii. 14, xxiii. 14).

Deut. xviii. 4, 5); but in the absence of a lawful sanctuary the " holy convocation " assembled about the Prophet, and his devout adherents brought the first-fruits to him as to one who for the time "ministered in the name of the LORD." II. Kings v. 7 borrows from Deut. xxxii. 39. The king, no doubt, recognized in the horrid transaction, vi. 28, 29, the fulfilment of Lev. xxvi. 29, Deut. xxviii. 53, and was the more exasperated against Elisha in consequence. "Make windows in heaven" (vii. 2, 19) alludes to Gen. vii. 11, and is equivalent to saying, " Send a deluge of bread." The law of leprosy was enforced even in a time of siege (vii. 3; comp. Lev. xiii. 46; Num. v. 2).

Now, it is not here affirmed that any one of these allusions, or all taken together, amount to an invincible demonstration of the existence of Deuteronomy and of the Levitical Law before the time of Elijah and Elisha, or that they admit of no other possible explanation; but it is safe to say that these allusions are as numerous and clear, as could reasonably be expected if Deuteronomy and Leviticus were then already known; that no prejudice can possibly arise against the common belief on this subject from any deficiency in such allusions; and that the presumption which they naturally create in its favor is not to be magisterially set aside, but only by the production of counter evidence of a decisive nature, and this does not exist.

The Doctor tells us further that " the main thread of the books of Kings ... knows nothing of the Levitical legislation." It has always been thought difficult to prove a negative; but the critics do it without the slightest trouble. Any witness who did not see the culprit commit the deed ought, in their judgment, to convince the jury of his innocence. It would certainly be very stupid in any one to adduce the absence of classical quotations from the volume before us in proof that the Doctor knows nothing of the classics. He abstained from such quotations simply because he found no occasion to make them in the course of his discussion. If the sacred historian had no reason for speaking of the distinctive requirements of the Levitical Law, the fact of his not mentioning them has no significance. His silence respecting them is no argument that he was not aware of their existence, or that he did not recognize their binding authority. No adverse conclusion can be drawn, unless something is positively said, which is incompatible with the existence of the Law or with the writer's knowledge of its existence.

But do the books of Kings, in fact, know nothing of the Levitical Law? The elaborate description of Solomon's Temple and its vessels (1. Kings vi., vii.), and the entry into it of the glory of the LORD (viii. 10, 11), presupposes the account of the Mosaic Tabernacle and its furniture (Ex. xxv. ff., xxxvi. ff.). The correspondence, not only in general plan but in a multitude of details, is so exact and pervading that one must of necessity have been derived from the other. The Temple is either an enlarged Tabernacle, built of more solid materials; or else the Tabernacle is reduced in size from the Temple, so as to be capable of being transported from place to place. The most radical critics do not shrink from the latter alternative. They do not hesitate to assert that the account in Exodus of the Mosaic Tabernacle is altogether fictitious; that it is a purely imaginary structure, to which no reality ever corresponded; that its measures and arrangements are mere deductions from the Temple of Solomon. But altogether apart from such a wholesale and unwarrantable challenge of the truthfulness of a narrative, which has every appearance of being historical, and has always been so regarded, no motive has ever been shown for such a fiction. It must surely have been a most dreary exercise of the imagination to figure out all the boards and curtains and coverings and loops and taches and pillars and sockets and bars and hooks and fillets and hangings, and to record them in long and wearisome detail, as though each minute particular was of the utmost consequence, when in point of fact the whole thing was utterly baseless; and the building, in regard to which so much pains was taken to invent and circulate a false account, had ceased to exist ages before, and was no longer of any present, practical interest. But if these details are real and genuine, and represent the actual Tabernacle of Moses, then this portion of the Levitical Law, at least, must have been in the possession not only of the author of Kings, but of the architect of Solomon's Temple.

Further, the altar in use before the Temple was built had horns (I. Kings i. 50, 51, ii. 28), and accordingly was conformed to the regulation, Ex. xxvii. 2. Solomon's Temple was completed in the eighth month of the year (I. Kings vi. 38); but in order to add impressiveness to its dedication, this was fixed at the time of the annual feast in the seventh month (viii. 2). Jeroboam changed the month in the Northern Kingdom, thus fixing the feast on the fifteenth day of the eighth month (I. Kings xii. 32, 33). The proper time for its celebration was therefore, according to the book of Kings, the fifteenth day of the seventh month, as it is defined Lev. xxiii. 34; Num. xxix. 12. Neither the month nor the day is named in Deuteronomy (see xvi. 13 ff.); and according to the critics this is one of the later innovations of the Levitical Law, the day of the observance having previously been free, and regulated by the season. We are also told that there is no indication of a priestly hierarchy in Deuteronomy, that all Levites could be priests and all stood upon a level. But II. Kings xii. 10, xxii. 4, 8, make mention of the high-priest; xxiii. 4, xxv. 18, of priests of the second order; and I. Kings viii. 4 of priests and Levites as distinct classes. We also read repeatedly of Abiathar the priest, Zadok the priest, Jehoiada the priest, Urijah the priest, Hilkiah the priest, who were successively at the head of the sacerdotal body. All this is manifestly governed by the Levitical Law. According to II. Kings xxiii. 9 the direction given in Deut. xviii. 6-8, as the Doctor interprets it,[1] was disobeyed, which is a fresh reason for questioning the accuracy of his interpretation. (See above p. 79.) But apart from this, unleavened bread is here spoken of as the provision of

[1] "The Old Testament in the Jewish Church," p. 362.

priests; of this Deuteronomy says nothing, but we find it stated over and over in Lev. ii. 10, 11, vi. 16–18, vii. 10, x. 12. In II. Kings xii. 16[1] the trespass and sin-offerings are spoken of, which are peculiar to the Levitical Law; so are the meat-offerings (1. Kings viii. 64), and the morning and evening daily sacrifice, and the sprinkling of sacrificial blood (II. Kings xvi. 13, 15). King Uzziah, when a leper, was dealt with (II. Kings xv. 5) according to the law, Lev. xiii. 46, which is alluded to but not given, Deut. xxiv. 8.

So far, therefore, from the books of Kings knowing nothing of the Levitical legislation, and accepting only the standard of the book of Deuteronomy, they follow the Law of Leviticus whenever they have occasion to mention anything which falls within the scope of that law. They show acquaintance with its sanctuary, its calendar, its priesthood, and its ritual. That critic must be hard to please who asks for anything more.

When, in the paragraph already quoted, the Doctor finds allusion in " the ancient law of Ex. xx.

---

[1] This passage speaks of "trespass-offering money and sin-offering money." The former admits of a ready explanation (Lev. v. 15–19; Num. v. 7, 8). What is meant by sin-offering money is more doubtful. It has been conjectured to be money given to the priest for the purchase of the victim, a portion of which became his perquisite in return for this service, or a gift voluntarily bestowed upon the officiating priest (Num. v. 10). But however this may be, the Doctor's idea, that it was a money-equivalent paid by the transgressor for his sin, is palpably false. This has no analogy in the whole Old Testament, is abhorrent to all Israelitish ideas, and is justly characterized by himself as "a gross case of simony" ("The Old Testament in the Jewish Church," p. 251).

24," to "the altars of earth or unhewn stone which stand in all corners of the land," he is plainly substituting his own interpretation of the law for the law itself. That surely would not be "closely modelled on the religion of the Patriarchs as it is depicted in in Genesis;" for the Patriarchal family was a unit and offered its worship at a single altar. Though in their wanderings altars were successively reared by them in various places, each was for the time their exclusive sanctuary. Nor does it correspond any better with the state of things in the time of Moses. The Ark of Jehovah then "led the march of Israel." The Doctor speaks of "the first beginnings of [Israel's] national organization centering in the Sanctuary of the Ark." "The Sanctuary of Jehovah" was "the final seat of judgment" (p. 36). And he strenuously insists upon the vast importance of the national sense of unity thus created in its contrast with "a multitude of local cults without national significance" (p. 40). If now this law was given to Moses at Sinai, as it claims to have been (Ex. xx. 22 ff.), and was written and acted upon by Moses himself (xxiv. 4), and specific injunctions were given by him in respect to it (Deut. xxvii. 5, 6) which were obeyed by his successor (Josh. viii. 30, 31,) and through all this period, by the Doctor's own admission, the host of Israel had but one central Sanctuary, the Sanctuary of the Ark, and if, furthermore, the consciousness of national unity thus produced was of vital consequence to Israel as a people, and as the people of Jehovah,— we surely have a right to assume that the law is to be interpreted in conformity with the circumstances in which it was enacted and with the practice of Moses himself under it.

If, further, the language of the statute be examined, there is nothing in it to require the assumption that a plurality of coexisting altars is intended. The terms are in the singular number throughout — an altar of earth, an altar of stone, mine altar, place[1] (not " places " as in the Authorized Version)

[1] Dr. Robertson Smith (p. 393) takes exception to the note (see above, p. 74) in which this circumstance has been before remarked upon. The collective use of the noun in such a construction is not denied. But attention is called to the significant circumstance that where the conception is that of a coexisting plurality, " all the places " is expressed in Hebrew by the plural noun (e. g. Deut. xii. 2; I. Sam. vii. 16, xxx. 31; Ezra i. 4; Jer. viii. 3, xxiv. 9, xxix. 14, xl. 12, xlv. 5; Ezek. xxxiv. 12); while in the other two passages, in which this phrase is used with a singular noun, the reference is not to places viewed jointly, but regarded successively (Gen. xx. 13; Deut. xi. 24). The words are used in a different sense, Gen. xviii. 26. And as to the objection that Ex. xxii. 30 could have no application to the desert, because ver. 29, with which it is associated, could only come into operation in Canaan, the fourth commandment was certainly operative in the Wilderness, though "the stranger that is within thy gates " looks forward to the occupancy of cities. The legislator from the first contemplated the settlement of the people in Canaan, but he did not for that reason leave them without law in journeying through the desert. Ex. xxi. 14 undoubtedly speaks of God's altar (in the singular number again) as an asylum, while even this must not be suffered to screen wilful murderers; but ver. 13, " I will appoint thee a place whither he shall flee," just as plainly anticipates the subsequent appointment of cities of refuge. (See above, p. 76, note.) The use of the altar for this purpose is here recognized as familiarly known; only it is limited to the unintentional manslayer, and the appointment of an additional place of like intent is promised. This promise is fulfilled Num. xxxv. 10 ff.; Deut. xix. 1 ff., and the privilege of the altar is not withdrawn. Where is the discrepancy?

— and are quite consistent with the view that but one altar at a time was meant at each successive place of encampment, or wherever God might subsequently appoint. If a multiplicity of altars, as opposed to one common sanctuary for all Israel, is denoted by this law, this cannot be inferred from the language used. It can only be established by proving that in actual fact Jehovah recorded His name at different places simultaneously. To what extent this was done by special theophanies, or separate altars were allowed in abnormal periods, has been sufficiently discussed already. (See above pp. 94 ff., pp. 137 ff.) The whole matter was governed by fixed principles and rigidly confined within plainly marked limits. Unlimited discretion was never accorded to men to build altars and establish sanctuaries at their own pleasure or convenience. And, apart from supernatural manifestations or extraordinary emergencies, there was from Moses to Malachi but one divinely sanctioned and permanent sanctuary, the Sanctuary of the Ark, and but one legitimate altar of sacrifice, the altar in its court.

But, we are told (p. 393), "the climax of absurdity is reached" when this law of an altar of earth or of whole stones is regarded as comprehending the brazen altar of the Tabernacle and the Temple. It is not easy to see wherein the absurdity lies. The construction of the altar remains unchanged. It is simply encased in a frame overlaid with brass, to mark it as belonging to the Tabernacle Court, of which brass was the dominant and characteristic metal; and likewise to suggest that the altar, renewed at each station on their march, was still substantially the same altar, for it had the same external covering, and stood in the same sacred surroundings. That neither priests nor worshippers saw any "absurdity" in this appears from the fact that the altar continued to be built of "whole stones according to the law" in each successive temple, and as long as the Temple stood (I. Macc. iv. 47; Josephus, Against Apion, i. 22; comp. also his Jewish War, v. 5, 6).

The Doctor, however (pp. 110–112), thinks himself absolved in his discussion of the work of the Prophets, from any "detailed inquiry as to how much of the Pentateuchal Law was already known." The Pentateuch, even if extant, "was practically a buried book." The question of its Mosaic authorship is accordingly of no significance in the history and religion of Israel, and may be left on one side while attention is directed to things that "had practical place and recognition in Israel."

"We have not found occasion to speak of Moses as the author of a written code, and to inquire how much his code contained, because the history itself makes it plain that his central importance for early Israel did not lie in his writings, but in his practical office as a judge who stood for the people before God, and brought their hard cases before Him at the Sanctuary" (Ex. xviii. 19, xxxiii. 9 *seq.*).

Can, then, the bare fact that Moses exercised the office of judge, and was the medium of divine communications to the people, be so important, and yet the judgments which he actually rendered, and the messages which he delivered to the people as from God, be of no account? Can the tribunal at the Sanctuary have been so weighty an affair, and the regulations which governed its decisions not worth considering? In order to estimate the value of that tribunal, and its influence in shaping the current life of Israel, precisely what we most need to know is what was the system of justice therein represented, what sort of cases came before it, and upon what principles they were settled. This will give an insight into the usages and ideas of the people and the management of their affairs that can be gained in no other way. The civil code introduced by Moses, and the ordinances of worship appointed by him, furnish the needed starting-point in the study of the institutions and life of Israel. There is just the same authority for referring these to Moses as there is for believing that he acted as judge and leader of Israel in their coming forth from Egypt. The whole subsequent history unfolds from this fixed point, is determined by it, and cannot be properly understood without it. The Pentateuch was not a "buried book" because some of its statutes may not have been rigidly enforced in all the troublous and degenerate periods that followed. The very statutes that were temporarily obscured are needed to set those periods of defection in their true light. What would be thought of that historian of Roman Law who should set aside all consideration of the code of Justinian, because in the disorders and distractions of later ages some of its provisions were temporarily overborne, and only slowly rose to full recognition again in later jurisprudence?

But the Doctor presents us with an *a priori* argument, which easily disposes of the whole matter and obviates the necessity of a laborious examination into the facts.

"It is perfectly clear that the great mass of Levitical legislation, with its ritual entirely constructed for the Sanctuary of the Ark and the priests of the house of Aaron, cannot have had practical currency and recognition in the Northern Kingdom. The priests could not have stultified themselves by accepting the authority of a code according to which their whole worship was schismatic. . . . The same argument proves that the code of Deuteronomy was unknown, for it also treats all the Northern sanctuaries as schismatic and heathenish, acknowledging but one place of lawful pilgrimage for all the seed of Jacob."

And so it might be argued that no rogue would ever stultify himself in a court of justice by admitting the validity of laws which make him a criminal and pronounce his doom. The Ten Tribes had undoubtedly the most powerful inducements to deny and to renounce the authority of the laws of Moses, if it was possible for them to do so. But if we find them living under these very institutions, only modified by being blended with their idolatry, if we find evidence, in their departures from Mosaic requirements, that they nevertheless confess their divine original and their binding obligation, then the strength of their motive to do otherwise but renders the confession that is wrung from them more significant. The question of the genuineness of the Mosaic legislation is all important in its bearing on all the subsequent stages of Israelitish history; and it is only to be settled by a direct appeal to the facts in the case.

We are referred in these Lectures (p. 117) to two chapters in the Bible as authority for the state of things in the Northern Kingdom, — Deut. xxxiii., "the so-called blessing of Moses," and Josh. xxiv. It is refreshing to find some firm footing in this dismal quagmire, to which everything has been reduced by the critics. And there are two points in these chapters which are well worthy of consideration. The priesthood is distinctly attributed to Levi (Deut. xxxiii. 8, 10), and notwithstanding this the fact is that in the Ten Tribes the priests were taken indiscriminately from all the people, and "were not of the sons of Levi" (1. Kings xii. 31, xiii. 33). And Josh. xxiv. 26 tells us of "the book of the Law of God," which was already in existence in the time of Joshua, for he wrote in it an account of that solemn day which was passed in Shechem. So that Israel, halting between Jehovah and Baal in the days of Elijah, was confessedly in possession of the book of the Law of God and of Joshua's serious and tender admonitions.

And here we must join issue with the statement on page 115: —

"In the time of Amos and Hosea the truest hearts and best thinkers of Israel did not yet interpret Jehovah's dealings with His people in the light of the Deuteronomic and Levitical laws; they did not judge of Israel's obedience by the principle of the one Sanctuary or the standard of Aaronic ritual."

This is not to be decided magisterially by one flourish of the pen. Let us put together the scattered hints which these Prophets afford us on this subject, that we may obtain, as far as we can, an accurate idea of the divine standard of duty which then prevailed. According to Amos ii. 4 the great crime of Judah, for which a terrible penalty awaits them that the LORD will not turn away, is that "they have despised the Law of the LORD and have not kept His commandments." Hosea (viii. 1) in the name of God, denounces swift vengeance upon Israel, "because they have transgressed My covenant, and trespassed against My Law." This "Law of Jehovah," then, to which both these Prophets alike appeal, was common to both kingdoms, and both were culpable and obnoxious to the severest judgments for violating it. In Hos. iv. 6, according to the Doctor's own understanding of the verse, the priests are charged with having forgotten the Law of their God; and in ver. 5 the Prophets are involved with them in a like condemnation. "Thus Hosea, no less than Amos, places himself in direct opposition to all the leaders of the religious life of his nation" (p. 156).

And yet both priests and Prophets are spoken of as charged with sacred functions, and are not the objects of an indiscriminate denunciation. The priests were entrusted with the administration of the Law. It was theirs to declare God's Law to the people, and exercise the highest judicial functions under it. Hence, when Hosea would by one stroke set forth the extreme of presumptuous daring and hopeless obduracy that possessed the people, so that it was useless to labor longer for their correction, he says (iv. 4) "Thy people are as they that strive with the priest."[1] The form of expression is peculiar and highly significant. The censure which he passes upon the people is not that of resistance to the priesthood; for, considering the character of the priests, as that is described immediately after, such resistance might be in many cases highly commendable. But they are " as they that strive with the priest;" they are compared to bold and reckless men, who resist the officers of law, and refuse submission to the authority of the supreme tribunal. It was in fact this prerogative of the priesthood which gave such fearful point to the charge already cited, that they whose duty it was to teach and to enforce the Law had themselves forgotten it, so that the people were destroyed in consequence, and God rejected these unfaithful priests from being priests to Him any longer. So, too, while the Prophets are rebuked and threatened, and there were those to whom prophecy was a trade and whose only concern was to get their bread (Am. vii. 12), — just as there were those who craved the priest's office for a living (I. Sam. ii. 36), — the sacred character and functions of Prophets are distinctly set forth. They are immediate messengers

---

[1] The text of this clause needs no correction, least of all any such bungling emendation as those which the Doctor gravely discusses (p. 406). The allusion to the priests' judicial function, coupled with the thought, which at once presents itself to the Prophet's mind, of their culpable unfaithfulness to this high trust, leads to the denunciation ver. 5, — the suppressed thought, which links vers. 4 and 5, coming to full expression in ver. 6.

of God, to whom He makes confidential disclosures of all His purposes (Am. iii. 7), and through whom He declares His will and purposes to men (Hos. vi. 5, xii. 10).[1] Amos ii. 11, 12 includes among God's distinguishing benefits to Israel His raising up Prophets of their sons, and charges them with the sin of having "commanded the Prophets, saying, Prophesy not." Amos, no doubt, intends to associate himself with the Prophets who were thus obstructed in the performance of their divine commission; for, though not by regular profession a Prophet, nor one of the Sons of the Prophets, he too had been sent by God to prophesy to Israel, and had been interdicted from doing it (Am. vii. 15, 16). While Hosea and Amos do not apply the term "law" to the utterances of the Prophets, it might be, and it was so applied; in Isa. i. 10, "the Law of our God" is an equivalent expression to "the Word of the LORD" spoken by the Prophet himself. (See also xxx. 9, 10.) But that the Law was something more than the oral instructions of the

---

[1] The Doctor tells us (p. 182): "The possession of a single true thought about Jehovah, not derived from current religious teaching, but springing up in the soul as a word from Jehovah Himself, is enough to constitute a prophet, and lay on him the duty of speaking to Israel what he has learned of Israel's God." If he means to efface the distinction between the inspiration of the Prophets and the illumination enjoyed by all pious men who are led to clearer views of truth and duty through their own devout experiences, enlightened by the Holy Ghost, — and further, if he means to deny to the Prophets any direct and immediate commission from God to speak in His name, beyond the general obligation resting on all to impart of that which they have received, — then his statement falls below the conception entertained by Hosea and Amos.

Prophets and the judicial decisions of the priests, delivered from time to time as occasion required, appears from the fact that they could be charged with forgetting it. There must, therefore, have been a fixed body of law, independent of and superior to those who were appointed to teach or to administer it, which neither priest nor Prophet could modify or set aside, and which was binding on them as on the people.

The obligation of obedience resting on Israel is further set forth by representing this Law in the light of a covenant (Hos. vi. 7, viii. 1) or solemn engagement between Israel and Jehovah, the breach of whose stipulations is a just ground of controversy to Jehovah with His people (xii. 2), and calls for the exercise of His righteous judgment (v. 1, 11, vi. 5). Hosea (i. 2 ff.) further presents it under the image of the marriage relation, of which sacred bond their sin was a gross and shameless violation. This covenant union is traced back to the Exodus: "I am the LORD thy God from the land of Egypt, and thou shalt know no god but Me" (Hos. xiii. 4, xii. 9; see also xi. 1; Am. iii. 1, 2, ii. 10). It is even traced beyond that to God's dealings with their pious ancestor Jacob (Hos. xii. 3, 4). The leader out of Egypt, to whose charge the people was committed, was a Prophet (ver. 13), which implies that God made known His will through him. And in its infancy the nation cordially responded (Hos. ii. 15).[1] The covenant between Jehovah and Israel was accordingly formed in

---

[1] For "sing," in the Authorized Version, read "answer;" the reference is to Ex. xxiv. 3.

the days of Moses; and of this there is, besides, monumental evidence in the existence of the Ark of the Covenant. The giving of the Law began with Moses; whether he gave the Law in full, or simply made a beginning which was added to and developed subsequently, may be left undetermined for the present.

Of what compass was this Law in the time of Hosea and Amos? and what did it contain? It is observable that neither of these Prophets thinks it necessary to expound the requirements of the Law or to argue their obligation. They assume throughout that these are well known and their binding force acknowledged. They deal chiefly in charges of transgression and threatenings of punishment. We may take it for granted that the sins with which the people are charged are violations of this Law, and that the virtues whose absence is deplored were enjoined by it. One comprehensive word used several times by Hosea, and variously rendered "goodness," "mercy," and "kindness" (Hos. vi. 4; see margin), embraces both love to God and love to man.[1] He heaps to-

[1] This word is admirably expounded by Dr. Robertson Smith (p. 162): "Jehovah and Israel form as it were one community, and *hésed* is the bond by which the whole community is knit together. It is not necessary to distinguish Jehovah's *hésed* to Israel, which we would term his grace, Israel's duty of *hésed* to Jehovah, which we would call piety, and the relation of *hésed* between man and man which embraces the duties of love and mutual consideration. To the Hebrew mind these three are essentially one, and all are comprised in the same covenant. Loyalty and kindness between man and man are not duties inferred from Israel's relation to Jehovah; they are parts of that relation; love to Jehovah and love to one's brethren in Jehovah's house are identical."

gether a number of particulars (iv. 1, 2): "There is no truth, nor kindness (or piety), nor knowledge of God in the land; swearing and lying and killing and stealing and committing adultery; they commit violence, and blood toucheth blood." It is plain that this Law must have embraced such duties of man to his fellow as chastity and sobriety (Hos. iv. 11, vii. 4, 5; Am. ii. 7, vi. 4–6); fidelity to engagements (Hos. x. 4); justice, kindness, and truth (Hos. x. 12, 13, xi. 12; Am. v. 7, 24, vi. 12); upright dealing as opposed to fraud and heartless oppression, particularly of the poor (Hos. vii. 1, xii. 6–8; Am. ii. 6–8, iii. 10, iv. 1, v. 11, viii. 4–6); and judicial integrity (Am. v. 10, 12, 15). The Doctor concedes (p. 113) the existence at this time of "the Book of the Covenant" (Ex. xxi.–xxiii.). "The ordinances of this code closely correspond with the indications as to the ancient laws of Israel supplied by the older history and the Prophets. Quite similar, except in some minor details which need not now delay us, is another ancient table of laws, preserved in Ex. xxxiv. These two documents may be taken as representing the general system of sacred law which had practical recognition in the Northern Kingdom."[1]

---

[1] The Doctor adds in the same sentence: "The very fact that we have two such documents conspires with other indications to make it probable that the laws, which were certainly generally published by oral decisions of the priests, were better known by oral tradition than by written books." We are not now dealing with the question whether the Law was oral or written, and simply remark that the history clearly states the mutual relation of these two series of laws. The second is not a varying tradition of the first. (See above, p. 279.) Moreover,

The Prophets, however, deal still more largely and emphatically with the criminality of the people against Jehovah. Duties toward God must, therefore, have had a prominent place in the Law. Israel is charged with being grossly unfaithful to her conjugal relation to Jehovah (Hos. i. 2, v. 7, vi. 7) and forsaking Him for other lovers (Hos. ii. 7 and *passim*); and, without a figure, with idolatry (Hos. iv. 12, 17, viii. 4, xi. 2, xiv. 3, 8); a lack of the true knowledge of God (Hos. iv. 1, 6, vi. 6); forgetting God (Hos. ii. 13, viii. 14, xiii. 6); not seeking God (Hos. v. 15, x. 12; Am. v. 4, 6); not waiting for Him (Hos. xii. 6); not hearkening to Him (Hos. ix. 17); rebelling against Him (Hos. xiii. 16); profaning His holy name (Am. ii. 7); not returning to God after the infliction of judgments (Am. iv. 6, 8-11, where there is distinct reference to Deut. iv. 30, xxx. 2); backsliding from Him (Hos. xi. 7, xiv. 4); transient piety (Hos. vi. 4); presumptuous trust in God in their wickedness (Am. v. 18, vi. 1); mixing themselves with heathen nations and becoming like them (Hos. vii. 8); placing their dependence in a heathen monarch instead of Jehovah (Hos. v. 13, vii. 11, viii. 9, xii. 1, xiv. 3). For this they had been visited with famine, drought, blasting, mildew and locusts, pestilence after the manner of Egypt (comp. Deut. xxviii. 27, 60), the sword, and overthrow like that of Sodom and Gomorrah (Am. iv. 6-11; comp. Deut. xxix.

does the Doctor think that Ex. xxxiv. 17 "had practical recognition in the Northern Kingdom?" What becomes, then, of his argument of the legitimacy of the golden calves?

23). And still heavier judgments were in store for them: the kingdom should come to an end (Hos. i. 4; Am. ix. 8), the land be utterly desolated (Hos. ii. 3, iv. 3; Am. iii. 11–15); their idolatrous sanctuaries destroyed (Hos. x. 2, 8; Am. iii. 14; comp. Lev. xxvi. 30), and the people exiled (Hos. ix. 3; Am. v. 27). See this identical catalogue of evils, Lev. xxvi. 14 ff.; Deut. xxviii. 15 ff. All this tends to create the impression that in the Law, to which these Prophets appeal, Israel's duty to Jehovah of worship and service had a greater proportional space accorded to it than is the case in Ex. xx.–xxiii.

Was "the principle of the one Sanctuary" included in the Law to which Hosea and Amos appeal, and by which they "judge of Israel's obedience"? The Northern sanctuaries are separately and by name denounced as centres of iniquity and false worship by both these Prophets; and, according to Amos i. 2 God's earthly seat was in Zion and Jerusalem. Hosea in express terms exposes the iniquity of the golden calves, as the Doctor concedes, though he maintains that this had always before been regarded in the Ten Tribes as a legitimate form of the worship of Jehovah, and sanctioned by all preceding Prophets, as Elijah, Elisha, and Amos. That the skirts of these Prophets were clear of any complicity in this idol-worship has already been abundantly shown. But it is further plain, from the language of Hosea himself, that he is making no innovation and announcing no new doctrine. His words are not those of a man proclaiming for the first time that what the people had all along considered right was outrageously wrong. He enters into no argument with these hereditary idolaters; he refutes no objections; he anticipates no opposition to his most startling statements. Confident of carrying the consciences and the convictions of his hearers with him, he calls their whole system of worship by the name of the grossest offence known amongst men. Their service nominally paid to Jehovah, he declares, was really rendered to Baalim (ii. 13). The indignant and contemptuous manner in which he speaks of the calves (viii. 5, 6, x. 5) and the stupidity of their worshippers (xiii. 2), and warns them of the wrath of God thus provoked and the judgment that should follow, shows that this is not some new light that has but recently dawned on his own mind; but that as the servant of Israel's God he is confronting those who were knowingly transgressors of His holy Law, while they willingly walked after a human commandment (v. 11), that of Jeroboam the son of Nebat.

When, now, Amos sharply contrasts seeking Jehovah and seeking Bethel (v. 4–6), and declares in the strongest terms the loathing that Jehovah feels for their services professedly offered to Him (vers. 21–23), the Doctor takes the meaning simply to be, "He is not to be found by sacrifice, for in it He takes no pleasure; what Jehovah requires of them that seek Him is the practice of civil righteousness" (p. 139). "The whole ritual service is to Amos a thing without importance in itself" (p. 140). Amos "shows a degree of indifference to all practices of social worship which is not uncharacteristic of an inhabitant of the desert" (p. 167). A worship which to Hosea was basely criminal, which was an atrocity to be punished by the direst judgments, — because Jehovah spurned the degrading homage offered to the calves, refusing to accept it as rendered to Himself, — cannot have been to Amos a matter of indifference. When Amos speaks of the god of Dan as the sin of Samaria (viii. 14); when he says of Israel's multiplied services, " Come to Bethel and transgress; at Gilgal multiply transgression" (iv. 4); when he makes the Northern sanctuaries the centres of iniquity and corruption that pervaded the kingdom, so that in the day that God visited the transgression of Israel upon him, He would also visit the altars of Bethel (iii. 14), — this is not simply because he attached no importance to ritual service. The service there paid was not merely of no account, inadequate as a substitute for the practice of virtue. It was abhorrent. It was a nuisance to be abated, and which the LORD would tolerate no longer. "I hate, I despise your feast-days, and I will not smell in your solemn assemblies. Though ye offer Me burnt-offerings and your meat-offerings, I will not accept them; neither will I regard the peace-offerings of your fat beasts. Take thou away from Me the noise of thy songs, for I will not hear the melody of thy viols." It is not feast-days as such that are thus abominable. It is not disgust at offerings and an outward ceremonial that is here expressed. It is "*your* feast-days" and "*your* solemn assemblies" that the LORD detests, because the worship itself was of a debased, idolatrous character, and it was coupled with the practice of iniquity.[1]

The Doctor seems at a loss to find a proper antithesis to these denunciations of Amos. "If we ask what Amos desired to set in the place of the system he so utterly condemns, the answer is apparently very meagre. He has no new scheme of Church and State to propose — only this, that Jehovah desires righteousness and not sacrifice" (p. 141). Would Amos, then, abolish ritual worship altogether? and not sacrifices only, but "songs" of praise as well? Are there to be no acts of adoration and homage, social or individual? Would he have no direct intercourse between Israel and his glorious King, no Temple, no altar, no prayer, no thanksgiving, no outward expression of devotion, — only "the practice of civil righteousness"? This would be a nearer approach to Confucianism than we can well imagine in a Prophet of Israel.

If, however, he is not aiming at the abolition of all forms of worship, then it must be urged again that

---

[1] The Doctor tells us (p. 139): "When Amos represents the national worship of Israel as positively sinful, he does so mainly because it was so conducted as to afford a positive encouragement to the injustice, the sensuality, the barbarous treatment of the poor, to which he recurs again and again as the cardinal sins of the nation." This statement is defective, since it does not penetrate deeply enough into the source of this moral degradation. It is not merely because of the manner in which the worship was conducted, but because of what it was. It was not the service of the pure and holy Jehovah, the giver of the moral law. It was a bestial nature-worship, to which the name of Jehovah was attached, but in which His attributes were disregarded.

the intense language of Amos cannot be accounted for on the hypothesis of indifference. It betrays the most powerfully excited feeling. His emotion is wrought up to the highest pitch. This could not arise from that which he held to be of small account, but only what was most precious and most dear. He cannot bear with the desecration of what was so sacred, the profaning of what was so holy. It is not that worship is so little worth, but because it rises in value and in awfulness above everything beside, that he cannot look with equanimity upon Israel converting the worship of Jehovah into a besotted mummery, the mimicry of devotion.[1]

Place now beside this that significant reference at the very beginning of his prophecy (i. 2) to the fact that the God whose warning message he bears,—the divine Judge of Israel and the nations,—utters His wrathful voice from Jerusalem and from Zion. Jehovah speaks from the Temple on that holy mountain; from thence He thunders with a mighty roar against all the wicked of the earth. If Jehovah is there, He dwells in a Temple erected for sacrifice and for ceremonial observance. He is there for the purpose of

[1] This consideration is of itself sufficient to show that the interpretation which the Doctor would put upon Amos v. 25 cannot possibly be correct. It cannot mean that "the Israelites offered no sacrifice in the Wilderness, and yet Jehovah was never nearer to them than there" (p. 140), as an argument that sacrifices are of small consequence. The real emphasis in the verse lies in the words "unto me." Their apostasy from God began even in the Wilderness, in idolatries perpetrated there. And this is no more inconsistent with Am. ii. 10 than Hos. ix. 10 is with Hos. ii. 15.

being worshipped and of receiving the adoration of His subjects. His presence there is the sanction of the purpose for which the house was built, and for which it was resorted to by those that feared His name. While Bethel and Gilgal and Beersheba are denounced (v. 5), as well as the High Places of Isaac and the sanctuaries of Israel generally (vii. 9), Zion was the spot where Jehovah might be found.

Add now to this, that in Hosea's eyes the multiplication of sanctuaries is of itself a sin. When Israel worships on the tops of mountains and upon the hills, and under oaks, poplars, and terebinths (iv. 13) she acts the part of an unfaithful wife, who leaves her lawful husband for the love of strangers. When she worships at Gilgal and at Bethaven (he will not call it Bethel, for it is no longer the "house of God") she does the same (iv. 15). Snares are set on Mizpah and Tabor (v. 1). Gilgal is a seat of detestable wickedness (ix. 15). Ephraim hath multiplied altars to sin (viii. 11),—each fresh altar not only a fresh occasion of sin, but its erection itself a sin. The vast number of his altars is also charged against him in x. 1, and perhaps in xii. 11 likewise; they are as devoid of all sacredness as ordinary stone-heaps, unless indeed the stone-heaps represent the state of utter ruin to which they shall be reduced. Consider further, that while the LORD declares that He will no more have mercy upon the house of Israel, He will have mercy upon the house of Judah, and save them by Jehovah their God (i. 6, 7); that for the present God refuses to recognize Israel as His people or to be Himself their God (ver. 9); but that hereafter Judah and Israel shall be joined again (ver. 11), as before the schism and apostasy of Jeroboam, and then (iii. 5) the children of Israel shall return and seek the LORD their God and David their king. And can there be a remaining doubt as to where the true place of worship was in the mind of Hosea?

With all this associate one more fact, and the chain of argument will be complete. The binding obligation of "the principle of the one Sanctuary" was recognized by Hezekiah (II. Kings xviii. 4, 22), as the critics confess, shortly after the time of Hosea, or perhaps even before his long ministry was ended. And conclusive proof has been furnished in the preceding pages, as we suppose (see above, pp. 85 ff., pp. 137 ff.), that its obligatory character was recognized in all periods of the history of Israel from the time of Moses downward. This was, then, we may affirm without hesitation, an integral part of the Law recognized by Hosea and Amos as the standard authority in both Israel and Judah in their day.

But, if this point is established, some further consequences follow. The fact that the principle of the one Sanctuary was enforced by Josiah with greater rigor than before is the staple argument of the critics for dating the book of Deuteronomy from his reign, or shortly before it. If, however, that principle, instead of being a recent invention of "the prophetic party" of that period, was already standard law in the time of Hosea, and in fact had been law in Israel ever since the days of Moses, what becomes of the critical argument, and what of the conclusion based upon it?

Much of Deuteronomy certainly was of ancient date. Dr. Robertson Smith correctly says [1]: —

> "The Deuteronomic Code is not a mere supplement to the First Legislation. It is an independent reproduction of its substance, sometimes merely repeating the older laws, but at other times extending or modifying them. It covers the whole ground of the old Law, except the law of treason (Ex. xxii. 28) and the details as to compensations to be paid for various injuries."

And he gives a very serviceable comparative table,[2] showing "how completely Deuteronomy covers the same ground with the First Legislation." Now, according to the Doctor's own theory, the First Legislation, or the Book of the Covenant, existed long before the time of Hosea. All this portion of Deuteronomy, then, belonged in substance, if not in form, to the Law in Hosea's days. And in regard to the remaining provisions of Deuteronomic Law, can the critics point out one which was introduced between the age of Hosea and that of Josiah? If not, what good reason can they give for questioning that the whole Deuteronomic Law was in the possession of Hosea and of Amos? In fact, what good reason can they give for questioning that it had been in existence ever since the days of Moses? The Doctor tells us (p. 35), "It is difficult for us to determine with precision how far Moses in person carried the work of giving to Israel

---

[1] "The Old Testament in the Jewish Church," p. 317.
[2] Ibid. p. 431.

divine ordinances." Is it not in fact so difficult that the safest way for us is to accept the explicit testimony of the sacred record, that both the Book of the Covenant and the Deuteronomic Law were given by Moses himself, confirmed as this is by the uniform belief of all post-Mosaic times and by all the tests which we are capable of applying to it. The advocates of development may be reluctant to concede this. But we do not really see what they have to stand upon, in refusing their assent, but their own *a priori* theory. The facts, so far as they are capable of being ascertained, are all the other way.

Had the Law, to which Hosea and Amos appeal, any ritual requirements? It will not be necessary to reproduce here the evidence already given (see above, pp. 115, 116) that Israel in the time of these Prophets had an extensive ceremonial. But was this of divine obligation? The Doctor reminds us that—

"Israel, like the other nations, worshipped Jehovah at certain fixed sanctuaries, where He was held to meet with His people face to face. The method of worship was by altar gifts, expressive of homage for the good things of His bestowal, and the chief occasions of such worship were the agricultural feasts, just as among the Canaanites. The details of the ceremonial observed were closely parallel to those still to be read on Phœnician monuments. Even the technical terms connected with the sacrifice were in great part identical" (p. 56).

If these heathen parallels are of any significance in accounting for the attitude of the Prophets toward the ceremonial worship in Israel, it might be supposed that they did so in one or the other of two ways. In the first place Israel's religious rites may be conjectured to have been of heathen origin and imported into the worship of Jehovah from the worship of heathen divinities, and thus may have been regarded as foreign to God's true worship and offensive to Him. Or, in the second place, it may be imagined that these rites, being common to Israel and the heathen, contained nothing that was distinctively characteristic of the religion of Jehovah in contrast with other systems, and may for this reason have been considered a matter of indifference. It was of no account whether men engaged in the ritual or not. Jehovah was to be served not by sacrifice but by righteousness. Upon either hypothesis the bare fact that Hosea and Amos refer to these ceremonies as observed in Israel, would not establish for them a place in the Law which was to these Prophets the standard of divine obligation.

Now as to the first supposition, it is evident that the ritual practised in their days was not regarded by the Prophets as heathenish importations which were in themselves criminal and offensive; for in all their censures of Israel's worship they never intimate anything of the kind. On the contrary, Hosea represents sacrifice by which pardon was obtained, and the ephod by which the will of God was consulted, as essential to the maintenance of Israel's intercourse with Jehovah; so that when he would depict the people in the seclusion of the Exile, — awaiting a happier future, but their relation to God and to idols both severed for the present, — he speaks of them

(iii. 4) as on the one hand without a sacrifice and without an ephod, and on the other hand without an image and without teraphim. As the latter were indispensable instruments and accompaniments of idolatry, so were the former of the true worship of Jehovah. When he says (v. 6) "They shall go with their flocks and with their herds to seek the LORD, but they shall not find Him," the antithesis implies that there was reason to expect that going with such offerings they would find Him. The real cause of their failure is immediately added: "He hath withdrawn Himself from them." When the Most High declares (vi. 6) that He desired "the knowledge of God more than burnt-offerings," it is implied that burnt-offerings were desired. When their petitions, offered at their sacrificial festivals, are contemptuously called "howling upon their beds" (vii. 14), it was not that this was a prohibited mode of entreating His favor, but because of their rebellion against Him and that they did not cry unto Him with their heart. The threatened captivity would be aggravated by their inability to observe the laws of ceremonial purity: "They shall eat unclean things in Assyria" (ix. 3). The acceptability of drink-offerings properly presented is taken for granted (ix. 4); and sacrifice must have been regarded as pleasing to God, when it is made the symbol of praise: "So will we render calves, our lips" (xiv. 2). So that when their predicted shame and disappointment is attributed to their sacrifices (iv. 19), it is not because sacrifices are in themselves criminal, but theirs are not what sacrifices ought to be. Amos speaks of it as a divine favor to Israel that their sons were led to take the Nazarite vow (ii. 11), and reproaches the people for a breach of the ceremonial in giving them wine to drink (ver. 12), and in adding leaven to their thank-offering (iv. 5). And if Jehovah dwells in Zion (i. 2) He necessarily sanctions that form of worship, for which His house on Zion was expressly built.

Sacrifice as such is not offensive to God, therefore; and the warmth of the language of Amos regarding it has already shown us that it is not a matter of indifference. It must, consequently, have been esteemed obligatory; and, as the intensity of the Prophet's feelings with regard to it reveals, the obligation must have been so solemn and imperative that a dereliction of duty in this particular awakened the most intense indignation. There is no escape from the conclusion that the developed ritual of their day was enjoined in the Divine Law.

And if this Law contained all that they describe, it must have contained much more; for their allusions are merely incidental, and not made with any view of covering the entire round of required observance; and there is the greater reason to believe that this was the case, because the scope and tenor of their teaching was mainly directed to a different matter,—not so much to the forms of worship, with which the people were sufficiently familiar, as to the spirit of piety which should animate them, and the life of uprightness which should accompany them. And, further, a Law containing these particulars must have likewise included other things which they necessarily imply. If there were priests and offerings and tithes and distinctions of clean and unclean, there must have been specifications under each of these heads, to enable the people to act intelligently with regard to them, and the ministers of religion to decide the questions which would be constantly arising about them. There must have been rules regulating the support of the priests and the contributions of the people. Directions must have been given with some detail as to the ritual to be observed in different kinds of sacrifice, and what were proper occasions for their presentation. And so in regard to other matters. The particulars positively stated by the Prophets not only justify but compel the assumption of an extended ceremonial Law. These few hints and allusions do not of course enable us to determine all its contents in detail. But all these allusions accord with the Levitical Law of the Pentateuch. They are just such as might be expected if that Law, in its full extent, was in the hands of these Prophets. There is not one statute of that Law which may not have been in it then, so far as we can gather from the intimations given by Hosea and Amos, or so far as we can infer from contemporaneous or subsequent history. They must have possessed the Levitical Law as we now have it, or one so closely resembling it that no critic can point out a single particular in which it must have differed from it.[1]

[1] As a further suggestion of the source of this ritual, it may be observed that the usage of the Feast of Tabernacles, alluded to in

So that Prof. Rudolph Smend,[1] though an advocate of Graf's hypothesis, uses the following language: —

"That purity and holiness, and the corresponding lustrations and atoning sacrifices, must at all times have played a great part in Israelitish worship, and this [worship] must, in the Temple of Jerusalem, have had essentially the form which is presented in Leviticus, cannot be denied, even though the casual intimations of the older prophetical writings do not suffice to prove it. For this reason we cannot see what essential alterations the conceptions hitherto entertained of the inner development of religion in Mosaism must undergo, even if a few particulars should be shown to be post-exilic." "Accordingly we do not know what objection can be made to the earlier composition of Leviticus on the ground of the older prophetical writings."

There is no reason in fact why the Levitical Law may not have been given by Moses, except the figment of development. There is nothing but this philosophical theory, unsupported by any Biblical facts, to outweigh the positive and repeated declarations contained in Leviticus itself — and accredited to us by the testimony of all subsequent ages, through which it has been handed down and by

---

Hos. xii. 9, finds its explanation neither in the Book of the Covenant nor in Deuteronomy, but only in Lev. xxiii. 42.

[1] In his elaborate and extremely able article "On the Stage of Development of the Religion of Israel presupposed by the Prophets of the Eighth Century," in the "Studien und Kritiken" for 1876, pp. 655, 661. This was written shortly after the appearance of Duhm's "Theology of the Prophets," and chiefly with the view of pointing out the serious errors of that work. I have been largely indebted to the suggestions of this article in the preceding discussion.

which it was esteemed most sacred — that these laws were announced by Moses as divinely communicated to him. That the absence of these ritual laws from Deuteronomy cannot be urged in support of the theory, as though Leviticus must be the development of a later age, is also confessed by Smend: —

"If a law-book, which professedly aims to give a complete order of the cultus, speaks of many things about which another, which has no such design, is silent, it nevertheless does not follow that the former, on account of the greater copiousness of its contents, must belong to a later time, in which the worship was further developed" (p. 654).[1]

We inquire further, was the Law, of which Hosea speaks, written or oral? The usage of the period is very clearly shown by his contemporary Isaiah, who speaks of it as a matter of course that enactments were committed to writing. "Woe unto them that decree unrighteous decrees, and to the scribes that write grievousness" (Isa. x. 1). The fact that Hosea and Amos wrote their prophecies not only implies an already existing literature, which is besides sufficiently attested in other ways; but, inasmuch as they were designed to enforce the divine Law, and were themselves regarded as a supplementary Law of the LORD (Isa. i. 10), if they were reduced to writing, it must have been because this was likewise the case with the

[1] Dr. Robertson Smith must acknowledge the cogency of what is here said by Smend, since he himself considers the aim of Deuteronomy to be different from that of Leviticus. See the passage cited from "The Old Testament in the Jewish Church," in note 2, page 76, above.

code to which they were virtually annexed. It was customary at that time to write whatever was to be carefully preserved (Isa. viii. 1, xxx. 8). Samuel wrote the manner of the kingdom (I. Sam. x. 25). David had a recorder and a scribe among the chief officers of his court (II. Sam. viii. 16, 17, xx. 24, 25); so had Solomon (I. Kings iv. 3) and subsequent kings (II. Kings xii. 10, xviii. 18). The commission, appointed by Joshua to divide the land, made their report in writing (Josh. xviii. 9). In the song of Deborah, whose antiquity is universally acknowledged, scribes marshal the troops (Judg. v. 14). Writing was in familiar use in ordinary matters. David wrote a letter about Uriah (II. Sam. xi. 14, 15), Jezebel about Naboth (I. Kings xxi. 8, 9), the king of Syria about Naaman (II. Kings v. 5–7), Jehu about Ahab's sons (II. Kings x. 1). Lots were inscribed (Num. xvii. 2; Lev. xvi. 8); writing by the priest was part of the ceremonial in the jealousy-offering (Num. v. 23); and an old Canaanitish city bore the name of Kirjath-sepher, (Book-town). The law of divorce (Deut. xxiv. 1) implies that men generally were able to write. Gideon required a young man, taken at random, to write out for him the princes of Succoth (Judg. viii. 14; see also Isa. x. 19). In such a state of things it would be utterly unaccountable if the Law, which was held to be of divine authority and believed to have emanated from God Himself, which lay at the foundation of public justice and regulated public worship, was suffered to remain unwritten and exposed to all the risks of oral transmission.

The Ten Commandments were not only written but engraved in stone in the lifetime of Moses himself. In Josh. xxiv., to which we are referred (p. 118) for a reliable exposition of Israelitish views, it appears (vers. 25, 26) that Joshua at once wrote the statute and ordinance which he gave to the people in Shechem; and further that " the book of the Law of God " was already in existence at that time.[1] The Doctor himself concedes (p. 113) that there were " ancient laws" which had "currency in a written form;" only he tells us that they must be sought not in Deuteronomy nor in Leviticus, but "in other parts of the Pentateuch, particularly in the Book of the Covenant (Ex. xxi–xxiii.)." And while he asserts (p. 114) that " neither Hosea nor Amos alludes to an extant written Law," he adds that " this fact does not prove that written laws did not exist." When, therefore, Hosea (viii. 12),[2] speaking in the name of God, says in express terms, " I write to him the ten thousand precepts of My Law; they have been counted as a strange thing,"

---

[1] The hasty inference that this chapter "speaks without offence of the sacred tree and sacred stone that marked this great Northern sanctuary, and is therefore quite ignorant of the Deuteronomic Law," is shown to be invalid, p. 162, above.

[2] The Doctor says, "Hos. viii. 12 is mistranslated in the Authorized Version." If this is to be settled by confident assertion we may balance his statement by the contrary one of Professor Smend (p. 633 of the article before cited), whom we may without disrespect presume that the Doctor will admit to be his peer in Hebrew learning. (See above, p. 114, note). Smend (p. 637) thinks that there were several written collections of laws; but of this there is no evidence. Hosea and Amos speak of but one Divine Law; and their words leave no room for the supposition of various rival codes with conflicting statutes.

this is just such a declaration as the facts already reviewed prepare us for and warrant us in crediting. The Law known to Hosea and Amos was an extensive code, embracing a multitude of requirements, and it was in written form; and although transgressed as though it were something foreign to the people, and which had no claim upon them, it had nevertheless proceeded from the LORD Himself.

One more question remains: Who wrote this Law, to which Hosea and Amos attach undoubted divine authority, and upon which they base all their denunciations? We have a right to ask, and to demand an answer, for it is universally allowed to be one of the great legal systems of the world. Such a body of law never grew up by accident. It is not the aggregate of judicial decisions rendered in the course of ages, at various tribunals by successive judges. In that case there would necessarily be conflicting and incoherent statutes, and the bare record of such decisions would be a tangled wilderness of disconnected utterances. Even if resting ultimately on such decisions, it must have been carefully codified. It is a systematic body of law, based on great fundamental principles, which are carried out to their logical results in a consistent and masterly manner.[1] Every part of it evidences clear thought, a high faculty of administration, and comprehensive views. Who produced this body of

---

[1] If, as has sometimes been alleged, some of these institutions — as, for example, the Year of Jubilee — were merely theoretical, and never came into practical operation, this but adds to the evidence that the whole sprang from one constructive mind.

law, or who digested it and reduced it to order? Whose thought reigns in the whole?

The critics have felt the pressure of this question, and sought at one time to fasten Deuteronomy upon Jeremiah, as they have assigned Leviticus to Ezra. But they have themselves abandoned the former as untenable; and even those who allege that Leviticus in its present form was written by Ezra, must concede that the chief provisions of that Law were much older. Both of these codes must have been substantially, at least, and in their main features, prior to Hosea and Amos, — long prior, for the Law of which these Prophets speak was no recent production, no modern innovation, but the old, established, authoritative Law. Could its author have been David? Of his reign we have a full account, — of his enterprises, of the measures which he carried into effect, of his schemes of government and of worship. But there is no record of his having prepared or introduced any such body of law; this is in fact not shaped upon the theory of a kingly government; and later ages never suggest that it is to be referred to him. Could it have been Samuel, the great reformer, prophet, and judge? But the chaotic period, in which he lived and labored, is just the one in which these laws were more in abeyance than in any other. Is the great legislator of Israel, then, buried in complete oblivion, his name forgotten quite, and no tradition, however faint, preserved respecting him? Did the master-mind that shaped these laws and institutions, which are the wonder of all who study them, leave no impress of himself upon his nation and his age?

One is involuntarily reminded of the story which used to be told of the Englishman making his first journey in France, who innocently inquired of one who sat next him in the coach, "Whose are these elegant grounds and buildings that we are passing?" The bewildered native, ignorant of English, simply replied, "Monsieur, je ne sais pas." Accepting this as the real name of the owner of this magnificent estate, the Englishman repeated his question from time to time, as fresh villas came into view, receiving uniformly the same response. At length, astonished at such vast possessions belonging to one proprietor, he exclaimed, "Monsieur Je-ne-sais-pas must be a very rich man." And the Unknown, to whom the critics would introduce us, must be a man without his equal in the whole history of Israel. Yet he has himself completely vanished out of history, and left no trace of his existence, no memory even of the age in which he lived. Nay, by the strangest of all freaks of fortune, a unanimous, persistent, and unvarying tradition has confounded this commanding spirit, this unique legislator, with a rude chieftain who never gave any laws, so far as the critics know, except in so far as he decided petty disputes between his followers, and whose only distinction is that of having led a horde of undisciplined nomads out of bondage into a desert many centuries before.

Is it the whole history of Israel that is at fault, or is it only that the critics have been dreaming? Possibly the real Moses of history may after all have been quite different from the fictitious personage substituted for him by the critics. And in the adopted son of Pharaoh's daughter, who intermarried with the Egyptian priesthood and was learned in all the wisdom of Egypt, who was fired with an enthusiastic attachment to his people and their God and was inspired by the Holy Ghost, — the great commander and organizer who shaped the institutions of his nation and impressed his own ideas ineradicably upon their entire subsequent history, — we may find a rational and sober answer to our question, which else must remain unanswered or land us in the most incredible of paradoxes.

The critics will smile incredulously at the suggestion of what they are pleased to call the traditional view, as though it were some unfounded opinion, which has come to be believed merely by dint of constant repetition, and which accordingly has no claim upon the faith of candid and honest inquirers in comparison with the so-called critical or scientific view, and is now only held in ignorance or defiance of advancing light. But let us understand the sort of tradition on which it rests. The Pentateuchal Law claims in the most unambiguous manner to have been given and recorded by Moses. The general character of the legislation, and the terms in which it is couched, accord with this claim. Its truth is further vouched for in the most direct and positive manner in the history of his trusted attendant and successor Joshua (i. 7, 8, viii. 31–34, xxii. 5, xxiii. 6); also by xxiv. 26, which the critics with unwonted clemency suffer to stand; further by Judg. iii. 4; I. Kings ii. 3; II. Kings x. 31, xiv. 6, xvii. 37, xviii. 6, 12, xxi. 8, xxii. 8, xxiii. 24, 25, not to speak of numerous testimonies of later date. The history and legislation of the Pentateuch lies at the basis of all the subsequent history of the Old Testament. It is presupposed in the Psalms.[1] It is presupposed in the Prophets. Moses' authorship has the explicit sanction of our blessed Lord Himself. The prior existence of the Pentateuch is shown by its being so interwoven with all subsequent portions of the history and literature of Israel that it cannot be torn from it without the destruction of the whole. It is upon this immovable foundation that the traditional view securely reposes. The tradition is imbedded in the Scriptures from first to last, and can only be surrendered when the inspired

[1] No prominence has been given in any of the preceding discussions to the testimony rendered by the Book of Psalms to the truth of the Pentateuch, and to the divine authority as well as the Mosaic origin of its institutions, for the simple reason that the critics exercise the same right of peremptory challenge in regard to unwelcome witnesses that Anglo-Saxon law allows in the case of jurors deemed unfriendly. The titles of the Psalms are set aside without ceremony; and each individual Psalm is arbitrarily assigned to whatever date best suits the critical theory which chances to be in vogue at the time. Under the operation of this rule the Psalter becomes merely the hymn-book of the Second Temple; the great mass of the Psalms are reckoned post-exilic, if not Maccabean; and nothing is allowed to be Davidic until the critics have first satisfied themselves by a thorough search that it contains nothing capable of being used against them. In fact it has been discovered that the safest course is to exclude David from the Psalter altogether, and to deny to him any devotional composition in the proper sense, allowing to him only "sportful forms of unconstrained mirth." "Melodies of the Temple service were borrowed from the joyous songs of the vintage, and so it was possible that David should give the pattern alike for the songs of the Sanctuary and for the worldly airs of the nobles of Samaria." ("The Old Testament in the Jewish Church," p. 205). Accordingly, any argument *ex concessis* from the Psalms is out of the question.

volume itself is abandoned as untrustworthy, and Jesus ceases to be trusted as an infallible teacher. When progress means marching over such a precipice as this, sensible men will be apt to call a halt, and prefer to abide on the *terra firma* of tradition a little longer, rather than adventure themselves upon the cloudland which lies beyond.

Besides Elijah and Elisha, who have already been spoken of, the Prophets whose work is particularly discussed in these Lectures are Hosea and Amos in the Ten Tribes, Isaiah and Micah in Judah. The aim of the whole is to exhibit them in their individual character and their mutual relations, and in their relations to the times in which they lived. What is known of each Prophet is briefly sketched, and the specific character of his times depicted, and the bearing of this upon his ministry is shown; special traits are pointed out, which distinguish the teaching or mode of thought of each of these Prophets; and the different aspects, under which they severally set forth the proximate or the ultimate future as they conceive it, are indicated and contrasted with one another. In all this there is much that is valuable and suggestive. The chief occasion of regret is that the bias derived from his critical prepossessions inclines him at every point to reduce the religious meaning of the Prophets to a minimum, to foist upon them inaccuracies with which they are not chargeable, and to represent them as in irreconcilable conflict, because of those differences in their portraiture by which they really supplement and complete each other.

It illustrates the facility with which the drift of events can be comprehended after they have actually taken place, that Dr. Robertson Smith can see no evidence of prophetic foresight in the disclosures of Amos. "The most ordinary political insight," he tells us (p. 131), could have seen the danger which threatened Israel from Assyria; "and what requires explanation is not so much that Amos was aware of it as that the rulers and people of Israel were so utterly blind to the impending doom." But it is obvious that Amos claims no political shrewdness above those whom he addresses. He points to no political causes that are at work; he makes no political deductions. It is not from this quarter that his inspiration proceeds. The one thought, that possesses his mind, is that of the moral causes which are at work. Israel has sinned and Jehovah has sent him to announce the penalty. The Doctor says, (p. 129,): "It is not Israel's sin that brings him forward as a preacher of repentance; but the sound of near destruction encircling the land constrains him to blow the alarm." Precisely the reverse is true, as appears from the whole tenor of the prophecy. The encroachments of Assyria had not yet affected Israel. The Northern Kingdom had never been more prosperous, and there seemed to be no reason to question the stability of this prosperity. Even after Assyria had pushed its conquests westward, until Damascus was overthrown, Israel's ancient rival and enemy, politicians still thought that Israel might be secure and prosperous in alliance with or in nominal subjection to the Great King. They were chiefly divided upon the question which of the rival empires, Assyria or Egypt, was the safer ground of dependence. But through all the fluctuating schemes of politicians, and their alternate hopes and fears, the steadfast word of the Prophet went on to sure accomplishment. And so did the prediction of Hosea (i. 6, 7), which no degree of political insight could have dictated, that while Assyria should overthrow the Northern Kingdom, its weaker sister, Judah, should be miraculously delivered. Their prediction can only be discredited by imputing to them what they do not say and what their language cannot be fairly interpreted to mean. Thus (p. 183), "To Hosea, as to Amos, the fall of the house of Jehu and the fall of the nation appear as one thing; both Prophets, indeed, appear to have looked for the overthrow of the reigning dynasty, not by intestine conspiracy, as actually happened, but at the hand of the destroying invader."

According to the Doctor's view of the matter (p. 184), the comparison of Hosea i. 4, with II. Kings x. 30 "places in the strongest light the limitations that characterize all Old Testament revelation. It shows that we can look for no mechanical uniformity in the teaching of successive Prophets." Hosea speaks of " a revolution accomplished with the active participation of older Prophets," as " the bloodshed of Jezreel, the treacherous slaughter of the house of Ahab." " Elisha saw and approved one side of Jehu's revolution. He looked on it only as the death-blow to Baal-worship; but Hosea sees another side and condemns as emphatically as Elisha approved." There is, however, no real discrepancy between these Prophets, as the Doctor himself suggests in the very act of urging it. What Elisha approves and what Hosea condemns are distinct things. By divine direction Jehu executed the just judgment of God upon the house of Ahab; so far he did right and was approved. There was, however, a converse to this, which is immediately added by the sacred historian (II. Kings x. 31), "But Jehu took no heed to walk in the Law of the LORD God of Israel with all his heart; for he departed not from the sins of Jeroboam, which made Israel to sin." Jehu had been explicitly told (II. Kings ix. 9), by the Prophet who gave him his commission, that the house of Ahab was to be made "like the house of Jeroboam the son of Nebat, and like the house of Baasha the son of Ahijah," who were punished for the criminality of the golden calves. This very criminality was subsequently perpetuated by Jehu. From an executioner of God's righteous sentence he thus became an accomplice and participant in the crime; and in judging the house of Ahab he pronounced a like doom upon himself. A slaughter, which found its justification only in its being inflicted in obedience to the declared will of God, ceased to be justifiable as performed by one who set that will at defiance (I. Kings xvi. 7; Deut. viii. 20). We have tacitly assumed that "blood" in this passage means "bloodshed" as the Doctor paraphrases it. It may, however, signify blood-guiltiness, and the sense of the passage be that a guilt equivalent to that contracted by Ahab in Jezreel should be avenged upon the house of Jehu, which by following in a like course of sin justified, and as it were assumed, the crimes of their predecessors.

In order to give a more precise idea of the method and aim of these Lectures, we quote a summary statement (p. 229) of the relation between Isaiah and the Prophets of Israel, as the author conceives it. The errors of the passage are too obvious to require further correction.

"Isaiah builds on the foundations laid by his predecessors, Amos and Hosea. But his treatment of the problem is more comprehensive and all-sided. The preaching of Amos was directed only to breaches of civil righteousness, and supplied no standard for the reformation of national worship; it left even the golden calves untouched. Hosea, on the other hand, has a clear insight into the right moral attitude of the religious subject to God; but that subject is to him the personified nation, sinning and repenting as one man, and therefore he has no practical suggestions applicable to the actual mixed state of society; his prophecy leaves an unexplained hiatus between Israel's present sin and its future return to Jehovah. Isaiah, on the contrary, finds in Jehovah's holiness a principle equally applicable to the amendment of the state and the elevation of religious praxis, an ideal which supplies an immediate impulse to reformation, and which, though it cannot be fully attained without the intervention of purging judgments, may at least become the practical guide of those within Israel who are striving after better things."

The allegation (p. 268) that Isaiah's prophecy to Ahaz (chs. vii., viii.) was "of the nature of a shrewd political forecast rather than of exceptional prediction, and, as the future actually shaped itself, his worst anticipations were not realized," is based on two unfounded assumptions, viz.: that viii. 4 describes the ultimate overthrow of Samaria, and that the pictured desolation of Judah belonged to a single campaign. The prediction in ch. xx. is allowed to have been accomplished; but he says (p. 282), "this result had not come about in the way that Isaiah anticipated"; which anticipation we learn not from the Prophet, but from his critic, who tells us that Isaiah had expected the Assyrian king to press forward against Egypt on the fall of Ashdod. In regard to Isaiah's predictions of the blissful future under the forms of the old dispensation, we are told (p. 337) that they have not only "received no literal fulfilment, but it is impossible that the evolution of the divine purpose can ever again be narrowed within the limits of the petty world of which Judah was the centre and Egypt and Assyria the extremes." He objects (p. 339) to a figurative interpretation of such prophecies, but nevertheless admits (p. 342): "It is plain from the very freedom with which Isaiah recasts the details of his predictions from time to time,—adapting them to new circumstances, introducing fresh historical or poetical motives, and cancelling obsolete features in his older imagery,—that he himself drew a clear distinction between mere accidental and dramatic details, which he knew might be modified or wholly superseded by the march of history, and the unchanging principles of faith, which he received as a direct revelation from Jehovah Himself and knew to be eternal and invariable truth."

Now, if the meaning of all this is simply that Isaiah did not understand, nor was it given to him to reveal, the divine plans in all their extent and fulness, this is readily conceded. And it is a very proper subject of investigation, What were the limitations of the revelation granted to him, and what is the exact conception expressed in his words? But if "the lion which eats straw like the ox, the seas and rivers dried up to facilitate the return of the exiles to Judah," are "plainly figurative" (p. 303), and if the Prophet clearly distinguishes substance and form in employing the symbolic institutions of the Old Testament to body forth the future, no correct exegesis can fasten upon the prophecy the inaccuracy of declaring, nor upon the Prophet the narrowness of supposing, that his picture was to be realized in the particular forms in which he has drawn it. These were more or less consciously used and accepted as figures of a reality more glorious, but as yet only partially disclosed and dimly understood; just as the vision of the New Jerusalem is to us the picture of a future whose magnificence impresses us, but in what precise form it shall be realized we cannot tell.

The "Branch of the LORD" (Isa. iv. 2) is referred (p. 248) to "the simple blessings of agricultural life." Immanuel (vii. 14 ff., p. 271) was simply an ordinary child, born at the time, and gave no such pledge to Ahaz of the stability of his royal house as an allusion to the promised and expected Son of David might have done. "It is by no means clear" (p. 306) whether the child with the remarkable names (ix. 6) is "one person or a race of sovereigns." At any rate no divine person is intended, for "there is no reason to think that they denote anything metaphysical." And Isa. ii. 2–4 "is far from implying a world-wide sovereignty of Israel" (p. 309). Micah, it seems (p. 290), did not predict the captivity; "thou shalt come even to Babylon" (iv. 10) is a gloss. So, while Isaiah is represented (pp. 259, 260) as declaring "the inviolability of Jerusalem," and Jeremiah the "captivity of Jerusalem," Micah is made to affirm, in contradistinction from both, and contrary to what actually occurred, that the city shall be taken, and its population driven forth into the open field; "there, and not within her proud ramparts, Jehovah will grant her deliverance from her enemies." "Jehovah's righteousness," as declared by the Prophets, is limited (p. 245) to "kingly righteousness," which "aims at, not the transformation of the hearts of men, but the removal of injustice in the state."

And thus by emptying words of their meaning, by attributing to the Prophets ideas which they never entertained, by representing them as in collision where there is nevertheless entire harmony, and by the application of the potent wand of criticism in a few obstinate cases where less summary measures would not avail, the revelation of God through the Prophets is made out to be a very different thing from that which it actually is.

INDEX OF SCRIPTURE TEXTS

QUOTED OR REFERRED TO.

GENESIS.	Page
iii. 15	236
v. 24	303
vii. 11	305
xii. 6, 7	161
xiii. 18	164
xiv. 22	270
xvii. 1	270
xviii. 1, 2	271
xviii. 10	303
xviii. 26	311 *note*
xix. 11	303
xix. 24	270
xx. 13	311 *note*
xxi. 31, 33	162
xxi. 33	270
xxiv. 3	270
xxiv. 32	282 *note*
xxvi. 23–25	162
xxvii. 7	96
xxviii. 10 ff	165
xxviii. 12, 13	270
xxxi. 19, 30	271
xxxi. 19, 32	276 *note*
xxxi. 49, 54	159
xxxii. 1, 2	303
xxxii. 2	159
xxxii. 24, 30	271
xxxiii. 18, 20	162
xxxv. 2	271, 276 *note*
xxxv. 4	162
xxxv. 9 ff	166
xxxvii. 14	164
xxxix. 1	106 *note*
xlix. 10	83, 237
xlix. 25	270

EXODUS.	
i. 11	68
i. 14	68
ii. 15	58 *note*
iii. 1	279

EXODUS (*continued*).	Page
iii. 2	279
iii. 5	94
iii. 14	43
iii. 18	119
iv. 6	303 *note*
iv. 10 ff	61 *note*
iv. 24–26	61 *note*
iv. 27	279
v. 7 ff	68
vi. 12, 30	96
xii. 3 ff	118 *note*
xii. 9	119 *note*
xii. 25	118
xiv. 21	303
xv. 25	303
xvi. 12	303
xvii. 14	49, 50
xvii. 15	95
xviii. 13–16	58 *note*
xviii. 19	313
xviii. 21, 22	70
xix., xx.	279
xix. 3–8	283 *note*
xix. 3–19	283 *note*
xix. 20–25	284 *note*
xx.	282, 285 *note*, 287, 296
xx.–xxiii.	324
xx. 1–20	283 *note*
xx. 2	299 *note*
xx. 4	294
xx. 5	113
xx. 6	299 *note*
xx. 10	299 *note*
xx. 11	299 *note*
xx. 21, 24–26	284 *note*
xx. 22 ff	51, 310
xx. 23	52, 113
xx. 24	74 *note*, 95, 131, 302, 310
xx. 24, 25	74
xxi.–xxiii.	50, 51, 284 *note* (bis), 322, 340

EXODUS (continued).	Page	EXODUS (continued).	Page
xxi. 6	70	xxxii.	283 note, 291, 292
xxi. 12–14	76 note	xxxii. 4	264 note
xxi. 13	311 note	xxxii. 19	282
xxi. 14	311 note	xxxii. 27, 35	100
xxii. 5, 6	68	xxxii. 30 ff	100
xxii. 8, 9	70	xxxiii. 1	284 note (bis)
xxii. 20	106 note	xxxiii. 1–6	57 note
xxii. 21–24	70	xxxiii. 1–11	283 note
xxii. 28	70, 304, 331	xxxiii. 3	58 note, 151, 284 note
xxii. 29	68	xxxiii. 4 ff	100
xxii. 30	74, 75, 118	xxxiii. 7	58 note, 100, 102
xxiii. 2, 3, 9	70	xxxiii. 7, 9, 11	58 note
xxiii. 10, 11	68	xxxiii. 7–11	57 note
xxiii. 12	68	xxxiii. 9 ff	313
xxiii. 12 ff	283	xxxiii. 11	58 note
xxiii. 12–33	52	xxxiv.	282 (bis), 284 and note, 285 note, 287, 322
xxiii. 14 ff	88 note		
xxiii. 14–18	118	xxxiv. 1	52, 282
xxiii. 15, 16	68	xxxiv. 4	282, 284 note
xxiii. 16	133	xxxiv. 5	284 note (bis)
xxiii. 17, 19	76	xxxiv. 6	284 note
xxiii. 18	287 note	xxxiv. 6, 7	282
xxiii. 19	68	xxxiv. 6–9	284 note
xxiii. 20 ff	101	xxxiv. 9	282, 284 note
xxiii. 24	106 note, 121	xxxiv. 10	283, 284 note
xxiv. 3	51, 320 note	xxxiv. 10–13	285 note
xxiv. 3–8	284 note	xxxiv. 10–26	52
xxiv. 4	49, 51, 74, 121, 310	xxxiv. 11–26	283
xxiv. 8	51	xxxiv. 12	118
xxiv. 12–14	283 note	xxxiv. 12, 13	285 note
xxv. ff	306	xxxiv. 13	121
xxv. 10 ff	88	xxxiv. 14–26	285 note
xxv. 10–22	66	xxxiv. 15, 16	106 note, 113
xxv. 21	88	xxxiv. 17	323 note
xxv. 21, 22	281	xxxiv. 18–20	75
xxv. 22	88	xxxiv. 19, 25	118
xxv. 30	140	xxxiv. 21	68
xxvii.–xxxi.	81 note	xxxiv. 22	87 note (bis), 133, 287 note
xxvii. 1 ff	74		
xxvii. 2	307	xxxiv. 25	287 note
xxvii. 20	90	xxxiv. 27	49, 282
xxviii. 6	92 note	xxxiv. 27, 28	52
xxviii. 30	67	xxxiv. 28	88, 281, 282 and note, 285 note (bis), 304
xxviii. 31 ff	92 note		
xxix. 4	90 note	xxxiv. 29–35	285 note
xxix. 30	81 note	xxxv. 25, 26	68
xxix. 36, 37	131	xxxv. 30 ff	68
xxix. 38–41	303	xxxvi. ff	306
xxx. 8	90	xl.	58 note
xxx. 10	134	xl. 20	281
xxx. 16	131	LEVITICUS.	
xxxi. 2 ff	68		
xxxi. 10	81 note	i.	58 note
xxxi. 18	283 note	i.–vii.	81 note

INDEX OF SCRIPTURE TEXTS. 357

LEVITICUS (continued).	Page
i. 5, 8, 11	80
i. 6–8	303
ii. 2	80
ii. 10, 11	309
ii. 14	304 note
iii. 1 ff	93 note
iii. 2	80
iv. 12, 21	60
v. 15–19	309 note
vi., vii.	287 note
vi. 11	60
vi. 16–18	309
vii. 10	309
vii. 28 ff	93 note
vii. 30 ff	93
vii. 37, 38	54
viii.–x.	81 note
viii. 2 ff	60
ix. 16	303
ix. 24	303
x. 12	309
x. 15	93
x. 19, 20	99
xiii., xiv.	77
xiii. 2	80
xiii. 46	60, 305, 309
xiv. 3	60
xiv. 7, 8	303
xiv. 8	60 (bis)
xiv. 34	59, 118
xiv. 34 ff	60
xvi.	81 note, 134
xvi. 8	339
xvi. 21, 22	60, 135 note
xvi. 26, 28	60
xvi. 32	81 note
xvii. 3	60
xvii. 3 ff	77
xvii. 3–7	157
xvii. 4, 5	78 note
xvii. 7	113
xviii. 3	59
xviii. 17	80 note
xix. 2	100
xix. 5	96
xix. 18	100
xix. 23	59
xix. 29	89 note
xix. 36	64, 117 note
xx. 3	117 note
xx. 5, 6	113
xx. 11	117 note
xxi. 1	80
xxii. 27	75

LEVITICUS (continued).	Page
xxiii. 3	304
xxiii. 10	118
xxiii. 14	304 note
xxiii. 26–32	134
xxiii. 34	308
xxiii. 42	337 note
xxiii. 44	54
xxiv. 8, 9	140
xxiv. 10, 14, 23	60
xxv. 2	59, 118
xxv. 8–10	134
xxv. 9	134
xxv. 23	304
xxv. 33, 34	83 note
xxv. 39, 40	304
xxvi.	101, 183
xxvi. 1	121
xxvi. 5	117 note
xxvi. 13	64
xxvi. 14 ff	324
xxvi. 22	304
xxvi. 29	305
xxvi. 30	324
xxvi. 40 ff	101
xxvi. 46	54
xxvii. 29	89 note, 304
xxvii. 34	54

NUMBERS.

	Page
iii. 3	80
iv.	129
iv. 5, 20	141 note
iv. 15	92 note
iv. 15, 20	92
iv. 15–21	59 note
v. 2	305
v. 2–4	60
v. 7, 8	309 note
v. 10	309 note
v. 23	339
vi. 1–5	89 note
vi. 2, 3	117 note
vii. 22	93
x. 2 ff	60
x. 8	80
x. 21	59 note
x. 33	59 note, 88, 283 note
x. 35	89
xi. 1	303
xi. 5	68
xi. 16	70
xi. 24, 26, 30	58 note
xi. 26–29	98
xi. 27	58 note

NUMBERS (continued).	Page
xii.	77
xii. 3	61 note
xii. 4, 5	58 note
xii. 10	303
xii. 13	303
xii. 14, 15	60
xiii. 32, 33	117 note
xiv. 4	64
xiv. 11 ff	100
xiv. 33	113
xiv. 44	88
xv. 41	64
xvi.	77
xvi. 35	303
xvii. 2	339
xviii. 2	130
xviii. 4	130
xviii. 7	134
xviii. 12, 13	304
xviii. 17	84 note
xviii. 18	84 note
xviii. 20	77
xix. 3, 4	60
xix. 3, 7, 9	60
xix. 14, 16	60
xix. 14, 22	117 note
xx. 5	68
xx. 8	303
xx. 12	61 note
xxv. 3, 5	117 note
xxv. 11–13	155
xxvii. 17	304
xxvii. 21	67
xxvii. 58, 59	92 note
xxviii. 11	304
xxviii. 19, 24	118 note, 124
xxix. 7–11	134
xxix. 12	308
xxix. 13 ff	125
xxxi. 27	56 note
xxxii. 2	70
xxxiii. 2	49
xxxiv. 8	117 note
xxxv. 10 ff	311 note
xxxv. 30	304
xxxvi. 1	70
xxxvi. 8, 9	304

DEUTERONOMY.	
i. 1	161
i. 43	65 note
iv. 23–26	151
iv. 29	101

DEUTERONOMY (continued).	Page
iv. 30	323
v.	282, 287
vii. 15	64
viii. 11	138
viii. 20	349
ix. 21	293
ix. 23	65 note
x. 1–5	88
x. 1–8	66
x. 4, 5	281
x. 6	79
x. 8	82, 89
x. 8, 9	77
xi. 6	77
xi. 10	68
xi. 16, 17	303
xi. 24	311 note
xii.–xxvi.	50, 53
xii. 1	138
xii. 1, 8, 9	59
xii. 2	311 note
xii. 2–5	157
xii. 5	74, 243, 267, 276 note
xii. 5 ff	155
xii. 5, 10 ff	60
xii. 6, 11	118
xii. 8, 9	118
xii. 9	59
xii. 15	77, 85 note
xii 27	118
xiii. 5	89 note
xiii. 5, 10	64
xiii. 9	304
xiii. 10	304
xiii. 12 ff	89 note
xiv. 23 ff	60
xiv. 24	84 note
xiv. 28	117 note
xiv. 29	79
xv. 4, 7	59
xv. 5, 6	70
xv. 19	118
xv. 19, 20	84 note
xv. 20	75
xvi. 2	118 and note
xvi. 2, 6 ff	60
xvi. 7	60, 118 note, 119 note
xvi. 13 ff	308
xvi. 14	82 note
xvi. 18	71
xvi. 19	65 note
xvi. 20	70
xvi. 21, 22	121
xvi. 22	121

INDEX OF SCRIPTURE TEXTS. 359

DEUTERONOMY (continued).	Page
xvii. 5	304 (bis)
xvii. 6, 7	304
xvii. 8–12	64, 71
xvii. 9, 18	79
xvii. 12	89 note, 116 note
xvii. 14	59, 65 note, 145
xvii. 14 ff	64
xvii. 15	65 note
xvii. 15, 16	64
xvii. 18	108
xviii. 1	78, 79, 82 note
xviii. 1 ff	82 note
xviii. 1, 2	77
xviii. 3	85 note, 133
xviii. 3–5	78, 82 note
xviii. 4, 5	305
xviii. 6	79
xviii. 6–8	78, 308
xviii. 8	82 note
xviii. 15	117 note
xviii. 15 ff	101
xviii. 18	57 note
xviii. 21, 22	181
xviii. 22	304
xix. 1	59
xix. 1 ff	311 note
xix. 8, 9	70
xix. 14	59 note, 116 note
xix. 15	304
xix. 17	64
xx. 1	64
xx. 10–15	63
xx. 16–18	63
xx. 17	89 note
xxi. 1, 23	59
xxi. 17	304
xxii. 21	89 note
xxii. 30	117 note
xxiii. 3, 4, 7, 8	63
xxiii. 7	64
xxiii. 21–23	89 note
xxiv. 1	339
xxiv. 8	79, 309
xxiv. 8, 9	77
xxiv. 9, 18, 22	64
xxiv. 13, 15	70
xxiv. 16	108
xxv. 4	117 note
xxv. 6	89 note
xxv. 13 ff	117 note
xxv. 17–19	63
xxvi. 11, 12	82 note
xxvi. 12	117 note
xxvi. 14	117 note

DEUTERONOMY (continued).	Page
xxvii. 3	53
xxvii. 5, 6	310
xxvii. 9	79, 81 note
xxvii. 9, 12, 14	79
xxvii. 17	116 note
xxviii.	101, 183
xxviii. 15 ff	324
xxviii. 27, 60	323
xxviii. 30, 39	117 note
xxviii. 53	305
xxviii. 60	64
xxviii. 68	116 note
xxix. 5	303
xxix. 23	324
xxx. 2	323
xxx. 3	117 note
xxxi. 9	52, 81 note
xxxi. 9, 22, 24	49
xxxi. 9, 25, 26	66
xxxi. 9, 26	107
xxxi. 24	54
xxxi. 24–26	53
xxxii. 37, 38	89 note
xxxii. 39	305
xxxiii.	279, 316
xxxiii. 1	279
xxxiii. 2–5	280
xxxiii. 8, 10	82, 316
xxxiii. 8–11	78
xxxiii. 18, 19	163

JOSHUA.

i. 7, 8	107, 344
iii. 3	80 note, 92 note
iv. 19	166
iv. 23	303
v. 2 ff	166
v. 5 ff	101
v. 15	94
vi. 6	92 note
viii. 30, 31	310
viii. 31	107
viii. 31–34	344
viii. 33	80 note, 92 note
ix. 27	128 note
xiii. 26	160
xviii. 1	87
xviii. 9	339
xix. 50	111 note
xix. 51	87
xx. 7	162
xx. 8	160
xxi.	82 note

INDEX OF SCRIPTURE TEXTS.

JOSHUA (continued).	Page
xxi. 4 ff	80 note
xxi. 13	164
xxi. 16	83 note, 92
xxi. 32	160
xxi. 38	160
xxii. 5	344
xxii. 8	57 note
xxii. 26 ff	95
xxiii. 6	344
xxiv.	316, 340
xxiv. 1	162
xxiv. 14	276 note
xxiv. 14, 23, 26	162
xxiv. 19	151
xxiv. 25, 26	340
xxiv. 26	107, 316, 344

JUDGES.	
i.	91
i. 17	89 note
ii. 1 ff	101
ii. 1–5	95
ii. 7	102
ii. 11–19	97
iii. 4	138, 344
iii. 9	97
iii. 11, 30	97
iii. 19	166
iv. 3	97
iv. 4	101
iv. 10	160
v.	296
v. 4, 5	279
v. 14	339
vi. 8	101
vi. 20, 21, 24, 25 ff	165
vi. 20–22	95
vi. 24	95
vi. 25	96
vi. 25 ff	95
viii. 14	339
viii. 27	138, 165
viii. 28	97
ix. 4, 27, 46	161
ix. 6	162
ix. 27	88 note
x. 14	89 note
x. 17	160
xi. 11	96, 160
xi. 13 ff	89 note
xi. 35, 36	89 note
xiii. 4, 5, 14	89 note
xiii. 16 ff	95
xvi. 17	89 note

JUDGES (continued).	Page
xvii.–xxi.	89
xvii. 2	106 note
xvii. 3	264 note
xvii. 5	138
xvii. 5, 12	106 note
xvii. 7	92
xvii. 7–9	91
xviii. 14 ff	117 note
xviii. 30	264 note (bis)
xviii. 30, 31	264 note
xviii. 31	87
xix. 1	91
xix. 18	87
xix. 23, 24	89 note
xx. 1	89 note, 96, 163
xx. 6	89 note
xx. 6, 10	89 note
xx. 12	163
xx. 13	89 note
xx. 18, 26, 27	164, 166
xx. 18, 26, 31	88
xx. 27	88 (bis), 281
xx. 31	88
xxi. 2	88
xxi. 4	89, 96, 164
xxi. 10, 13	89 note
xxi. 11	89 note
xxi. 12	89
xxi. 17	89 note
xxi. 19	88 and note
xxi. 21	87 note

I. SAMUEL.	
i. 1	92
i. 3	91 (bis)
i. 3, 9	80
i. 7	90
i. 9	90 note
i. 11	89 note
i. 20, 21	87 note
i. 22	139
i. 24	90
ii. 11	93
ii. 11, 18	79 note
ii. 12 ff	93
ii. 13	96
ii. 14, 22, 29	91
ii. 14, 29	139
ii. 18	92 note, 106 note
ii. 22	90 note
ii. 27, 28	91
ii. 29	91, 139
ii. 29 ff	139
ii. 30 ff	155

INDEX OF SCRIPTURE TEXTS. 361

I. SAMUEL (continued).	Page
ii. 36	318
iii. 1	79 note
iii. 3	90
iii. 11 ff	139
iii. 15	90 note
iii. 20, 21	139
iv. 1	279
iv. 3	89
iv. 4	90, 139, 148
iv. 11	102
vi. 13	141
vi. 14, 18	83 note
vi. 15	92, 128
vi. 19	92, 141 note
vii. 1	103, 106 note
vii. 2	103, 142
vii. 3	104
vii. 5, 9	163
vii. 6	164
vii. 9, 17	105 note
vii. 12	279
vii. 13–17	143 note
vii. 16	166, 311 note
vii. 17	140, 164
viii.	143 note, 144
viii. ff	143 note
viii. 3	65 note
viii. 5	65 note
viii. 7	145
viii. 7, 8	65 note
viii. 19, 20	146
ix. 12	164
ix. 12, 13	105 note
ix. 13	104
x. 3	105, 166
x. 5	105
x. 8	105 note, 166
x. 17	163
x. 18, 19	65 note
x. 24	65 note
x. 25	339
xi. 14, 15	105 note, 166
xii. 14	65 note
xiii. 8, 13	152
xiii. 8–14	105
xiii. 9 ff	166
xiv. 3	140
xiv. 18	103 note
xiv. 35	105 note
xiv. 47–52	143 note
xv. 15 ff	166
xv. 15, 21	105 note
xv. 22	109
xv. 22, 23	151

I. SAMUEL (continued).	Page
xv. 23	276 note
xv. 26	147
xv. 35	147
xvi. 2	152
xvi. 2 ff	164
xvi. 2–5	105 note
xix. 16	276 note
xx. 6	105, 164
xxi. 1, 6	103
xxi. 6	140
xxii. 11	140
xxii. 19	140
xxii. 20	91
xxiii. 18	160
xxv. 1	143 note
xxvi. 19	96
xxx. 24, 25	56 note
xxx. 31	311 note

II. SAMUEL.	
ii. 1	164
ii. 4	164
ii. 8	160
iii. 3	106 note
v. 3	164
v. 12	153
vi. 1	148
vi. 2	148
vi. 3	92 note
vi. 6, 7, 13	92 note
vi. 7	92
vi. 13	106 note
vi. 14	106 note
vi. 17	154
vi. 18	106 note
vi. 21	148
vii.	154
vii. 6	90 note
viii. 11	154
viii. 15–18	144 note
viii. 16, 17	339
viii. 17	154
viii. 18	106 note
ix.	144 note
x.	144 note
xi. 13	282 note
xi. 14, 15	339
xiv. 24	147
xv. 7–9	164
xv. 24	128
xv. 24, 29	92 note
xv. 24–29, 35	154
xvii. 24	160
xix. 24 ff	144 note

II. SAMUEL (continued).	Page
xx. 23	127 note
xx. 23–26	144 note
xx. 24, 25	339
xx. 25	154
xxii.	110
xxiv. 16–18	94

I. KINGS.

	Page
i. 50, 51	307
ii. 3	108, 138, 344
ii. 26, 27	155
ii. 27	91
ii. 28	307
ii. 35	130 note
iii. 1	111 note
iii. 2	105, 106 note, 155
iii. 4	164
iii. 6	160
iv. 3	339
vi., vii.	306
vi. 5	90 note
vi. 12	138
vi. 38	308
vii. 51	154
viii. 2	308
viii. 3	92 note
viii. 4	80 note, 128, 308
viii. 6–9, 21	298
viii. 9, 21	281
viii. 10, 11	306
viii. 53, 56	108
viii. 62	131
viii. 63	106 note
viii. 64	309
ix. 4, 6	138
ix. 15	111 note
ix. 25	106 note, 133
xi. 7, 8	155
xi. 29 ff	265
xi. 33	267
xi. 33, 38	138
xi. 40	267
xii. 1, 25	162
xii. 2	264 note
xii. 25	111 note
xii. 26 ff	108
xii. 28, 29	264 note
xii. 29	166
xii. 31	316
xii. 32, 33	308
xiii. 2	265
xiii. 32	265
xiii. 32, 33	155

I. KINGS (continued).	Page
xiii. 33	108, 316
xiv. 8, 9	108
xiv. 9	265, 271
xiv. 10, 11	271
xiv. 22–24	155
xv. 14	155
xv. 17	111 note
xvi. 1, 2	265
xvi. 2–4	271
xvi. 7	349
xvi. 25, 26	272
xvi. 31–33	269
xvii. 1	303
xvii. 6	303
xvii. 12, 14, 24	270 note
xvii. 14	303
xviii. 13	269
xviii. 17	269
xviii. 18	272
xviii. 21, 24	271
xviii. 23, 33	303
xviii. 24, 38	303
xviii. 27	271
xviii. 29, 36	133, 303
xviii. 30	165
xviii. 31	271
xviii. 36	119 note, 152, 164, 270
xviii. 40	304
xix. 3 ff	270 note
xix. 6	303
xix. 8	273, 304
xix. 10	119 note
xix. 14	165, 269
xix. 15	272
xx. 42	304
xxi. 3	304
xxi. 8, 9	339
xxi. 10	304
xxi. 21–24	271
xxi. 22	294
xxii.	266
xxii. 17	304
xxii. 28	304
xxii. 43	155

II. KINGS.

	Page
i. 10, 12	303
ii. 3 ff	303
ii. 8, 14	303
ii. 9	304
ii. 21	303
ii. 23, 24	295
ii. 24	304

INDEX OF SCRIPTURE TEXTS.

II. KINGS (*continued*).	Page
iii.	266 *note*
iii. 2, 3	294
iii. 10, 13	295 *note*
iii. 13, 14	295
iii. 17	303
iii. 20	303
iv. 1	304
iv. 16	303
iv. 23	304
iv. 42	304
v. 5–7	339
v. 7	305
v. 10	303
v. 27	303
vi. 17	303
vi. 18	303
vi. 23, 24	143
vi. 28, 29	305
vii. 2, 19	305
vii. 3	305
viii. 12, 13	272
ix. 9	294, 349
x. 1	339
x. 28, 29	267
x. 29	108
x. 30	348
x. 31	344, 349
x. 32	272
xi. 4	127 *note*
xi. 12	108
xii. 3	155
xii. 7, 10	133
xii. 10	308, 339
xii. 16	309
xiii. 3, 22	272
xiii. 6	293
xiv. 4	155
xiv. 6	108, 344
xiv. 22	111 *note*
xv. 4	155
xv. 5	309
xv. 35	155
xvi. 13, 15	309
xvi. 15	133
xvii. 9	155
xvii. 13	266
xvii. 37	344
xviii. 2	231 *note*
xviii. 4	107
xviii. 4, 22	330
xviii. 6	108
xviii. 6, 12	344
xviii. 12	108
xviii. 13	231 *note*

II. KINGS (*continued*).	Page
xviii. 18	339
xviii. 22	156
xix. 34	120
xx. 16–18	182
xxi. 3	155
xxi. 4 ff	128 *note*
xxi. 7–9	108
xxi. 8	344
xxii. 4	133
xxii. 4, 8	308
xxii. 8	107, 344
xxiii. 3, 25	138
xxiii. 4	133, 308
xxiii. 9	156, 308
xxiii. 13	155
xxiii. 24, 25	107, 344
xxv. 18	308
xxv. 25	133

I. CHRONICLES.

iv. 41 42, 43	63 *note*
vi. 8	130 *note*
vi. 28	92
vi. 53	130 *note*
ix. 2 ff	129
xiii. 3	103
xv. 2	79 *note*
xvi 39	155
xviii. 17	106 *note*
xxii. 5	154
xxiii. 25, 26	154
xxiv. 3	91, 130 *note*, 155
xxvii. 17	130 *note*

II. CHRONICLES.

i. 3, 13	164
v. 5	80 *note*
v. 7–10	298
vi. 11, 41	298
vii. 9	132
viii. 2	111 *note*
viii. 13	133
xiv. 3–5	156
xiv. 13	160
xvii. 6	156
xix. 5, 8	71
xxiii. 4	130
xxiii. 18	80 *note*
xxiv. 6	35 *note*
xxviii. 6	160
xxx. 17	130
xxx. 19	100
xxx. 27	80 *note*
xxxi. 20	160

INDEX OF SCRIPTURE TEXTS.

II. CHRONICLES (*continued*). Page

xxxiii. 12, 23	160
xxxiii. 17	156
xxxiv. 2, 3	227
xxxv. 3	299
xxxv. 13	119 *note*, 130
xxxv. 21	208
xxxvi. 20	39
xxxvi. 22	239

EZRA.

i. 1	239
i. 4	311 *note*
ii. 36 ff	129
ii. 58	128 *note*
ii. 63	67
iii. 7	196 *note*
vii. 7, 24	129
viii. 15 ff	129
viii. 20	128 *note*
ix. 5	135 *note*
ix. 11	57 *note*

NEHEMIAH.

i. 4	160
vii. 39 ff	83 *note*, 129
vii. 65	67
viii.–x.	132
viii. 1, 14	127
ix. 13	280
x. 28, 29	128 *note*
x. 29	127
x. 32	131
xi. 20	78
xii. 1–9	129
xii. 45	127

ESTHER.

i. 3, 14, 18	228
i. 19	228

JOB.

xxxvii. 6	42

PSALMS.

i.–xli.	109
iii. 4	110
v.	109
vi.	109
ix.	110
x.	110

PSALMS (*continued*). Page

xi. 4	110
xi. 6	110
xiv.	109
xv.	110
xv. 1	110
xviii.	110
xviii. 6	110
xviii. 10	110
xviii. 22	110
xix.	110
xix. 7	108
xix. 7–10	110
xx.	145
xxi.	145
xl.	110, 111 *note*, 112
xl. 1, 5	112 *note*
xl. 6	110, 111 and *note*
xl. 7, 8	112
l. 8–15	111 *note*
li.	111 *note*
li. 16, 17	111 *note*
lxviii. 8, 17	279
lxviii. 16 ff	148
lxxviii. 5	108
lxxviii. 56–61	140
lxxviii. 60, 68	102
lxxviii. 61 ff	264 *note*
lxxxvii. 4	221
xcix. 6	153
ciii. 7	115 *note*
cxvi. 9	96

CANTICLES.

vi. 13	160

ISAIAH.

i. 10	215, 319, 338
i. 11 ff	99, 111 *note*, 118, 121
i. 11–20	241
i. 15	121
i. 24 ff	220
ii. 2	123
ii. 2, 3	120
ii. 2–4	241, 353
ii. 3	120
ii. 6, 7	65 *note*
iii. 10, 11	220
iv. 2	352
iv. 5	120
v. 19	185
v. 26–30	183
vi. 1 ff	1–0

INDEX OF SCRIPTURE TEXTS.

ISAIAH (continued).	Page
vi. 13	220
vii. 3 ff	61
vii. 5–8	183
vii. 7, 8	232
vii. 14 ff	352
vii. 15, 16	232
vii. 16	232
viii. 1	50, 339
viii. 2	117 *note*
viii. 4	351
vii., viii.	350
ix. 6	237
x. 1	338
x. 5–34	183
x. 19	339
x. 20–22	220
x. 21	237
x. 24–34	213
x. 32	120
xi. 9	157
xi. 14	198
xi. 15	214
xii. 6	157
xiv. 31	186
xvii. 8	120
xvii. 12–14	213
xviii 7	157
xix. 19	120
xix. 21	121
xix. 23	214
xix. 23–25	221
xix. 25	245
xx.	351
xx. 4	213
xxiii	188, 194
xxiii. 6, 7, 12	194
xxiii. 15–18	195
xxiii. 18	221
xxiv. 23	157
xxv. 10	198
xxvii. 9	120
xxvii. 13	157
xxviii. 16	157
xxix. 1, 8	157
xxix. 13	121
xxx. 1 ff	64
xxx. 8	50, 339
xxx. 9, 10	319
xxx. 20	157
xxx. 31 ff	213
xxxi. 1	64
xxxi. 4, 9	157
xxxi. 8, 9	213
xxxiii. 20	120

ISAIAH (continued).	Page
xxxiv.	199 *note*
xxxvi., xxxvii.	231 *note*
xxxvi. 1	231 *note*
xxxvi. 7	156
xxxviii., xxxix.	231 *note*
xxxviii. 1	231 *note*
xxxviii. 5	231 *note*
xxxviii. 6	231 *note*
xxxix. 5–7	232 *note*
xxxix. 6	232
xl.–lxvi.	237
xl. 3	146
xli. 8	243
xlii. 5	115 *note*
xliii. 9–12	181
xlviii. 21	214
xlviii. 22	220
liii. 8, 9, 10, 11	238
lv. 3	238
lvi. 3	245
lvi. 3–8	221
lviii. 6	134
lxi. 1 ff	134
lxiii. 1–6	63
lxvi. 1–3	127, 242
lxvi. 23	242

JEREMIAH.

ii. 18, 36	64
iii. 2	157
iii. 16	243, 299
vii. 12	140
vii. 12, 14	102
vii. 12–14	243
vii. 14	221
vii. 21 ff	118
vii. 22	91 *note*, 110
vii. 31	157
viii. 3	311 *note*
xi. 3 ff	221
xii. 16	221
xv. 1	153
xvii. 1–3	157
xvii. 15	185
xxiv.	221
xxiv. 9	311 *note*
xxv. 11	195
xxv. 11, 12	209, 239
xxv. 12, 13	183
xxv. 22	195
xxvi. 6	102, 243
xxvi. 6, 9	140
xxvii. 3	198

INDEX OF SCRIPTURE TEXTS.

JEREMIAH (continued).	Page
xxvii. 7	39
xxviii.	234
xxviii. 9	181
xxix. 10	239
xxix. 14	311 note
xxxi. 31 ff	243
xxxi. 32, 33	299
xxxv. 2, 4	90 note
xxxvi. 4 ff	61
xl. 12	311 note
xl. 14	198
xli. 2, 15	198
xliii. 2 ff	126
xliii. 8–13	200
xliv. 12–14	200
xliv. 15 ff	126
xliv. 29, 30	201, 202
xlv. 5	311 note
xlvi. 2	195
xlvi. 13–28	200
xlvi. 26	202
xlvii. 2	186
xlviii. 47	63
xlix. 6	63
xlix. 17, 18	63
xlix. 23–27	197
l., li.	39, 183
l. 1	183
li. 59–64	183

EZEKIEL.

	Page
i.	244
vi. 3, 6	157
viii. 3 ff	128 note
xi.	221
xi. 15	245
xi. 16	243
xi. 23	243
xvi. 16	157
xvi. 53, 55, 61	215
xvi. 53–61	244
xvii.	244
xvii. 22, 23	123
xx. 7, 8	276 note
xx. 27–29	157
xxi. 20	198
xxiii.	244
xxiii. 3	276 note
xxv. 14	199
xxv. 15–17	185
xxvi.–xxviii.	188
xxvi. 10	194
xxvi. 12	194

EZEKIEL (continued).	Page
xxviii. 24–26	197
xxix. 10, 11	210
xxix. 11–16	200
xxix. 16	211
xxix. 17–21	203
xxix. 18–20	193
xxxiii. 21	199 note
xxxiv. 12	311 note
xxxv.	199 note
xxxvi. 5	199 note
xxxvii. 1 ff	124
xxxix. 9 ff	124
xl.–xlviii.	122
xl. 1	134
xl. 2	123
xl. 39	110
xlii. 16 ff	123
xliii. 2–4	123
xliii. 18 ff	131
xliv. 5 ff	128
xliv. 7	130
xliv. 11	130
xliv. 28 ff	133
xlv. 19, 20	132
xlv. 21, 25	133
xlv. 23–25	124
xlvi. 13 ff	133
xlvi. 24	130
xlvii.	244
xlvii. 1–12	123
xlviii. 11–13	131

DANIEL.

	Page
ii.	227
iv. 30	111 note
v. 2 ff	227
v. 10	226
v. 28	228
v. 30	226
vi. 8, 12. 15	228
vii.	227
vii. 6	228
vii. 13	238
viii. 8, 22	228
viii. 14	225
viii. 20	228
ix. 2	40, 239
ix. 24 ff	239
ix. 24–27	229, 239
x. 1	225
xi.	240
xi. 2	225
xi. 40–45	225

INDEX OF SCRIPTURE TEXTS. 367

DANIEL (continued).	Page
xii. 1, 2	229
xii. 7	225
xii. 11, 12	225

HOSEA.

i.–iii.	113
i. 2	323
i. 2 ff	61, 320
i. 4	324, 348
i. 6, 7	329, 348
i. 9	221, 245, 330
i. 10	143
i. 11	230, 330
ii. 3	324
ii. 5, 8, 13	271
ii. 7	323
ii. 11	115
ii. 13	323, 325
ii. 15	113, 320, 328 note
ii. 19, 20	113
iii. 4	117 note, 334
iii. 5	159, 330
iv. 1	114
iv. 1, 2	322
iv. 1, 6	323
iv. 3	324
iv. 4	116 note, 318
iv. 4, 5, 6	318 note
iv. 5	317
iv. 6	115, 317
iv. 8	116
iv. 11	322
iv. 12, 17	323
iv. 13	114, 163, 329
iv. 15	158, 166, 294, 329
iv. 16	114
iv. 19	334
v. 1	158, 161, 329
v. 1, 11	320
v. 6	334
v. 7	113, 323
v. 10	116 note
v. 11	325
v. 13	323
v. 15	147, 323
vi. 4	321, 323
vi. 5	319, 320
vi. 6	111 note, 116, 323, 334
vi. 7	113, 320, 323
vi. 11	117 note
vii. 1	322
vii. 4, 5	322
vii. 8	323
vii. 11	323

HOSEA (continued).	Page
vii. 14	334
viii. 1	115, 317, 320
viii. 4	159, 323
viii. 5, 6	293, 325
viii. 6	294
viii. 9	323
viii. 11	116 note, 158, 329
viii. 12	114, 340 and note
viii. 13	115, 116 note
viii. 14	230, 323
ix. 3	116 note, 324, 334
ix. 3, 4	116
ix. 4	116 and note, 334
ix. 5	115
ix. 9	114
ix. 10	117 note, 328 note
ix. 15	158, 166, 329
ix. 17	323
x. 1	158, 329
x. 2, 8	324
x. 4	322
x. 5	325
x. 8, 15	158
x. 9	114
x. 11	117 note
x. 12	323
x. 12, 13	322
xi. 1	320
xi. 2	323
xi. 7	114, 323
xi. 12	322
xii. 1	323
xii. 2	320
xii. 3, 4	320
xii. 6	323
xii. 6–8	322
xii. 9	115, 320, 337 note
xii. 10	319
xii. 11	116 note, 158, 166, 329
xii. 13	57 note, 320
xiii. 1, 2	113
xiii. 2	325
xiii. 4	320
xiii. 6	323
xiii. 16	323
xiv. 2	334
xiv. 3	323
xiv. 3, 8	323
xiv. 4	114, 323

JOEL.

ii. 1, 15, 32	157
ii. 15 ff	119

INDEX OF SCRIPTURE TEXTS.

JOEL (continued).

	Page
iii. 4–8	186
iii. 16, 17, 21	157
iii. 18	244
iii. 19	63
iii. 19, 20	199
iii. 21	119

AMOS.

i. 2	117 note, 159, 294, 324, 328, 335
i. 6–8	185
ii. 4	115, 317
ii. 5	230
ii. 6–8	322
ii. 7	117 note (bis), 322, 323
ii. 9	117 note
ii. 10	118, 320, 328 note
ii. 11	335
ii. 11, 12	117 note, 319
ii. 12	335
iii. 1, 2	320
iii. 2, 3	151
iii. 7	319
iii. 10	322
iii. 11–15	324
iii. 14	158, 294, 324, 326
iv. 1	322
iv. 4	116, 117 note, 158, 166, 294, 326
iv. 5	116, 335
iv. 6, 8–11	323
iv. 6–11	323
v. 4, 6	323
v. 4–6	158, 325
v. 5	161, 294, 329
v. 7, 24	322
v. 10, 12, 15	322
v. 11	117 note, 322
v. 18	185, 323
v. 21	115
v. 21 ff	99, 118
v. 21–23	325
v. 22	115
v. 25	118 (bis), 328 note
v. 26	294
v. 27	324
vi. 1	323
vi. 4–6	322
vi. 12	322
vi. 14	117 note
vii. 9	158, 329
vii. 12	318
vii. 15, 16	319

AMOS (continued).

	Page
viii. 4–6	322
viii. 5	115, 117 note
viii. 14	158, 161, 293, 326
ix. 8	324
ix. 10	220
ix. 11	159, 230
ix. 13	117 note
ix. 14	117 note (bis)

OBADIAH.

vers. 16, 17, 21	157
ver. 18	199

MICAH.

i. 5	157
iii. 10	111 note
iii. 12	230
iv. 1 ff	119
iv. 1, 2, 7	157
iv. 10	182, 232, 353
v. 5, 6	213
vi. 8	99, 110, 118
vii. 14	165

NAHUM.

iii. 8–10	201, 213

HABAKKUK.

i. 5–10	233
ii. 2	58 note
ii. 3	185
ii. 12	111 note
iii. 3	279
iii. 3, 4	280

ZEPHANIAH.

i. 8, 9	127 note
ii. 4–7	186
ii. 9, 10	198

ZECHARIAH.

i.–viii.	237
ii. 11	221
vii. 5	132
viii. 19	132
ix.–xi.	237
ix. 5–7	186
xii.–xiv.	233

INDEX OF SCRIPTURE TEXTS.

ZECHARIAH (continued).

	Page
xiv. 8	244
xiv. 21	221

MALACHI.

	Page
i. 3, 4	198
i. 11	120, 245
ii. 4-8	128 *note*
iii. 3	128 *note*
iii. 7	148
iv. 4	280

MATTHEW.

	Page
ix. 9	61
xxiv.	212

LUKE.

	Page
xiv. 26	91 *note*
xix. 40	210

JOHN.

	Page
xiii. 23	61
xxi. 25	210

ACTS.

	Page
xxi. 3-6	196

I. TIMOTHY.

	Page
iv. 3	290

REVELATION.

	Page
vii. 5 ff	124
xi. 8	215
xxii. 1 ff	124

I. MACCABEES.

	Page
iii. 46	163
iv. 47	313
vi. 53	133

II. MACCABEES.

	Page
viii. 28, 30	57 *note*

JOSEPHUS.

	Page
Antiq., x. 9. 7	198, 199, 206
Antiq., x. 11. 1	197
Antiq., xiii. 10. 3	133
Antiq., xiv. 16. 4	133
Against Apion, i. 19	187, 205
Against Apion, i. 21	196
Against Apion, i. 22	313
Jewish War, v. 5. 6	313

HERODOTUS.

	Page
ii. 58	209
ii. 177	200
ii. 177 (Rawlinson's Notes)	204
iii. 2, 16	201

University Press: John Wilson and Son, Cambridge.

www.ingramcontent.com/pod-product-compliance
Lightning Source LLC
Chambersburg PA
CBHW020305240426
43673CB00039B/709